THE ACTIVE MANAGER'S TOOL KIT

Other Books by Mel Silberman

The Consultant's Big Book of Organization Development Tools (0071408835)

The Consultant's Toolkit (0071362614)

THE ACTIVE MANAGER'S TOOL KIT

Edited by Mel Silberman, Ph.D.

McGraw-Hill

New York   Chicago   San Francisco
Lisbon   London   Madrid   Mexico City   Milan
New Delhi   San Juan   Seoul   Singapore
Sydney   Toronto

**Important Guidelines for Photocopying or Downloading Pages
from This Publication**

This book is printed on recycled, acid-free paper containing a minimum of 50 percent recycled de-inked fiber.

McGraw-Hill books are available at special quantity discounts to use as premiums and sales promotions, or for use in corporate training programs. For more information, please write to the Director of Special Sales, Professional Publishing, McGraw-Hill, Two Penn Plaza, New York, NY 10121-2298. Or contact your local bookstore.

CONTENTS

PART II: REPRODUCIBLE TOOLS FOR COACHING AND MANAGING EMPLOYEE PERFORMANCE

PART III: REPRODUCIBLE TOOLS FOR BUILDING COLLABORATION AND TEAMWORK

PART IV: REPRODUCIBLE TOOLS FOR FACILITATING PLANNING AND PROBLEM SOLVING

INTRODUCING THE ACTIVE MANAGER'S TOOL KIT

Do active managers outperform traditional managers? You bet they do. Let me tell you why.

Traditional managers are *reactive*. They wait for problems to occur and then try to put out the fires. In the meantime, they take care of "business as usual"—scheduling, assigning tasks, checking on employee activity, and writing reports. Their vision is also short-term. They focus on immediate results. In the worst of practices, they simply arrange to get rid of those employees that aren't cutting the mustard. Needless to say, these kinds of managers are becoming expendable when organizations need to downsize or embrace flatter, more team-based structures.

Nontraditional managers are *active*. They don't wait for problems, they anticipate them. They don't sit around merely watching what the troops are doing. Instead, they take care of "business as *un*usual"— developing their employees, both to do their current jobs as effectively as possible and to be in a position to do new jobs when change inevitably occurs. Active managers are indispensable to already great organizations and those that want to be.

Active managers are indeed "active," doing many things that the traditional managers gives scant attention to. They understand that inspiring and managing top performance is a continual process, not something left to the occasional event such as a performance review. They seek opportunities to empower their direct reports and encourage personal responsibility and self-initiative rather than simply telling people what to do and monitoring the outcome.

Active managers not only develop individual employees but also mobilize and coordinate teamwork. They appreciate that getting the job done is seldom the task of soloists, but the joint effort of the entire orchestra. Therefore, they take on the job of being team leaders who develop not just high performing individuals but high-performing teams.

Active managers are busy seeking information and obtaining data. This activity is not solely for the purpose of writing reports but to be close to the action, to understand the issues and concerns their charges are facing, and using that information to identify problems and to solve them.

Even in the training and coaching of employees, active managers take an active role. They don't leave it to others. In some cases, they partner with human resources and training professionals. In other instances, they lead staff development activities themselves, sensing that this involvement moves their relationship from being a boss to being a mentor. At the same time, active managers are intent on finding creative ways to express appreciation and praise good performance.

You might ask how any one manager can do it all. The key to being a successful active manager is being strategic and resourceful. The strategic part is establishing priorities—which activities will provide the most long-range payoff? This book will help you do that. It defines five arenas in which to allocate your energy. They are:

- Assessing and developing your own leadership skills
- Coaching and managing individual employee performance
- Building collaboration and teamwork
- Facilitating planning and problem-solving meetings
- Leading change

Look over the tools in each section and get a feel for the needs and issues they address. Use this information to guide your identification of what you need to address right away and what you can afford to put on the back burner for a while.

Once you decide on priorities, the task gets easier when the tools and resources to do these activities are located. It's silly to reinvent the wheel and develop everything on your own, from scratch. That's why this kit was created. With it, you have, at your fingertips, tools to make your job as active manager feasible.

For over 30 years, I have been a consultant who seeks to help others improve their current effectiveness and to facilitate change. I can't tell you how many times I wished that I could have at my fingertips a variety of tools, designed by expert consultants, that I could freely use to meet the needs of my clients. To expect such resources would have been unthinkable at a time when they were limited to proprietary use or would cost the user a small fortune. Times have changed. Many consultants view other consultants, such as myself, as their partners, not their competitors. Fortunately, I know a lot of them. And so, I have invited a talented and willing group of consultants to offer their tools to guide your efforts.

These include *questionnaires* that assess how well you are currently doing, *job aids* that help you to lead new initiatives, and step-by-step *exercises* that enable you to train your own teams.

Here's what you do. First, use the *questionnaires* to push and challenge yourself to take an honest look at what you believe, what you do, and what you accomplish.

Many of these instruments are ideal to utilize as input for team discussion. Your team can complete the instrument you have selected prior to or during your get-together. After completion, ask participants to score and interpret their own results. Then, have them compare outcomes with other teammates. Be careful, however, to stress that the data from these instruments are not "hard." They *suggest* rather than *demonstrate* facts about people or situations. Ask participants to compare scores to their own perceptions. If they do not match, urge them to consider why. Encourage your team to open themselves to new feedback and awareness.

Second, use the **job aids** as if you were reading advice from your own personal consultant. Highlight points that are important to you or push you to do further thinking. Reflect on the advice you're given and consider the tips that most apply to you and your situation. Above all, try them out. Experiment. That's what active managers do. They don't just do things the way they were told or the way they've always done them. They stretch their managerial muscles in new ways and become really flexible.

All of the job aids are formatted for quick, easily understood reading. (You may want to keep these handouts handy as memory joggers or checklists by posting them in your office.) Urge your people to be active consumers of these handouts, as well. You can also use them as reading assignments in team-building and staff-development sessions you might conduct.

Third, use the **exercises** as the basis for training activity to be shared with your team. All of these exercises are highly participatory. They are designed with the belief that learning and change best occur through experience and reflection. As opposed to preaching or lecturing, experiential activities place people directly within a concrete situation. Typically, participants are asked to solve a problem, complete an assignment, or communicate information. Often, the task can be quite challenging. Sometimes, it can also be a great deal of fun. The bottom line, however, is that participants become active partners in the learning of new concepts or in the development of new ideas.

The experiences contained in the activities are of two kinds: simulated and real-world. Well-designed simulations can provide an effective analogy to real-world experiences. They also have the advantage of being timesaving shortcuts to longer, drawn-out activities. Sometimes, of course, there is no substitute for real-world experience. Exercises that engage teams in actual, ongoing work can serve as a powerful mechanism for change.

All of the exercises have been written for ease of use. A concise overview of each exercise is provided. You will be guided, step-by-step, through the instructions. All of the necessary participant materials are included. For your photocopying convenience, these materials are on separate pages. Any materials you need to prepare in advance have been kept to a minimum. A special physical arrangement or piece of equipment is seldom needed.

So, you see that *The Active Manager's Tool Kit* is a book to be used and disseminated. Not only are you free to reproduce its contents without further permission but you can also download and customize important sections to be reprinted or e-mailed to the people with whom you work.

Be smart and courageous. Use these tools to give a professional touch to your performance as an active manager. You'll be recognized as a leader rather than a person mired "in the middle."

PART I

REPRODUCIBLE TOOLS FOR ASSESSING AND DEVELOPING YOUR LEADERSHIP SKILLS

1

HOW HIGH IS YOUR PEOPLE QUOTIENT (PQ)?

Mel Silberman

Overview   How smart are you with the people you manage?

Based on the book, *PeopleSmart: Developing Your Interpersonal Intelligence* (Berrett-Koehler, 2000), the PeopleSmart Rating Scale can be used to obtain an estimate of your interpersonal intelligence as a manager. Just like an IQ test, it is scaled so that the average score is 100. Because it is a self-test, however, your answers will be subjective. Therefore, the more honest you are when you take the test, the more accurate your PQ score will be. Also, your standards may be different from those of other readers. Use other managers you know as your benchmark. Finally, you might find it difficult to make an overall judgment of yourself at all times and with all people. For example, your PQ may be higher with some of your direct reports than with others. As you take the test, consider choosing two or three of your direct reports as your frame of reference.

Next, ask yourself how effective you are in your relationships with whomever you choose. Better yet, invite some of these people to give you their views about your PeopleSmart skills. Either ask them to rate you on the PeopleSmart Rating Scale, or ask them to look over the content of each skill and discuss their perceptions of your interpersonal effectiveness in each area. Whatever approach you use, you will find that focusing on a particular relationship is the best way to take stock of your PeopleSmart skills.

Contact Information: Mel Silberman, Active Training/PeopleSmart, 303 Sayre Drive, Princeton, NJ 08540, 609-987-8157, mel@activetraining.com, www.activetraining.com

PEOPLESMART RATING SCALE

PeopleSmart Skill 1: How would you rate your ability to understand people?

Excellent = 4, Good = 3, Fair = 2, Poor = 1

___ 1. I listen attentively to grasp what someone is thinking.
___ 2. I take notice of other people's body language to understand them better.
___ 3. To avoid misunderstanding, I ask questions that clarify what the speaker is saying.
___ 4. I am able to sense what another person is feeling.
___ 5. I can decipher the underlying reasons why people I know act the way they do.

Skill 1 score: _____

PeopleSmart Skill 2: How would you rate your ability to express your thoughts and feelings clearly?

Excellent = 4, Good = 3, Fair = 2, Poor = 1

___ 1. I give only enough detail so that I'm understood.
___ 2. People enjoy listening to me.
___ 3. I can take something complicated and explain it clearly.
___ 4. I say what I mean and what I feel.
___ 5. When I'm not clear, I let the other person ask questions rather than go on and on explaining myself.

Skill 2 score: _____

PeopleSmart Skill 3: How would you rate your ability to assert your needs?

Excellent = 4, Good = 3, Fair = 2, Poor = 1

___ 1. I am decisive about what I will do or not do for others.
___ 2. I speak up when my needs are not being met.
___ 3. I keep calm and remain confident when I get opposition.
___ 4. I stand my ground.
___ 5. I can say no with grace and tact.

Skill 3 score: _____

PEOPLESMART RATING SCALE (CONT.)

PeopleSmart Skill 4: How would you rate your ability to exchange feedback?

Excellent = 4, Good = 3, Fair = 2, Poor = 1

___ 1. I give appreciation and compliments freely.
___ 2. When I criticize people, I offer suggestions for improvement.
___ 3. To get different perspectives, I ask for feedback from a wide range of people.
___ 4. I ask others for feedback to improve myself, not to fish for compliments.
___ 5. I listen to feedback I receive from others.

Skill 4 score: ___

PeopleSmart Skill 5: How would you rate your ability to influence how others think and act?

Excellent = 4, Good = 3, Fair = 2, Poor = 1

___ 1. I establish rapport with people before trying to persuade them to do something.
___ 2. I explore other people's viewpoints before trying to convince them of my own.
___ 3. I give compelling reasons for adopting my viewpoint.
___ 4. People are not defensive when I give advice.
___ 5. I give people time to mull over what I've presented to them.

Skill 5 score: ___

PeopleSmart Skill 6: How would you rate your ability to get conflict resolved?

Excellent = 4, Good = 3, Fair = 2, Poor = 1

___ 1. I get the tensions between the other person and me out on the table.
___ 2. Right from the start, I seek agreement over victory.
___ 3. I learn all I can about the other person's needs and interests when negotiating.
___ 4. I work to solve problems, not blame others, when we hit a stone wall.
___ 5. When I reach an agreement with someone, I make sure we both stick to it.

Skill 6 score: ___

PEOPLESMART RATING SCALE (CONT.)

PeopleSmart Skill 7: How would you rate your ability to collaborate with others?

Excellent = 4, Good = 3, Fair = 2, Poor = 1

___ 1. I request help from others and give them assistance in return.
___ 2. I pitch in when the group needs something done.
___ 3. I focus on other people's welfare as much as my own.
___ 4. I keep others informed about what I'm doing if it affects them.
___ 5. I help to facilitate and coordinate the efforts of others.

Skill 7 score: ____

PeopleSmart Skill 8: How would you rate your ability to shift gears?

Excellent = 4, Good = 3, Fair = 2, Poor = 1

___ 1. When a relationship is not going well, I take the initiative to do something about it.
___ 2. I can see the patterns I fall into with other people.
___ 3. Even if I'm not at fault, I am open to making significant changes in my behavior when necessary.
___ 4. I am willing to take risks when they are called for.
___ 5. I am resilient. If things don't work out, I bounce back.

Skill 8 score: ____

Your People Quotient [the sum of each individual skill score]: ____

Interpreting Your Scores

Look over your own scores for each PeopleSmart Skill and the feedback you receive from other people. Identify some skills where you are less effective than others. (Interpret a score of 10 or lower on any one skill as an indication that you have a lot of work to do.)

If your overall PQ rating is over 150, you have superior PeopleSmart intelligence. Keep it up! A score between 125 and 150 indicates that you have very good PeopleSmart skills, but you should keep working on them. If you scored between 100 and 125, your PeopleSmart skills need some improvement. Remember, the scale is designed for 100 to be average or typical. A score under 100 suggests that you need considerable improvement.

2

HOW DO YOU RATE AS A LEADER?

Joan Cassidy

Overview As organizations embrace the notions of empowerment and team building, they must also stress the need for better leadership. Some individuals need a structured, controlled environment with continuous feedback to feel secure and to be productive. Others need a flexible, open, creative environment with little or no supervision. Successful leaders recognize these differences in themselves and others and then learn to adjust to optimize the performance of all individuals. The question is, "How do you determine your own leadership competencies?"

This 360° instrument identifies 20 characteristics or competencies attributed to successful leaders. It is important to recognize that not everyone will be exceptional or even very good in all 20. Based on their own innate qualities and preferences, most individuals feel more comfortable engaging in some activities, and prefer to avoid others. On the other hand, highly successful leaders understand their own strengths and weaknesses. They engage in developmental activities and also supplement and complement their weaknesses by drawing on others. This instrument helps individuals to determine their strengths and weaknesses as well as the relevance of those strengths and weaknesses to current and future leadership roles. It also helps them develop an action plan for improvement.

Contact Information: Joan Cassidy, Integrated Leadership Concepts, Inc., 901 Nanticoke Run Way, Odenton, MD 21113, 410-672-5467, DrJoanC@aol.com, www.DrJoanCassidy.com

360° LEADERSHIP DEVELOPMENT ASSESSMENT INSTRUMENT

Name of person being rated: _____

Name of person doing the rating: _____ **Date:** _____

Following are 20 competencies that represent knowledge, skills, abilities, and attitudes of successful leaders. Please read the description of each competency and then rate the individual identified above, using the following key:

5 = Exceptional; 4 = Very Good; 3 = Good; 2 = Needs Improvement; 1 = Very Weak

___ 1. **Creating a Vision and Setting Goals.** Without clear goals, followers perceive their work to have less purpose and impact and are less inclined to participate. A good leader has a clear vision about what needs to be accomplished and is able to set realistic goals to achieve that vision.

___ 2. **Explaining and Communicating Expectations.** Employees want to know and understand expectations for individual and group performance. Without these expectations, feedback is not as meaningful as it could be, making it difficult for individuals or a group to achieve goals and successes. Good leaders are clear about reporting relationships, and they establish evaluation criteria that are fair and appropriate.

___ 3. **Written Communication.** The successful leader writes clearly and concisely at the level needed by the person(s) receiving the information. In other words, the leader writes to *express*, not *impress*.

___ 4. **Oral Communication.** Good leaders inform others about what is going on and why. The leader engages in frank discussion about issues and how those issues affect individuals, and structures meetings to provide for needed dialogue.

___ 5. **Personal Integrity.** Personal integrity is becoming more and more an issue in the workplace. Good leaders demonstrate and model integrity in day-to-day interactions by:
  • establishing a relationship of trust;
  • being honest (even if it means making a different decision than the one recommended);
  • treating everyone fairly;
  • delivering on promises and meeting commitments;
  • placing personal needs (ego) in second place to needs of the overall group; and
  • admitting mistakes and accepting constructive criticism.

360° LEADERSHIP DEVELOPMENT ASSESSMENT INSTRUMENT (CONT.)

___ 6. **Creativity and Experimentation.** Great leaders value and establish an organizational climate built on trust and openness in order to ensure that creativity and new ideas flourish. Leaders encourage others to experiment and learn from mistakes, without fear of retribution. They are known for their out-of-the-box thinking.

___ 7. **Nurturing.** Good leaders demonstrate that they care about and are interested in others' individual growth by:
- noticing the work and accomplishments of the individual as a person;
- exhibiting understanding and empathy for a variety of personality types;
- saying "thank you" for a job well done;
- caring about individuals' personal and professional growth; and
- seeking input on decisions that others will be affected by.

___ 8. **Decisiveness.** Leaders make decisions in a timely and effective manner and explain the basis for their decisions. Ideal leaders base decisions on facts and priorities, rather than trying to please everyone. They know when to seek consensus as part of the decision-making process.

___ 9. **Making Appropriate Interventions.** Leaders must trust subordinates. Good leaders know when to leave a subordinate or team member alone to get the job done and when to make an intervention to resolve issues that are beyond the subordinate's or team member's span of control.

___10. **Active Listening.** Good leaders are available, attentive, unbiased, and responsive. They recognize the need to allow input as well as to follow up on the input given. Good leaders are open-minded and encourage other points of view. They frequently paraphrase what is being said to ensure that they understand the speaker's point.

___11. **Assertiveness.** Most people will acknowledge that the leader's role is not an easy one, especially in dealing with conflict. Conflict is a daily occurrence in the workplace. Good leaders understand that personality and other work conflicts do not go away, that they typically get worse if not addressed. Thus, leaders deal with conflict in a timely, straightforward manner. They are assertive and honest with all parties in dealing with any type of conflict.

___12. **Delegating.** The ability to delegate effectively and focus on performance and results is a key element of leadership. Leaders demonstrate trust by delegating authority along with responsibility. However, the leader must know subordinates and their capabilities in order to delegate effectively. Good leaders understand that effective delegation enhances team members' and subordinates' skills and ultimately leads to a higher success rate.

____13. **Fostering Team Building.** The best leaders are known for promoting team efforts. They recognize and reward individuals for outstanding performance. However, they work to minimize and eliminate harmful competitiveness that may undermine the team. Leaders continuously discourage we–they attitudes.

____14. **Acting as an Advocate.** Leaders are expected to be the "point persons" and to be responsible to the needs of the team. They have a dual loyalty, to team members as well as to others, particularly upper management. Leaders are advocates not only for an individual, but also for the team, the department, and the organization as a whole.

____15. **Appraisal and Feedback.** Good leaders are knowledgeable about what is required to get the job done and who is doing it. They engage in "management by walking around" to learn about work status. They also solicit input from internal as well as external customers concerning satisfaction. They use this data to provide appropriate and timely feedback to everyone concerned. Good leaders also distinguish between good and poor work and take the appropriate action (e.g., reward or recognition for good performance; coaching or corrective action for poor performance).

____16. **Coaching.** An ideal leader spends considerable time in devising professional development guidance for staff. The leader engages in the following types of activities, as appropriate:
- Tell the purpose and importance of the activity.
- Explain the process to be used (or allow freedom to design one).
- Show how it is done, completely and accurately (if it must be done a specific way).
- Ask whether the person has any questions and clarify if necessary.
- Observe while the person engages in the process.
- Provide immediate and specific feedback (coach again or reinforce success).
- Express confidence in the person's ability to be successful.
- Agree on follow-up action(s) as necessary.

____17. **Learning.** The ideal leader is a lifelong learner who:
- is open to change;
- engages others in problem solving;
- views ideas from different perspectives;
- experiments and learns from mistakes;
- continues to build his or her own skills as well as the skills of staff members.

___18. **Mediating.** Leaders must be able to mediate problems between people fairly. Ideal leaders are assertive in using mediation skills when warranted. However, the leader does not take sides, but keeps an open mind, gathers all the information in a thorough manner, and makes decisions based on facts.

___19. **Dealing with Critics.** Every leader gains some critics. Successful leaders, however, do not tear others down in public. They remain objective. They learn to distinguish between those who are attempting to provide constructive advice and those who have more selfish agendas. They then take the appropriate steps to deal with the situation.

___20. **Technical Competence.** Leaders are expected to have technical competence. This does not mean that they can do the actual work better than their team members. Rather, it means that they have a basic understanding of what is required and can make informed decisions.

SCORING INTERPRETATION

1. Use the attached **Individual Feedback Analysis Worksheet**. Collect the assessments, record the results, and compare the ratings (i.e., self versus others). Is there congruence? How varied are the results? Try to understand these differences. Congratulate yourself on any 4s or 5s! Make a note to continue engaging in these successful activities.

2. Next, concentrate on any 1s and 2s. For example, who rated you as a 1 or 2? Prioritize the 1s and 2s in terms of relevance to what you currently do or aspire to do.

3. Seek out the individual(s) who rated you as a 1 or 2 and discuss the rating. Ask for **specific** feedback (i.e., why they think you are a 1 or 2). Next ask for **specific** strategies or actions that you might take to improve. If you gave yourself a 1 or a 2, discuss with others how you might improve.

4. Focus on one to three of the relevant competencies that are in most need of improvement. Develop an action plan that includes the competency, an improvement goal, strategy, or action for improvement, resources needed, time frame, and method of evaluation. (See the **Individual Action Plan Worksheet** for suggestions.)

5. Share your strategies and action plan with those who rated you and ask for their continuing support. Set up a tickler system to periodically elicit feedback (e.g., about once every six months). Reward yourself each time you reach an important milestone!

360° LEADERSHIP DEVELOPMENT ASSESSMENT INSTRUMENT

INDIVIDUAL FEEDBACK ANALYSIS WORKSHEET

Name of Person Being Rated: _____ **Date:** _____

Insert numerical rating from each of the Raters*

Competency	Raters' Scores				Notes
	1	2	3	4	
1. Creating a Vision and Setting Goals					
2. Explaining and Communicating Expectations					
3. Written Communication					
4. Oral Communication					
5. Personal Integrity					
6. Creativity and Experimentation					
7. Nurturing					
8. Decisiveness					
9. Making Appropriate Interventions					
10. Active Listening					
11. Assertiveness					
12. Delegating					
13. Fostering Team Building					
14. Acting as an Advocate					
15. Appraisal and Feedback					
16. Coaching					
17. Learning					
18. Mediating					
19. Dealing with Critics					
20. Technical Competence					

* Raters:

1. _____ 3. _____

2. _____ 4. _____

360° LEADERSHIP DEVELOPMENT ASSESSMENT INSTRUMENT (CONT.)

Individual Action Plan Worksheet

Name: _____ **Date:** _____

It is important that you use a systematic process to ensure that you reach your improvement goal(s). After you have completed your Individual Feedback Analysis Worksheet, select one, two, or three competencies to work on. Use one sheet for each competency. Share your plans with others and encourage them to help you reach your desired goals.

Competency: _____
(Identify the competency that you need to work on.)

Goal for Improvement: _____

_____

(Be as specific as possible about what you want to improve.)

Strategies or Actions to Take for Improvement:
(Identify several strategies or actions you will take. To the extent possible, answer: Who, What, When, Where, How, and Why. This will help you to focus on resources that might be needed. Note: It is perfectly acceptable to delegate certain competencies that a subordinate may perform better than you. However, you need to be clear about what you are doing and why.)

_____

_____

_____

_____

Resources Needed: _____

Begin By: _____ **Target Completion Date:** _____

Evaluation: _____
(What data will you collect? From whom? When? How? What are significant milestones?)

_____

_____

_____

3

HOW DO YOU EMPOWER YOUR EMPLOYEES?

Gaylord Reagan

Overview People working in today's complex, bureaucratic organizations often feel manipulated, cautious, and vulnerable. In order to help themselves feel more in control, these same people use favored influence strategies to get what they want from others. Unfortunately, when used in this manner these strategies actually mark the actors' dependency and weakness. The Empowerment Patterns Inventory that follows will help you identify your favored patterns, and then learn to use them in an authentic manner.

EMPOWERMENT

Human beings are driven to satisfy a variety of needs. We eat to satisfy our hunger and drink to satisfy our thirst. We rest to overcome fatigue. On the interpersonal side, we assert our autonomy and individuality by demonstrating favored patterns of empowerment behavior. Just as our food and drink preferences say certain things about us, our favorite empowerment pattern (or strength) tells others about who we are and what our possible contributions might be.

Consultant Peter Block contends that we are acting in an empowered manner only when we use our favorite pattern purely for its own sake, not because of its impact on other people or as a way of getting what we want. On the other hand, when we use our pattern as a means to seek a reward or manipulate others, then we are not behaving like empowered people. Used in the latter manner, Block contends that our pattern actually marks our dependence and lack of empowerment. In other words, we are not satisfying our needs for autonomy and indi-

Contact Information: Gaylord Reagan, Reagan Consulting, 5306 North 105th Plaza, #9, Omaha, NE 68134, 402-431-0279, greagan@attglobal.net

viduality. This disappointing outcome is produced whenever we allow other people's actions to define our own.

In contrast to the situational models favored by training and development professionals, Block calls on his readers to avoid adapting their preferred patterns to the demands of particular situations. Instead, he urges people to be authentic and courageous as they assert their independence and take reasonable risks. Contrary to what a surface reading might suggest, Block's nonsituational model doesn't ask people to commit career suicide or to be uncooperative and inflexible. Instead, we are challenged to be authentic and courageous as we walk along the path of true empowerment. We need to speak our minds, own our part of the problem, confront harsh realities facing us, avoid "I" illusions, offer no excuses, and say what needs to be said to those who need to hear it. In this way, empowered people signal their unwillingness to become entangled in politically charged bureaucratic cycles.

Attempts to change our favorite pattern usually fail, since our effort represents what Block refers to as "a futile attempt to change what is unique about us." Instead, we should focus on learning to use our favorite pattern for its own sake, not for effect or out of mere habit. Managers and employees seeking to strengthen their sense of empowerment should first identify the patterns they prefer, and then examine the manner in which they use them.

THE EMPOWERMENT PATTERNS INVENTORY

Instructions: In each of the five groups below, write an 8 on the line preceding the sentence that best describes you. Then write a 1 on the line preceding the sentence that least accurately describes you. Finally, write the numbers 2 through 7 on the appropriate lines within each cluster. Do not leave any lines blank, and do not use any number more than once.

Group 1

_____ 1. I am very sensitive to other peoples' discomfort.

_____ 2. I have high standards, and make sure that everyone knows about them.

_____ 3. I often smile even when I may not feel like doing so.

_____ 4. I have a somewhat blank face that doesn't betray my feelings.

_____ 5. Other people say that my clothes are unusual.

_____ 6. I have lots of battle scars and bruises.

_____ 7. My desk is piled high with papers, but they are all neatly stacked.

_____ 8. I am very successful.

Group 2

_____ 9. I am willing to postpone getting what I want.

_____ 10. Other people often describe me as being an overachiever.

_____ 11. I usually nod when other people are speaking.

_____ 12. I am usually very quiet or even silent in meetings.

_____ 13. My personal style makes me fun to be around.

_____ 14. My communication is energetic and easy to understand.

_____ 15. I tend to be very respectful toward people in positions of authority.

_____ 16. Someday, I would like to be a teacher.

Group 3

_____ 17. I believe that my reward may not come until my next job.

_____ 18. I quietly judge other people who don't meet my standards.

_____ 19. I often use humor to connect with other people at work.

_____ 20. I believe in minimal sharing of information.

_____ 21. When it comes to meetings, I'm the last to arrive and the first to leave.

_____ 22. I don't like evaluating others peoples' performance.

_____ 23. My pictures frequently show me wearing dress clothing.

_____ 24. I generally arrive early at meetings.

THE EMPOWERMENT PATTERNS INVENTORY (CONT.)

Group 4

____ 25. If I help others with their problems, I believe that they will then give me what I need.

____ 26. I like my clothes to be color coordinated, so that mismatching is impossible.

____ 27. My main concern is to be like the person who supervises me at work.

____ 28. I use very little humor at work.

____ 29. I am technically bright, and have enough talent to survive problems.

____ 30. Any kind of "touchy-feely" stuff makes me very uncomfortable.

____ 31. I like lots of order and structure in my life.

____ 32. I have an elaborate filing system for my office.

Group 5

____ 33. Other people are somewhat fragile, and they often need me to rescue them.

____ 34. I want everything around me (desk, clothes, car, home) to be kept clean.

____ 35. I never make strong, explicit demands to get what I want.

____ 36. I try to avoid offending other people.

____ 37. I prefer to be my own person.

____ 38. Other people generally know exactly where I stand.

____ 39. I believe that being formal and polite is a way of showing sensitivity toward others.

____ 40. I like subjects like math, accounting, and engineering.

SCORING

1. Using the scoring grid below, record the number that you assigned to each sentence.

2. Calculate the total for each of the eight groups of five questions. Your score for each group can be no lower than five and no higher than thirty-five.

3. Finally, identify which group of questions, or pattern, received your highest total and which received the lowest. In many cases your totals will indicate your preference for, or lack of use of, more than one pattern.

Scoring Grid							
1.	2.	3.	4.	5.	6.	7.	8.
9.	10.	11.	12.	13.	14.	15.	16.
17.	18.	19.	20.	21.	22.	23.	24.
25.	26.	27.	28.	29.	30.	31.	32.
33.	34.	35.	36.	37.	38.	39.	40.
Pattern A	Pattern B	Pattern C	Pattern D	Pattern E	Pattern F	Pattern G	Pattern H

My most preferred pattern is: _____

My least preferred pattern is: _____

INTERPRETING YOUR RESULTS

1. Notice which of the eight patterns above received your highest total. This is the pattern that you prefer to use. Given your preference for this pattern, it is also the one that you are most in danger of using in inappropriate settings. In this sense, your strength can become your area of vulnerability.
2. Next, notice which of the eight patterns received your lowest total. This is the pattern that you use least frequently. Since this pattern isn't included in your normal repertoire, situations that are best handled by using this approach will pose a difficult challenge for you to overcome. In this sense, you have a blind spot in this area.
3. Finally, take a few moments to read the brief description of each pattern.

Pattern A: Lifesaver

People who favor this pattern find that for them getting what they want is simply a matter of saving other people. If they help other people resolve their problems, then those people will see that the *Lifesaver* gets what he or she wants—a classic quid pro quo approach. Of course, this means that *Lifesavers* must perceive themselves as being slightly superior to the people they save. It also means that in order for *Lifesavers* to feel empowered they first need a constant supply of people to save. If the person being rescued doesn't demonstrate an appropriate level of gratitude, then the *Lifesaver* must deal with a resulting sense of disappointment and cynicism: "After all I did for them, this is how they thank me!?"

Pattern B: Precisionist

People who favor this pattern believe that if they appear to be free of all faults, then they will get what they want from other people. Being perfect, behaving correctly, meeting all goals, being respectful toward authority figures, presenting a flawless appearance, making no mistakes, and being the perfect employee combine to mark the path to entitlement. This pattern makes it difficult for others to find fault with the people who use it, thereby disempowering those who may potentially pose a threat. Unfortunately, the pattern also makes it difficult for *Precisionists* to learn from their mistakes, since they don't make any.

Pattern C: Delighter

People who favor this pattern get what they want from other people by making them happy. Smiling a lot, being quick to apologize, behaving pleasantly, using humor, fitting in, using good interpersonal skills, always being positive, and adopting a compatible appearance are all means to the end of empowering the *Delighter*. On the other hand, this pattern requires its adherents to deny natural feelings such as conceit, arrogance, anger, and contempt. It can also lead *Delighters* to feel that they give something to others that others don't give in return.

INTERPRETING YOUR RESULTS (CONT.)

Pattern D: Distancer

People who favor this pattern perceive threats all around them. Bosses expect the impossible, jobs are downsized, employers are taken over by larger organizations, and interpersonal relationships exert a variety of pressures. *Distancers* feel that in order to survive and get what they want, they need to distance themselves from conflict and spend time alone so that they simply disappear from others' radar screens: If they can't see me, then they can't harm me. While using this pattern does lower one's profile, it also frustrates the human need to experience intimacy and a sense of connectedness with other people.

Pattern E: Mutineer

People who favor this pattern get what they want by rebelling against authority, rules, norms, and structure imposed by others around them. They create their own rules, and proclaim their freedom and independence. They are drawn to conflict and disagreement, and love to argue with other people. However, beneath their contentious surface *Mutineers* are dependent on others to impose rules and structure on them since those efforts give rebels something to react against. The *Mutineer* pattern attempts to deny the normal human need to receive approval from others and commit to something outside of oneself.

Pattern F: Attacker

People who favor the *Attacker* pattern believe that only the strong survive and get what they want, hence they pursue power. *Attackers* fear that at the deepest level nothing is really worth holding onto. As a result they continually drive themselves to gain control over new and unfamiliar things. In a sense, they are trying to fill an emptiness within themselves that cannot be filled. This pattern can produce a profound level of personal isolation since it attempts to deny the wish many people have to be dependent and controlled—to "escape from freedom," as Erich Fromm put it.

Pattern G: Bureaucrat

People who favor this pattern are drawn to rules, policies, structure, and order. They avoid conflict and are polite, respectful, and interpersonally distant. Their exacting approach demonstrates the bureaucrat's objectivity, detachment, precision, and impartiality. *Bureaucrats* get what they want by being hyper-aware of the rules imposed by others, which they strictly and faithfully observe. This pattern attempts to deny the confusion and chaos surrounding *Bureaucrats*, and produces a loss of passion, excitement, active commitment, willingness to change, and love.

Pattern H: Intellectual

People who favor this pattern prefer a "hard" world composed of complex ideas, abstractions, logic, theoretical models, designs, data sets, and research studies. They turn away from "soft" areas such as intuition, feelings, emotions, and subjectivity. This pattern helps *Intellectuals* get what they want by making it difficult for others to prove them wrong. It also ignores the emotional side of other people, thereby making it difficult for the patterns' adherents to make intimate connections with other people.

ACTION PLANNING

What should I know about using empowerment patterns?

Block contends that we truly act in an empowered manner only when we choose the empowerment pattern that we use in a given situation, and do so without using that pattern purely as a means to get what we want. We must also be careful to not allow other people's actions to trigger our actions, since doing that is a sure sign of our nonempowered state. When we consciously *choose* our empowerment pattern for its own sake, and do so in a way that is not a reaction to someone else's actions, then we are well on the way to empowering ourselves.

Some people feel uneasy about empowerment, since they interpret it as possibly hindering team effectiveness. From this perspective, empowered team members view themselves as being autonomous and are not able to subordinate their perceived individualism to the needs of the group. Block believes that this fear is misplaced. When people join a team because they fear that they cannot succeed on their own, he notes, that severely undermines the team's potential success. Simply put, a team composed of dependent members is a weak team. In contrast, empowered team members come together feeling strong and carry out their assigned tasks in a corresponding manner. A strong team has strong individual members.

On the other hand, Block cautions, there are times in our work lives when we are appropriately dependent. These include such normal activities as soliciting information about the basics of our business; asking for feedback from our bosses, customers, and colleagues; establishing a sense of connectedness with our coworkers; and establishing relationships with high-level benefactors or mentors. In these and other similar instances, it is appropriate for us to allow others' input and wishes to shape our thinking and behavior.

Finally, Block discusses three "acts of courage" that can help empowered people act courageously and with compassion instead of indulging themselves with aggressive, rebellious, or uncooperative behavior:

1. See things as they really are. Avoid making excuses, offering explanations, or pursuing illusions. It takes too much energy to feel crazy, weak, and powerless.

2. Own your contribution to the problem. The only thing we can control is our actions. Blaming others for our problems simply makes us feel helpless, and solves nothing.

3. Put into words what you see happening, and say what needs to be said to those who need to hear it.

23

ACTION PLANNING (CONT.)

How do I put what I learned here into practice?

1. What is your preferred empowerment pattern? How do you use that pattern: for its own sake, or as a means to get what you want from other people?

2. Are you satisfied with the way in which you use your preferred pattern? If so, how can you build on your success? If not, how can you improve the way in which you use the pattern?

3. What empowerment pattern appears to get the best results in your organization? Which appears to work least well? In both cases, why? What does your answer tell you about your organization?

4. What challenges will you have to overcome in implementing Block's model of authentic empowerment in your organization? How will you go about overcoming these challenges?

5. Is your preferred empowerment pattern the same in work and non-work settings? What differences can you see in the patterns that you use in these two settings? Does either pattern feel more natural to you when you are using it?

4

WHAT IS YOUR LEADERSHIP STYLE?

Deborah Hopen and Laura Gregg

Overview The leader role requires a diverse set of skills. No individual is naturally skilled in all of the required areas, so it's a good idea to assess your strengths and develop an improvement plan. This exercise will help you identify your interests and talents.

The Leadership Style Self-Assessment lists 16 characteristics that are generally considered desirable for leaders. The list comes from *Management Audits* by Allan J. Sayle. For each characteristic, the authors show statements that describe how you might respond in different situations. The choices range between two possible behaviors. The statement on the left more closely matches the dictionary definition of the behavior associated with that characteristic.

As you complete the assessment, think about each description and develop specific criteria for determining when it would be appropriate to exhibit the behavior described by the statement on the left and when it would be appropriate to exhibit the behavior described by the statement on the right.

The interpretations were developed by the authors after discussions with representative people who lead at different levels in a variety of organizations.

Contact Information: Deborah Hopen, 1911 S.W. Campus Dr. #764, Federal Way, WA 98023, 253-927-6668, debhopen@aol.com

Laura Gregg, 10445 NE 15th Street, Bellevue, WA 98004, 425-453-7210, wizel-jay@aol.com

LEADERSHIP STYLE
SELF-ASSESSMENT

Look over each of the following statements carefully. Which point on the scale best reflects your day-to-day behaviors and beliefs about leadership? There are no "right" answers to this questionnaire, so don't put down answers you think are best. Be prepared to share situations in which each end of the continuum applies.

1. I usually make decisions based on

facts and data	❶	❷	❸	❹	❺	feelings and opinions

2. To meet a specific objective, I believe that it's best to

be open to a variety of processes	❶	❷	❸	❹	❺	rely on a standardized process

3. When I encounter a setback, I usually

focus my attention on finding alternatives	❶	❷	❸	❹	❺	shift my attention to a more fruitful area

4. When making a point, I intend for my words to

improve the relationship	❶	❷	❸	❹	❺	improve the outcome

5. When I am faced with goals and deadlines, I believe it's more important to

keep on schedule and follow the plan	❶	❷	❸	❹	❺	sense the environment and make necessary adjustments

6. Other people would characterize my style during tense situations as

restrained	❶	❷	❸	❹	❺	expressive

LEADERSHIP STYLE
SELF-ASSESSMENT (CONT.)

7. I believe that my communications should be candid and forthright

regardless of the situation	❶	❷	❸	❹	❺	unless the situation will generate conflict or hurt relationships

8. When listening attentively to another person, I usually

disregard time	❶	❷	❸	❹	❺	keep an eye on the time

9. I get to know new contacts

quickly by "stepping into their shoes"	❶	❷	❸	❹	❺	steadily by "building the castle one brick at a time"

10. When I'm trying to learn about a new topic, I'm more inclined to

diligently gather details, tolerate delays, and build a complete picture	❶	❷	❸	❹	❺	quickly gather information, plow through delays, and extrapolate my findings

11. Those who work with me would say that I'm

always at work, like the "busy beaver"	❶	❷	❸	❹	❺	a deep thinker, like the "wise owl"

12. I'd like to be remembered as

a specialist—a person who mastered the concepts and tools in my field	❶	❷	❸	❹	❺	a generalist—a person who integrated the concepts and tools from many fields

LEADERSHIP STYLE
SELF-ASSESSMENT (CONT.)

13. Learning new subjects is worth my time if I believe that I'll be able to

increase my overall knowledge	❶	❷	❸	❹	❺	apply the information in the near future

14. It's natural for me to

be curious and ask a lot of questions	❶	❷	❸	❹	❺	be circumspect and listen for information

15. Give me some information and I'll

break it down to find its essential features	❶	❷	❸	❹	❺	pull it together to find its essential self

16. When I speak, my "umm..." factor is

less than 10%—I've always got words on the tip of my tongue	❶	❷	❸	❹	❺	over 10%—I sometimes have to pull my words together as I speak

17. My language arts skills, such as public speaking and writing, are

fine-honed; I take great pleasure in using the best words in well-structured sentences	❶	❷	❸	❹	❺	competent—I focus on making my point

18. Fairness and equality can be achieved most easily by

the consistent application of rules and guidelines	❶	❷	❸	❹	❺	careful analysis of the situation and application of customized solutions

SCORING THE LEADERSHIP STYLE SELF-ASSESSMENT

Count the number of times you selected each of the following ratings.				
❶	❷	❸	❹	❺

Use the following key to match the statements with desirable characteristics for leaders.				
Characteristic	**Statement(s)**		**Characteristic**	**Statement(s)**
Good judgment	1		Patient	10
Open-minded	2		Industrious	11
Resilient	3		Professional	12
Diplomatic	4		Interested	13
Self-disciplined	5 and 6		Inquiring mind	14
Honest	7		Analytical	15
Good listening	8		Articulate	16 and 17
Relational	9		Egalitarian	18

INTERPRETING THE LEADERSHIP STYLE
SELF-ASSESSMENT

Good Judgment

A key tenet of leadership is that decisions are based on facts and data, which help you improve your judgment. Under normal circumstances and whenever possible, you should rely on observable, objective evidence.

You may on occasion, however, need to tap into your feelings and opinions to help you interpret your observations. Almost every decision made in life is based on comparisons to other circumstances you have encountered previously. Opinions and the feelings associated with specific situations are based on these earlier experiences.

Open-Minded

Leaders need to be open to a variety of processes, or they become too prescriptive. This is particularly true when they are pressed to accomplish goals in different locations or work groups within a short time.

On the other hand, it's usually a good idea for some processes to be standardized within a particular location and, if possible, between different locations of the same work group. In this case, if you observe variations, you may want to point them out without insisting that all the processes be conducted in the same way. Remember, there often is more than one road that will get you to your intended destination!

Resilient

When a leader is unable to gather the necessary information to determine performance in a particular area, he or she will usually search for alternative sources of data.

Time management may become an issue if the leader spends too much effort trying to track down information about one of many processes. That's why leaders frequently seem to be jumping from one area of investigation to another. You might think of this as the best combination of both approaches.

Diplomatic

Words are powerful tools for building relationships and achieving outcomes. All too often, words are chosen without thoughtful consideration of their potential effect.

When acting in a leadership role, maintaining and improving the relationships are key concerns. That's why it's better to suggest than to demand. That's also why when an associate irritates you, you need to ask yourself if silence or confrontation will most effectively achieve the goal *and* build the relationship.

If diplomacy will put the success of the work at risk, however, you need to choose careful words that will assert your requirements without damaging the relationship.

Self-Disciplined
Keeping on schedule and following the action plan are critical requirements for successful leaders. These outcomes require a great deal of discipline because it's easy to become distracted and get off track.

Being too pushy is not a good idea, though. To build relationships, you must show care and concern for each associate's situation—everyone knows that Murphy's law is a reality of life. This means that you may have to adjust your action plan on occasion, but you should do this without sacrificing the quality of the desired outcome.

Responding to conflict also requires self-discipline. All too often, the natural tendency is to become quite verbal and to accent one's opinions with strong body language. This rarely will be effective for leaders unless they are being physically harassed.

Restraint allows you to remain in control. When you become too expressive or agitated, the other person gains control. Leaders really want to control the process without being autocratic.

Honest
Honesty is always the best policy. There are many situations, however, in which silence is golden! That is really the choice you must make. Nit-picking and wordsmithing are very counterproductive behaviors.

Never lie. If asked a direct question that has an unpleasant answer, choose your words carefully but speak the truth. If the goal truly will be at risk if you don't mention your concerns, bring them up for discussion—but set the stage by emphasizing that you are confident your associate has a good reason for the existing situation or is unaware of its importance to you.

Good Listening
Although questioning and listening are the two primary skills of successful leaders, neither can be done without a focus on time. Most work efforts require that much be accomplished in a short period. Time pressure sometimes causes leaders to be abrupt or to convey a subliminal message that the associate's input is not valued or necessary, which can hurt relationships and hinder progress toward your goals.

Relational
You have all met the person who approaches you directly, begins to talk with you in a comfortable way, and makes you feel as if you've been friendly acquaintances for years. To an associate who is struggling with

his or her assignment, this may convert fear and trepidation to comfort and sharing.

You've also met people who are more aloof when they meet strangers. They start by discussing the weather, moving into more serious subjects slowly over time. Although well-intentioned, this can leave the impression that you are withholding comment or are dissatisfied, which can increase the other person's anxiety about the situation. If you're not naturally outgoing, work with a trusted peer to practice warm introductions and questioning styles.

Patient

Patience is a virtue in almost every job, and leadership is no exception. Under normal conditions, you should remember that "slow and steady" wins the race. Certainly, you should be able to explain your decisions by showing solid facts and data that support them most of the time.

Occasionally, however, you may be forced to move forward with insufficient information and to extrapolate findings. In this case, you always should note that you have less confidence in your findings and explain why you took this approach.

Industrious

There's no doubt that leadership is a high-activity task. Sometimes you will feel like the "busy beaver" or a hamster on the treadmill. It's important that you stop on a regular basis to assimilate your findings, develop hypotheses, and determine what additional information you need to collect.

Professional

The word "professional" and the concept of "professionalism" are changing. Today businesses are encouraging employees to increase scope and take over more generalized job tasks. This increases flexibility for the organization and enriches the job for the employee.

Leaders, however, must be knowledgeable about any process they are evaluating. This is clearly more of a specialist's task. This demand for expertise is one of the reasons that leadership teams are more effective than individual leaders—they make it possible for each person to investigate a few processes for which he or she has more in-depth knowledge and experience.

Interested

It's tough to be a good leader if you're not naturally curious! If you can consider your mind to be a database, the processes and approaches you observe can be archived for permanent use. What you learn today may be invaluable to you under the same or a different circumstance years later.

This is quite different from the "just in time" approach to learning, which relies on the concept of "use it or lose it." Although much of what you observe will be useful for evaluating a given process, you should not ignore any information because it isn't relevant to the current situation—it usually will come in handy in the future!

Inquiring Mind

This characteristic usually brings a chuckle because of the famous (or infamous, depending on how you look at these things) advertising associated with the phrase! As described above, curiosity and a zest for learning are great attributes for leaders.

There are two exceptions, however. First, never let your interest make your mouth start moving when your ears should be listening. Second, never listen to gossip or ask about confidential personal information.

Analytical

To maximize trust and increase the effectiveness of your leadership, you need to focus on learning whatever process you are evaluating. This may require you to rise above more mundane details and to accept some work procedures without a thorough analysis. For example, if all the lower-level procedures seem to work together effectively, you might not need to stop to investigate them individually.

In many ways, this leaves the impression that you are trying to understand the approach, rather than to pick it apart. For leaders who are naturally analytical this may be quite difficult. In the end, there must be an appropriate balance between being sure that the parts do fit together well and being sure that the outcomes are being achieved as desired.

Articulate

Leaders need to be able to listen carefully, think quickly, and respond with questions that help them interpret and verify their observations. People who have trouble maintaining a continuous flow of conversation may find discovery interviewing very difficult.

Beware of focusing on developing your next question while a person is still answering the first one. This is a typical communication style that decreases understanding and shows a lack of respect for the other person's viewpoint.

The ability to be clear and concise in questioning, presenting findings, and writing final reports is invaluable to a leader. In fact, successful leaders often take continuing education courses to improve these skills.

Egalitarian

This is the trickiest characteristic on the list, and it's one that you'll rarely get right from an associate's perspective.

The dictionary defines fairness and equality in terms of consistency in applying rules and guidelines. On the surface, this sounds like a good approach, but think about the many atypical situations that occur in life. Is it really fair to apply the same rules the same way in every case? Doesn't good judgment require that you use "common sense" and work out an alternative approach? If you do that in one case, however, you must ask yourself if you've been fair in all the other cases when you've required adherence to the rules.

As you can see, this is a circular discussion that might best be left to philosophers. Unfortunately, it's a serious factor for leaders, too. You should try to be consistent without being rigid about a process or an individual's approach—try to use the same decision-making process and criteria.

This may mean that you consistently require processes and job performance to adhere exactly to your requirements for one system because it is critical to the achievement of a particular goal. You might be much more lenient in another area because the risks are lower. Clear definitions of what constitute deviations can help you in this troublesome area.

5
MOTIVATING OTHERS

Brooke Broadbent

Overview Motivation generates success. Therefore we pay attention to motivation. If you are in a leadership role as a manager, chances are you're preoccupied with how to motivate others.

Can we motivate others? The answer seems to be that we cannot motivate others, but we can create conditions for people to motivate themselves. This practical guide explains six easy-to-use principles for motivating others and contains two tables with specific advice for your examination.

WHAT IS MOTIVATION?

Motivation, according to the dictionary, is a noun under the word *motivate*. If you look up *motivate* you will discover it means "to stir to action; to provide with a motive." *Motive* is defined as "an impulse that causes one to act in a particular manner." What is that "impulse" and how do we get it to work for us? Why do some people work harder than other people? Why do some strive for promotions and others reject them? What motivates people?

Many things influence our behavior and our motivation. Some of those things are: current personal situation, past experiences, present work situation, the reward system, the managerial system, group relationships, the company culture, perception, and personal values. Each of us is motivated by different things at different times.

MOTIVATION COMES FROM WITHIN

The most important thing to keep in mind about motivation is that we cannot motivate others. Motivation comes from within—people moti-

Contact Information: Brooke Broadbent, Broadbent Associates, 867 Explorer Lane, Orleans, Ontario, Canada, K1C 2S3, 613-837-6472, brooke.broadbent@ottawa.com, e-LearningHub.com

vate themselves. The only thing a supervisor, a committee chairperson, an instructor, or anyone else can do is to create the conditions for people to motivate themselves.

SIX PRINCIPLES FOR MOTIVATING OTHERS

1. **Positive thoughts motivate.** What conditions motivate people? Recall the teacher, friend, or parent who motivated you to do well by telling you that you could succeed. This is an example of our first principle of motivation: Positive thoughts motivate.

2. **Enjoyment motivates.** Maybe you recollect the sheer enjoyment that came from an activity, something you did on your own or with others. You were motivated to succeed and you did. Enjoyment motivates.

3. **Feeling important motivates.** Perhaps in a wistful stroll down memory lane your mind harkens back to a time when your opinions were sought. Your ideas were important. People listened to you. Were you motivated? I bet you were! This is an example of our third principle of motivation: Feeling important motivates.

4. **Success motivates.** For many people, motivation occurs when they do something well. You feel part of a worthwhile endeavor and you work hard to ensure continued success. This illustrates principle four: Success motivates.

5. **Personal benefits motivate.** Another source of motivation is the famous radio station WIIFM—what's in it for me. When employees, course participants, or any people see how they can benefit personally, they become motivated. They tune in, an example of principle five: Personal benefits motivate.

6. **Clarity motivates.** Our sixth and last principle of motivation is best understood if you think of a situation in which you were not motivated. Chances are that the task you were to do was unclear. Instructions were ambiguous. Flip this over and we get the sixth principle of motivation: Clarity motivates.

What can you do as a leader to create situations that motivate?

There's nothing earth-shattering in our six principles of motivation. But how do you put them to work? The following table suggests common-sense ways for leaders to use the six principles. What you do in your particular situation will depend on your creativity.

Principles of Motivation	What Leaders Can Do to Motivate Others
1. Positive thoughts motivate.	When the group you lead attains its goals, advertise your success. Thank individuals for the success of the group.
2. Enjoyment motivates.	Find out what people like to do and when possible have them do the tasks they enjoy. Demonstrate your pleasure when people and the team succeed. Build in enjoyable social activities for everyone, such as having coffee or lunch together.
3. Feeling important motivates.	Ask people for their opinions. Listen intently to what they say. Consider their thoughts carefully. Give credit when you use somebody's idea.
4. Success motivates.	Set clear, reasonable goals with the group. Make certain that stakeholders help set goals, understand what the goals mean, and agree to them. Thank individuals for successfully contributing to the group.
5. Personal benefits motivate.	Identify and state how group members can personally gain from an activity. Monitor and report on success.
6. Clarity motivates.	Plan your messages, oral and written. Take time to ensure you communicate clearly. Check with others to ensure they understand your messages.

What can everyone do to create situations that motivate?

If you are not in a formal leadership position there is still plenty you can do to heighten motivation among colleagues and fellow participants in a training session. In our increasingly participative workplace, opinions are sought. If you identify what motivates you personally and share your thoughts with an enlightened team leader, committee chairperson, or supervisor, chances are they will respond positively.

Principles of Motivation	What Everyone Can Do to Motivate Others
1. Positive thoughts motivate.	Compliment people on their success.
2. Enjoyment motivates.	Smile. Your enjoyment will be contagious. Demonstrate your pleasure when people and the team succeed. Participate enthusiastically in social activities such as having coffee or lunch together.
3. Feeling important motivates.	Ask people for their opinions. Listen intently to what they say. Consider their thoughts carefully. Give credit when you use somebody's idea.

4. Success motivates.	Set clear, reasonable goals for yourself and with others. When you attain your goals, advertise your success. Compliment individuals on their contributions to the group.
5. Personal benefits motivate.	Identify how you can personally gain from an activity. Keep these benefits in mind. Evaluate your level of success. If you don't succeed, determine why—so you will know what to do to succeed next time.
6. Clarity motivates.	Plan your messages, oral and written. Take time to ensure that you communicate clearly. Check with others to ensure that they understand what you say.

PERSONALIZED MOTIVATION

Each of us has motivational hot spots. We need to keep this in mind when we try to create situations that motivate others. What motivates you or me may be different from what motivates someone else. If you are motivated by clarity, you might assume that it would motivate someone else. Be careful. Don't force your motivation preferences on someone else. The safest way is to include all six motivational elements in your undertakings. That way you will connect with everyone's motivational hot spots.

DIFFERENT STROKES...

This guide is like a toolbox. The tools or ideas you find inside have to be selected—the right one for each situation. You need to learn to use these tools. How? Through structured practice. Set goals. Select techniques. Use them. Assess the results. Determine whether you hit the targets you set. If you missed a target, identify why—maybe you should consider changing tools. Give yourself feedback about how well you created conditions to motivate others. Identify what you did well and what you can improve, and map out a plan for improvements. This personal feedback will help you develop motivational techniques that energize apathetic, bored, and unmotivated colleagues, course participants, or anyone else.

A FINAL WORD ABOUT YOUR SUCCESS

We said at the outset that motivation comes from within. People motivate themselves. Since motivation comes from within, supervisors, committee chairpeople, instructors, for that matter all of us, are limited in our power to motivate someone else.

Keep that in mind when measuring your individual success. Using these six principles, you will be able to create conditions to motivate others. It may take time to motivate others. Stick with it. You will succeed. You will personally benefit from the results. Everyone else will benefit, too—your committee, your colleagues, your team, and your course participants.

6

IMPROVING YOUR COMMUNICATIONS

Scott Parry

Overview　Here are 25 tips that describe actions that can be taken to improve the level of the understanding between you as a manager and those with whom you communicate. As you read the list, put a check mark in front of every action that you haven't done enough of and would like to work on to improve your communication skills repertoire. The checked actions can be developed into an action plan for improving communication.

Contact Information: Scott Parry, 100 Bear Brook Rd., Princeton, NJ 08540, 609-452-8598, jsparry@erols.com

25 TIPS FOR IMPROVING YOUR COMMUNICATIONS

1. **Listen actively.** Look at the person speaking. Control any distractions. At the end of any message that contains more than two or three points (steps, ideas, phases, etc.), summarize by saying something like this: "Let me make sure I understand what you've just told me. I believe you made three key points, namely .... Have I missed anything?"

2. **Use illustrations.** There are thousands of anecdotes, historic situations, proverbs, parables, and analogies you can cite to make a point or to confirm understanding of a point someone else has made. Such illustrations help both parties to visualize a point and remember it.

3. **Confirm attention.** When you start talking, the other person's mind is usually on other matters. His or her priorities and needs are probably different from yours. Begin by stating your purpose (topic, need, objective) and asking for a specific amount of time. Example: "I need to get your views on .... Have you got ten minutes now, or should I come back?"

4. **Plan the interaction.** You have a purpose, information to give, information to get, an appropriate sequence (game plan, strategy) for combining the give and get, and a desired reaction that will tell you whether you have or haven't achieved your purpose. Take time to plan each of these steps in advance. Load brain before firing mouth.

5. **Cancel lost causes.** If the person you're talking to about something important is distracted (e.g., taking phone calls, reading something, or simply preoccupied with another matter), cancel the interaction: "I can see that you're busy. When would be a good time for me to come back?" This should get the person's attention, either immediately or when you come back.

6. **Give prior notice.** When possible, let the other person know in advance that you'd like ten minutes "to discuss the Wykoff project." Set the time. Even if the person says, "Right now is okay," it's sometimes better to say that now is not good for you. This gives the other person time to think about the issue and to take it seriously when you come back to discuss it.

7. **Select time and place.** Should you meet in your office (workplace, location) or a conference room or a corner of the cafeteria? Morning, afternoon, or end of the workday? Depending on your purpose, the other person's availability and comfort level, and the physical layout, you should plan when and where you are most likely to achieve your objective.

---

25 TIPS FOR IMPROVING YOUR COMMUNICATIONS (CONT.)

8. **Anticipate the "What if ...."** Forewarned is forearmed. Plan for the different directions your interaction could take—the questions, suggestions, objections, and digressions that might come up. You might even want to rehearse (role play with yourself) or to write out a script of the ideal interaction as a way of being better prepared for different reactions.

9. **Maintain aim.** Stay on target. It's easy for either person to digress or bring up information that is not relevant to the purpose of the communication. By steering your comments and questions toward your objective, you will be able to meet your aim and accomplish your objective.

10. **Control bias.** At times you want to influence (bias) the other person's thoughts and actions (e.g., when selling, teaching, persuading). At other times, you want unbiased opinions and feelings, in which case you must work hard to use unstructured questions and to avoid showing your own opinions and feelings.

11. **Set a positive climate.** Some situations are difficult to handle: a reprimand, a denial, a termination. However challenging the communication, keep it rational and not emotional, adult to adult and not parent to child, win–win and not win–lose, so that both parties see the action as necessary and fair.

12. **Interact, don't dominate.** Your communications are generally effective to the degree to which the other party was participating and not merely listening. Keep the other person involved with questions and requests for information. The more interactive your dialogue, the more successful you are likely to be.

13. **Use the Funnel Technique.** When eliciting facts and feelings, start with broad (open-ended, nondirective) questions, such as, "Why is Team B lagging behind the others?" and move down the funnel into more structured, directive questions, such as, "Have their two new members reached full productivity yet?" and, "Is there a morale problem?"

14. **Separate replies from responses.** Unless they are deaf, people will usually reply to your questions. But the reply may not be the response you were looking for (the person didn't understand, is being cautious, or has other things in mind). Be ready to rephrase your question to get a response after getting a reply.

15. **Keep your words short.** Studies have shown that when we write or speak, we are much more likely to be understood and remembered if we keep our words short, with a least 65 percent of them kept to one syllable. Bear this in mind as you talk or write. (This paragraph has 88 percent one-syllable words. So if you fear that you will sound like a small child, think again!)

---

16. **Allow time to digest.** Pauses are welcome. Give your listener time to absorb and to anticipate with comments like, "Think for a moment of three or four obvious benefits of the new system." Then, after a brief pause, outline them. Listeners are much more attentive when given time to think for themselves. When writing, keep your paragraphs short. White space gives reader time to digest and helps to avoid information overload.

17. **Use vocal dynamics.** When you speak, vary your rate, pitch, and volume. Slow down to make a key point. Speed up on anecdotal or supportive material. Change your volume to emphasize an idea. Use humor when it comes naturally and offends no one. Use accents when relating dialogue, because this helps your listener keep two or more characters separate. If you don't vary your delivery, people may "burn out" or "tune out."

18. **Signal for turns.** A driver's hand signals help avoid accidents. Words like *however, moreover, in contrast, for instance, and, but, or* are signals that help your listeners know where you're going. Sometimes a phrase or sentence is needed: "Now let me cite three reasons why..." or, "The flip side is equally compelling. Let me explain ...." A writer uses paragraphs, chapter titles, and subtitles to alert readers. A good speaker will do the same for listeners.

19. **Use probes.** When others speak to you, they may stop short of telling you the full story. Several useful probe techniques will keep them going. Example: In an employment interview, you ask why the applicant left his last job and he replies with, "I felt I wasn't getting anywhere." You need to know what this means, so you might use: the echo probe: "Not getting anywhere?"; the neutral probe: "That's interesting. Tell me more."; the silence probe: You say nothing, look at him, and wait.

20. **Confirm their understanding.** When you want to know if another person understands after you've taken 5 to 10 minutes to relate something, ask the person to summarize. Avoid the parent-to-child command: "Now tell me what I just said." Instead, keep it adult to adult: "I've been doing a lot of rambling and don't know if I've made sense or covered everything. It might be helpful to both of us if you could take a minute to summarize what you just heard."

21. **Use questions deductively.** When you're instructing someone, you can either deliver the information or ask questions that will lead your listeners to deduce the correct procedure (concept, reasons, etc.). The use of questions is usually more effective. The other person is more participative, you're building on that person's level of understanding rather than yours, and your listener's comprehension and retention will be greater.

22. **Apply the Layer Method.** Professional writers and speakers bring their messages to life by alternating between abstract and concrete, between a concept and its application, between rule and example, between things and people. In short, they create layers of human interest in a message that might otherwise be dry or technical. If the first paragraph describes a new policy or procedure, the next paragraph shows how Marge Smith in accounting is affected. The third paragraph describes another aspect of the new policy or procedure, and the fourth paragraph illustrates how our customers are benefiting from it.

23. **Avoid sex bias.** Your references to groups of people should show no preferences for male or female pronouns. It is no longer acceptable to say, "Each employee should check with his supervisor" or, "The customer knows that he can always get his money back." The easiest way to avoid sex bias is to put your references in the plural: *employees* and *customers* require the plural, unisex pronouns *their, they, them.*

24. **Test your assumptions.** When your ability to influence the other person depends heavily on the accuracy of your assumptions, test them. Example: "With all the recent talk about quality improvement, I'm guessing that you've heard this tune before during your many years with the company, and you might be thinking that this is nothing new. How about it?"

25. **Answer the "WIIFM?"** "What's in it for me?" This is what other people are thinking as you deliver your message. Your ability to answer this question to their satisfaction will lead them to accept or to be cautious and reserved, or possibly even to reject. You need to draw on your empathy, putting yourself in their shoes, addressing their needs and concerns, as early in the communication as possible.

7

TEN STEPS TO BECOME AN EFFECTIVE MANAGER

George Truell

Overview Many people who are promoted into the position of manager have little or no opportunity to prepare in advance for this significant transition. The change from being a doer to being a leader of others is a challenging one! Unfortunately, many managers have had to learn through difficult trials and errors how to be effective in this new role.

This guide describes ten key steps you can take to improve your own effectiveness. They will help you translate your present knowledge of management policies and principles into sound daily practices on the job.

Contact Information: George Truell Associates, 495 North Forest Road, Williamsville, NY 14221-5036, 716-634-3491, gtabuffny@aol.com

TEN STEPS TO BECOME AN EFFECTIVE MANAGER

Are you an effective manager? If you see some room for improvement, there are practical steps you can take to increase your effectiveness. Answering the following questions will help you translate your knowledge of management policies and principles into sound operating practices.

1. **What are the goals and objectives of the organization? Do your team members know what they are?**

   In many companies, employees don't understand the overall purpose, function, or goals of the company, department, or unit in which they work. Unless employees understand where they are headed, agree with their department's or unit's goals and objectives, and believe that those goals are attainable, they won't be able to commit themselves to them. In effect, they won't be motivated.

   The best way for people to become committed to a company's goals and objectives is for them to participate in setting those goals. When this is not possible, the manager or supervisor should make sure that each employee fully understands where the department is headed and how it plans to get there.

2. **What is your role in attaining these goals and objectives? What are your team members' roles?**

   Once people understand their department's goals and objectives, they will want to know what their duties and responsibilities are in relation to these goals. A common practice in many organizations is to use job descriptions to define duties and responsibilities. Unfortunately, many job descriptions are too long and overstuffed with *how*-to-do-it phrases (methods) instead of *why*-to-do-it phrases (objectives). Too often, the descriptions are out of date and fail to indicate the relative importance or priorities of duties and responsibilities.

   If you are wondering how useful an employee's job description is, try this test. Ask the employee to write down his or her three or four most important duties and responsibilities and then rank them in the order of importance. Then do the same thing yourself for that employee's job. Compare the two lists. If they are not identical, you have pinpointed a problem area that needs correcting. Unless a person and his or her manager see that person's job in the same way, a great amount of slippage will occur in the department or organization.

   You can streamline job descriptions by arbitrarily limiting duties and responsibilities to three or four categories. This flushes out many of the *how to*'s and focuses on the *why*'s. In most jobs, duties and responsibilities can be clustered together under several major headings. Once you have identified these, it is easy to rank them and to relate them directly to the goals and objectives of the organization or department. Employees who can see this relationship often utilize more initiative and creativity in carrying out their responsibilities.

TEN STEPS TO BECOME
AN EFFECTIVE MANAGER (CONT.)

To keep job descriptions lean, group all duties and responsibilities for each job under four categories. At first this may seem impossible, particularly if the present description is several pages long. But keep asking: "What is the reason or purpose for this activity?" You will find that most duties and responsibilities fall easily under such broad terms as *quality, quantity, cost, service, control,* and *timeliness.* These are the major tasks that differentiate one job from others in the organization. Once you've done this grouping, you can easily rank all tasks according to their importance.

3. What tools or resources will you have to work with in order to fulfill your role?

The resources allocated to a manager are often found in budgets, schedules, and timetables—essential tools for the overall planning process. Unless a manager knows the amount of money, materials, machinery, equipment, personnel, space, and time he or she will have, the manager can't use them effectively.

Participation in the initial process of allocating resources, establishing budgets, and setting up timetables and schedules would help answer this question. For this reason, many companies today involve managers at all levels in the overall planning process. If a manager is to be held accountable for assets and resources and evaluated on his or her ability to use them, that person should know precisely what they are. Only than can he or she assume full responsibility for the effective utilization of those assets and resources.

4. What procedures and rules will you have to follow?

Once a target has been set, with your part in reaching it clearly defined, and once you know what resources you will draw upon in reaching it, find out what the rules of the game are. Policies (ground rules) and procedures (the application and implementation of ground rules) define the limits within which you can operate. They control your own actions and eliminate the need for continuous surveillance by your manager. As companies and organizations get larger, they increasingly need to replace a superior's "imposed control" with the manager's "self-imposed control."

An effective way to help your own employees understand the ground rules governing their jobs is to have them participate in establishing, reviewing, and modifying those rules and relating them to the changing goals and objectives of their own departments. Increased involvement makes for greater understanding and commitment.

5. How much authority do you have? How much do your team members have?

One problem that managers frequently encounter is a difference of opinion with an employee over the amount of authority that person can use in carrying out his or her duties and responsibilities. Employees often complain that their managers keep them under tight control, don't let them make decisions, and don't let them act on their own. They say that they have responsibility but no authority. On the other hand, some managers complain that their employees don't stand on their own two feet, don't make decisions on their own, and don't take responsibility for their actions. Instead, these managers say, employees keep running to them for answers. A lot of talent and effort are wasted when managers and employees can't agree on the scope of authority each person has.

One way to resolve this dilemma is for the employee and the manager to define ahead of time just how much authority the employee will have in carrying out his or her three or four major duties and responsibilities. Many organizations use the following simple code to indicate the level of authority an employee has been given:

A   The employee can act on his or her own.

AA The employee can act on his or her own, but is required to advise the manager about what he or she has done.

SR The employee is expected to check with his or her manager for suggestions and recommendations before acting.

In getting together with an employee to discuss the amount of authority he or she has been given, the manager can also let the employee know how well he or she is growing and developing on the job. Although an employee's duties and responsibilities may stay the same, changes in levels of authority for a given duty or responsibility may indicate growth in that employee's knowledge, skill, and competence in performing his or her assigned tasks.

6. What are your relationships inside and outside of your department or organization?

Formal organization charts and diagrams give some clues to the working relationships that exist in a company, but they show only one aspect of these relationships. For a true picture of your position in the network of company relationships, look beyond your reporting relationships up and down the line. Look at all the people with whom you must interact and coordinate activities. These people make up the informal organization and the various "publics" with whom you must deal. Clarifying these relationships in advance—finding out who is involved, what functions are involved, and the nature of the relationships—will help improve your effectiveness as a team member and as a manager.

7. What criteria will be used to measure your performance?

Jim Green, a manager, found out how well he had been performing his job—after he was fired. Ideally, this should not have happened. But many times employees are unaware of the performance standards that are being applied to them. Even when employees *think* that they know the standards, those standards may actually be different from the ones their managers are using.

Performance standards are predictions of conditions that reflect satisfactory job performance. These conditions include results, symptoms, or efforts that can be measured in terms of such factors as quantity, quality, cost, and timeliness. Activities that fall below a performance standard reflect failure; those that exceed it reflect excellence.

Today, many companies make certain that all employees know not only their assigned duties and responsibilities, but also the specific standards of performance expected from them, *before* they actually begin performing their jobs. In addition, many companies also provide opportunities for employees to participate in setting the standards they will be measured against. When employees have played an active part in setting these standards, they usually consider them to be fair and see them as factors over which they have some control. Because they understand the system of measurement that will be used, they can keep their own scores as they go along instead of waiting for their manager to give them feedback.

When new goals and objectives are established or when responsibilities change, new standards of performance may be needed to fit changing conditions. Whatever the changes, there should be no surprises. The manager and his or her employees must know "before the game starts" exactly how their performance will be measured, so they can continue to keep their own scores.

8. Will you receive feedback on how you are doing? Where, when, and how?

Many companies have formal performance appraisal systems that provide periodic feedback on how an employee is doing on the job. Unfortunately, these are often once-a-year events—such as the end of a calendar year or the anniversary of a person's employment—that require the completion of formal documents and involved paper processing.

People involved in any sport want to know how they are doing while they are playing the game. They aren't content to wait until the game is over before they get feedback on their performance. Likewise, people in a company want feedback while they're doing their jobs. Only by receiving ongoing feedback can they continue to fine-tune their efforts and improve their level of performance.

If you have been able to answer the first seven questions for your own job, you are now in a position to be able to stop at any time and assess where you are compared to where you had hoped to be, what aspects of your job you are performing well, and in what areas you should continue to improve. Ongoing feedback is the key, not a formal, once-a-year performance appraisal event.

TEN STEPS TO BECOME
AN EFFECTIVE MANAGER (CONT.)

9. **Where and from whom can you or your team members receive help and support when it is needed?**

    Valuable resources for any manager are the advice, counsel, assistance, and support from his or her own manager and from others with whom he or she works, both inside and outside the organization. Too often, however, such resources are not tapped. The manager is not viewed as a coach or counselor; staff groups are seen as threats or obstacles that get in the manager's way.

    How can managers solve this particular problem with their own employees? If you want to change this image so that your employees begin to look to you for coaching and counseling, periodically ask them this question: "What can I do more of, do less of, or do differently to be of help to you?" In addition, define the roles and availability of others in the organization who could also help them. After a while, your employees will begin to realize that your primary role is to do whatever you can to make each and every one of them successful.

10. **What rewards or recognition will you receive?**

    This may be the most important question: "Is it worth it?" Having performed effectively, you may justifiably wonder, "What can I expect to receive?" Continuity of employment and the possibility of receiving a wage increase are only two of the possible rewards and recognition that employees seek today. They also want the ability to see the results of their work contributions, more responsibility, a greater sense of achievement, the chance to acquire additional knowledge and skills, and knowledge about the opportunities that are available to them.

    With this in mind, many companies are revamping their wage and salary plans to make sure that they directly reflect the accomplishments and contributions employees are making, rather than the energy they have expended or "time in grade." One-time bonuses for specific accomplishments in a given time period have become more common in many organizations. Salary and wage systems are beginning to be more widely publicized so employees know where they stand and what's ahead for them. In addition, widespread posting of advancement and transfer opportunities has become a common practice in many companies today.

....

Have you been able to answer all ten questions? If so, you are on your way to becoming a more effective manager. Why? Because it's one thing to know theories about how to manage, and it's another to know exactly what's expected in every facet of your job. Both are important, and both will help you accomplish your goals more effectively.

8
BUILDING ORGANIZATIONAL TRUST

Barbara Pate Glacel and Emile Robert, Jr.

Overview   Trust is both a people issue and a substantive business reality. Whenever people come together to perform work, the success and productivity of the effort is related to the amount of trust in the relationship. This kind of trust does not mean whether or not one will steal items from another's work space. Rather, it means that a person is reliable in information, performance, and follow-through. Trust in the workplace is the belief that one can count on another to do what has been promised, to provide accurate information, to pick up the pieces when systems fail.

Sometimes even the most foolproof systems fail. Through no fault of one's own, trust is broken by the circumstance at hand, whether it be mechanical failure or human failure. This can have an impact on people, teams, and the organization as a whole. One must have a back up, a contingency plan, people to turn to. In this world of constant change and overwhelming amounts of information, a single person cannot go it alone. There is no substitute for the trusted team of people who work together to achieve higher productivity than could ever be achieved by a group of individuals.

The glue that binds the team together and provides the backup is trust. More than a feeling, it is money in the bank, which is difficult to measure unless you don't have it. Trust is about people. In the end, it is the people we trust who guarantee our success.

Contact Information: Barbara Pate Glacel, The Glacel Group, 12103 Richmond Lane, Oak Hall, VA 20171, 703-262-9120, BP Glacel@glacel.com, www.glacel.com

TIPS FOR BUILDING ORGANIZATIONAL TRUST

1. *Keep your word and always follow through on promises and commitments.* Your word represents your integrity and your ethics in doing what you say you will do. Failing to follow through on a commitment may have devastating consequences for others who depend on you. Rebuilding trust after such an omission is a difficult if not impossible task.

2. *Share information widely.* Be open about all issues that do not require confidentiality. Information is power, and one who withholds information may be suspected of hidden agendas, personal competition, or turf-building. By sharing information, you will also gain information from others and build the basis for a trusting relationship.

3. *Keep confidences about sensitive matters.* Confidential or personal information must be held in strictest confidence in order not to damage another's reputation or career. Sharing confidences, even with a single person, may be seen as self-serving or denigrating to others and will raise the question: Could I trust this person to hold my confidences?

4. *Demonstrate your belief in what you say by behaving consistently with your message.* In other words, do as you say. The consistency and integrity of your own behavior allows others to know what to expect from you. If others are not surprised by actions that seem contrary to your words, trust in who you are and the beliefs you represent will build.

5. *Go beyond what is expected by performing above the norm.* Achieving excellent results from all your efforts will build trust in your work and confidence that you will come through all situations to the best of your ability.

6. *Meet deadlines.* Another's deadline may be more important to him or her than to you, but by helping another meet that requirement, you build a trusting relationship that assures the other will help you when you have a need.

7. *Share who you are as a person.* Show your vulnerability and humanness. State when you do not have all the information you need or know the answer to a question. Describe your values, your ethics, and your priorities. Your personal statements speak volumes about your honesty and suggest that you do not hide behind a professional facade.

8. *Give and receive honest feedback often.* Maintain a learning relationship with others so that trust continues to grow as you improve your interpersonal relationships with others.

9. *Stay in tune with the informal communication within the organization.* By acknowledging and using informal communication networks through opinion leaders, you can achieve congruence between the formal and informal communiqués within the organization, relieving suspicions about motives and actions.

TIPS FOR BUILDING ORGANIZATIONAL TRUST (CONT.)

10. *Tell the truth.* Always be honest and open or explain why you cannot tell everything. The information explosion guarantees that the truth will eventually be revealed. Your telling less than the whole story without explanation undermines your foundation of trust.

11. *Admit your mistakes and apologize for them.* Others see your behaviors whether you want them to or not. Therefore, publicly admitting mistakes and apologizing makes you more human, shows your vulnerability, allows you to tell the truth, and builds trust.

12. *Acknowledge others' pain when things go wrong.* Organizational and individual actions inevitably cause pain at one time or another. Acknowledging others' pain, whether you caused it or not, is a key to building trusting relationships that will be even stronger when things go well.

13. *Be fair in your exercise of authority.* Fairness does not mean making everyone happy. However, demonstration of well-thought-out and fair decisions allows for trust in the process, even when leadership decisions are difficult for others to accept.

14. *Be consistent in your behavior with others.* Acknowledge both individual circumstances and consistency in your treatment of others. Do not play favorites. If your behavior may look inconsistent, explain your rationale.

15. *Demonstrate your personal values and your belief in organizational values.* Be explicit in your explanations about what is important to you and how it helps you to meet the organizational mission and ethic. This is a powerful motivator and trust-builder.

16. *Communicate from the heart as much as from the head.* Compassion and empathy have a place in organizational life. Demonstrating your heartfelt feelings, sorrows, joys, disappointments, or celebrations shows your personality, allows others to know you better, and allows their trust in you to grow.

17. *Respond to others' good ideas and requests for help.* Being available to others, recognizing their contributions, and helping them when they need you means that they will be more available to you, sharing credit, providing assistance, and creating a mutual trust to move your efforts forward.

9

A CASE STUDY OF AN ATTEMPT AT EMPOWERMENT

Paul Lyons

Overview
Here is a case study about a well-intentioned manager who wishes to share decision making with employees. The setting is a unit in a manufacturing operation. The manager wants to involve employees in participative decision making and use some of her MBA program ideas to create change. She views her actions as a win–win proposal, that is, she enhances her management skills at the same time she helps employees to be more effective as organization participants and learners.

You should find the case study to be an interesting activity for yourself. Or you might choose to discuss it with other managers in your organization. Finally, you might consider leading a management development session around the case.

The analysis of this case may take any one of several directions. Also, the paths or directions the case opens may be examined in combination. Case users may need to have some information and understanding regarding several concepts, including:

✓ participative management,

✓ the introduction of change,

✓ involving people in change processes,

✓ the motivational aspects of involvement, and

✓ the effective use of delegation.

The delegation feature is most important. Skillful delegation practices are not normally part of management education or training courses. Effective delegation is grounded in several important considerations. First, the manager has to know the skill and ability levels of the employees. Second, he or she has to gauge the readiness of the

Contact Information: Paul Lyons, MBA Program, Frostburg State University, Frostburg, MD 21532, 301-687-4179, plyons@mail.frostburg.edu

employees to accept delegation and their willingness to perform. Finally, the manager has to convey to employees that the manager will be supportive and helpful throughout the process.

Suggested Time 60 to 90 minutes

The case may be assigned as reading in advance of discussion or may be read as a handout. Reading the case, creating discussion, using small groups for deliberation of key points or questions, etc., may cause the time needed to vary greatly.

Materials Needed

✓ Form A (The Case of Avalanche, Inc.)

Procedure

1. Have participants read and study the case (Form A). They can do this as preparation (homework) or during the session.

2. Ask participants to review the questions at the conclusion of the case and to prepare written responses.

3. Have participants meet in small groups to share their responses. You may or may not request that each group develop a consensus position for each question.

4. In the larger group, focus on the concepts presented in the case (e.g., motivational consequences, resistance to change).

5. Invite the participants to present "minority reports" of suggestions and ideas that surfaced in the small groups but that did not receive support from colleagues.

6. Work together in the larger group to problem-solve regarding:

    (a) What Angela or others might have done in the first place, and

    (b) What Angela can do now.

Variations The case has several uses and is limited in its use only by the imagination of the instructor or trainer. The case could be used for:

✓ problem solving,

✓ mentor training,

✓ a homework assignment,

✓ a role-play activity, or

✓ an example of delegation practice.

THE CASE OF AVALANCHE, INC. FORM A

Background

Angela Carp was the manager for the snowboard production department at Avalanche Inc., a company that manufactures skiing equipment, ice skates, snowboards, snowshoes, and a variety of snow-related accessories, gear, and clothing. Angela was enrolled in an MBA program in nearby Ogden, Utah. She had read a lot about participative management and was impressed by the results of case studies and consultant reports. It seemed to her that there were many benefits to be had in production-type departments like hers where employees were really involved in decision making. Angela decided to experiment with participative management to find out if employees would respond positively to it. The employees are not in a union, hence, she knew she could make changes in decision-making practices without having to get approvals and assorted sign-offs. Angela chose the topic of job rotation to introduce participative management in her department.

Job Rotation

In the snowboard production department at Avalanche, job rotation was a standard practice. That is, the company expected each department manager to use job rotation of employees for purposes of cross-training, reduction of boredom on the job, creation of within-department flexibility, and so on. The rotation of jobs was believed to be an important element of employee motivation. Angela's boss, Hans Volk, the plant superintendent, did not specify to Angela nor to any department manager specifically how to conduct job rotation. It was generally expected that each department manager would do it and do it in a way that fit the needs of the department and the group of employees. Department managers were required to prepare a brief report every six months in which they explained how the job rotation was achieved.

For the past two years, Angela has made all of the job rotation assignments. She keeps a calendar of assignments and on an average of about every three weeks she makes some new assignments and changes in the work and tasks of the employees. The department does not have shift work; all employees in the department work on one shift. Since March of 1996, the employees at Avalanche are the best-paid employees in the snow recreation (goods production) industry. The firm is very successful and many local people seek to be employed at Avalanche. When there is a job vacancy, it is not unusual for dozens of people to apply for the job. The job rotation idea is one that people seem to accept and take for granted. In Angela's department, there have been very few complaints about the rotation of jobs and tasks. Most of the complaints have been from people who liked what they were doing and didn't want to move to something different.

On Wednesday morning, Angela told her 17 production employees to shut down all production activities at 2:45 Thursday afternoon and report to a conference room in the administrative section for a 3:00 p.m. meeting. The meeting was about job rotation. At 3:00 on Thursday all the employees were assembled in the conference room. Angela told them that she was really pleased with the way the job rotation was working out as far as flexibility gained and the interest that the employees seemed to take in their jobs and the quality of output and so on. She said that it was working out so well that she thought she could delegate the whole job rotation program to them, for them to manage as they saw fit. After all, everyone understood the nature and purposes of job rotation and if they could self-manage the program perhaps even greater benefits could result. Also, successfully performing this kind of supervisory or management task could help them in applying for a promotion in the future. Finally, the time savings for Angela in having delegated the job rotation planning and scheduling would allow her to spend more time training employees in the computer-aided manufacturing equipment.

To Angela, the employees seemed genuinely enthusiastic about taking over the job rotation program to manage on their own. She asked if there were any questions or comments. There were very few comments from the group. Since there were about 30 minutes left in the workday, Angela told the group she was going over to the work area to finish a project she had started earlier that day and that the next 30 minutes was theirs to do some initial planning regarding how to assume the job rotation tasks. She left the meeting feeling pretty good; maybe she was even a bit smug. She thought to herself, "This participative management experiment is going to be a big success. I'm really glad I decided to do this."

Results

About one week later, when the normal job rotation changes would take place in accordance with the schedule that Angela had put in motion, she noted that virtually no one was shifting to different tasks. She thought this was strange but said or did nothing. Another week passed. Everything was going well in the department, yet there were no changes in the rotation of jobs or tasks. Angela quietly asked the senior fiberglass technician, Harry, what was going on with the rotation plans. Harry told her that basically nothing was going on with the plan. He said there were three things going on for various people in the department with regard to her delegation: First, many people were tired of rotating jobs and would just as soon be left alone; second, no one would step forward and take responsibility for the initial planning, not even a small committee; and third, some people didn't like the idea of doing Angela's job for her. After all, she's paid to do administrative tasks, they aren't. Stunned is a good word to describe how Angela felt when she heard Harry's comments.

THE CASE OF AVALANCHE, INC. FORM A (CONT.)

Questions

1. What are some benefits of empowerment, especially as it is represented in this case? For the employee? For the organization?

2. Could Angela have introduced empowerment (as per the practices she suggested) differently? Explain.

3. Is what Angela proposed a delegation of authority?

4. What can Angela do now?

PART II

REPRODUCIBLE TOOLS FOR COACHING AND MANAGING EMPLOYEE PERFORMANCE

10

WHAT ARE YOUR COACHING STRENGTHS?

Scott Martin

Overview   In today's learning environment, it is every employee's responsibility to continuously improve personal performance development. As an active manager, one of your principal functions is the development and support of those who report to you. How well you fulfill the role of coach is crucial to your own success and that of your associates. These two instruments will help you to asses your strengths and discover undeveloped or underdeveloped areas in your coaching activities, behaviors, and philosophies. The first instrument is to be completed by you, the second by your direct reports. Comparing the results of the two will provide the means for developing an action plan that addresses the underdeveloped areas and reinforces the strengths.

Contact Information: Scott Martin, Organizational Solutions: S. Martin & Associates, 14 Heather Rd., Turnersville, NJ 08012, 609-582-7666, scottmartin14@comcast.net

COACHING INVENTORY: <u>SELF</u>

The Coaching Inventory (<u>Self</u>) has been developed to help managers assess the extent to which they engage in coaching activities and behaviors, embody coaching philosophies, and create a climate conducive to coaching. It is intended as a method for managers to get a general idea of the extent of their coaching, but not necessarily as a scientifically precise measurement. Managers can use the results, along with other learning and experience (e.g., the Coaching Inventory (<u>Employee</u>), etc.), to begin to determine what areas of coaching may need more of their attention.

Directions: The Coaching Inventory (<u>Self</u>) consists of 35 statements related to coaching. In Part I, please circle the number of the response that best identifies the extent to which you engage in this activity or behavior, according to the following three-point scale:

- I rarely or seldom engage in or display this behavior or activity.
- I sometimes or occasionally engage in this behavior or activity.
- I frequently engage in this behavior or activity.

Part II is a self-scoring key with directions.

Please fill out this inventory and score yourself. The plotted profile will indicate areas that you may want to work on improving.

PART I: COACHING INVENTORY (Self)

Directions: Circle the number of the response that best identifies the extent to which you engage in this activity or behavior.

	Rarely or Seldom	Occasionally or Sometimes	Frequently
1. I spend time with my employees to help them develop professionally and in their careers.	1	2	3
2. I spend time with my employees discussing with them how to perform to their highest abilities.	1	2	3
3. I observe my employees and target any skills or behaviors for further development.	1	2	3
4. When giving feedback to an employee, I prefer to guard the feelings of the employee by softening the feedback.	3	2	1
5. When meeting with an employee, I ensure privacy and uninterrupted time.	1	2	3
6. In a developmental meeting, I encourage an employee to tell me as much as he or she can about the issue.	1	2	3
7. I revise development plans that have previously been agreed upon with the employee as needed, and provide further coaching.	1	2	3
8. I resist losing my best employees to other opportunities within the company.	3	2	1
9. During a formal performance appraisal or employee progress review, I devote time to discussing plans to further improve performance.	1	2	3
10. I identify and communicate the consequence of an employee not developing to his or her potential.	1	2	3
11. In a performance or development discussion, I describe to the employee specifically what the ideal performance or behavior is.	1	2	3
12. In a developmental or performance discussion, we concentrate on my perspective rather than the employee's.	3	2	1

PART I: COACHING INVENTORY (<u>Self</u>) (CONT.)

	Rarely or Seldom	Occasionally or Sometimes	Frequently
13. I encourage a two-way discussion by asking employees for their perspective on areas for development or improvement.	1	2	3
14. I periodically review with employees their progress toward established development goals.	1	2	3
15. I set time aside throughout the year, outside of performance appraisal and other formal processes, to discuss each employee's professional development and advancement.	1	2	3
16. I create a work environment that allows employees to change and improve their performance over time.	1	2	3
17. When I identify a development need for an employee, I just discuss it with them without worrying about any formal advance planning for the meeting.	3	2	1
18. I provide specific feedback to the employee on performance and development and suggest changes for improvement.	1	2	3
19. In a development or performance discussion, I pay attention to and consider the employee's perspective.	1	2	3
20. In a meeting with an employee, I tend to concentrate so much on what I want to say that I don't always hear what the employee is saying.	3	2	1
21. I evaluate my employee's development and reinforce any increase in competence.	1	2	3
22. During a formal performance appraisal or employee progress review, I devote time to discussing development and career advancement goals.	1	2	3
23. I leave performance discussions to performance appraisal meetings only.	3	2	1
24. Before actually conducting a developmental meeting with an employee, I determine specifically what I want the employee to do differently and why.	1	2	3

PART I: COACHING INVENTORY (Self) (CONT.)

	Rarely or Seldom	Occasionally or Sometimes	Frequently
25. In a developmental meeting, I help the employee to identify barriers to future development and ways to overcome them.	1	2	3
26. When meeting with an employee, I show that I am interested and attentive through my nonverbal behaviors, such as facing the employee directly, making eye contact, etc.	1	2	3
27. I make sure I have understood everything an employee has said through behaviors such as concentrating, paraphrasing, and checking for understanding.	1	2	3
28. It is not appropriate for me to assist employees in implementing development plans, so I leave them on their own for the most part.	3	2	1
29. I help my employees to better understand the expectations of our organizational culture and environment, and how they can impact their professional aspirations.	1	2	3
30. I actively identify performance improvement opportunities for individual employees.	1	2	3
31. If and when I note a development need or opportunity for an employee, I take time to analyze the situation and to determine the root causes and barriers to improvement.	1	2	3
32. I give honest feedback that helps employees to better understand how their behaviors and performance are perceived within the organization.	1	2	3
33. I convey a positive attitude throughout a coaching session that communicates my belief in the employee's ability to reach agreed-upon goals.	1	2	3
34. I probe for further information from an employee through behaviors such as concentrating and paraphrasing and checking for understanding.	1	2	3
35. I monitor the employee's use of a skill or behavior that was targeted for improvement on the job.	1	2	3

PART II: SCORING (Self)

Directions: Transfer the numerical values (1, 2, 3) you have given to each item to the spaces in the columns below. (Please record each individual number carefully, as some of the numerical values change within each column or category.) Add the numbers in each column for a total score for each category.

Commitment toward Professional Development	Commitment toward Performance Development	Assessment, Diagnosis, and Planning
1.	2.	3.
8.	9.	10.
15.	16.	17.
22.	23.	24.
29.	30.	31.
Total:	Total:	Total:

Meeting Face-to-Face and Giving Feedback	Attending	Listening and Responding	Implementation and Follow-Up
4.	5.	6.	7.
11.	12.	13.	14.
18.	19.	20.	21.
25.	26.	27.	28.
32.	33.	34.	35.
Total:	Total:	Total:	Total:

INTERPRETATION

Look at your scores in each category as one indication of the degree to which you use or are committed to this coaching philosophy, behavior, or skill.

Scores in the 12- to 15-point range indicate use of or commitment to these coaching areas.

Scores in the 5- to 8-point range indicate areas of coaching on which you may want to focus more attention.

PLOTTING YOUR PROFILE

To create a profile of your coaching strengths and highlight opportunities for improvement, plot the scores from each of the seven categories on the graph below. Create a plot line by connecting the circled numbers.

	Commitment toward Professional Development	Commitment toward Performance Development	Assessment, Diagnosis, Planning	Meeting Face-to-Face and Giving Feedback	Attending	Listening, Responding	Implementation, Follow-Up
MOST	15	15	15	15	15	15	15
	14	14	14	14	14	14	14
	13	13	13	13	13	13	13
	12	12	12	12	12	12	12
	11	11	11	11	11	11	11
	10	10	10	10	10	10	10
	9	9	9	9	9	9	9
LEAST	8	8	8	8	8	8	8
	7	7	7	7	7	7	7
	6	6	6	6	6	6	6
	5	5	5	5	5	5	5

You may also want to plot your employees' scores (from the "Employee" inventories) on the graph in a different color to compare to your own scores.

COACHING INVENTORY: <u>EMPLOYEE</u>

Name of Person Being Rated: _____   **Your Name (optional):** _____

The Coaching Inventory (<u>Employee</u>) has been developed to help your Coach or Manager to better assess, through your perceptions, the extent to which he or she engages in coaching activities and behaviors, embodies coaching philosophies, and creates a climate conducive to coaching. Coaches can use the results, along with other learning and experience (e.g., the Coaching Inventory, <u>Self</u>) to begin to determine what areas of coaching may need more of their attention. Please be candid in your responses to the following items to help ensure that your Coach or Manager obtains the maximum benefit from the inventory.

Directions: The Coaching Inventory (<u>Employee</u>) consists of 35 statements related to coaching. In Part I, please circle the number of the response that best identifies the extent to which the Coach or Manager engages in this activity or behavior, according to the following three-point scale:

- Rarely or seldom engages in or displays this behavior or activity.
- Sometimes or occasionally engages in this behavior or activity.
- Frequently engages in this behavior or activity.

Part II is a self-scoring key with directions.

PART I: COACHING INVENTORY (Employee)

	Rarely or Seldom	Occasionally or Sometimes	Frequently
1. My manager spends time with me to help me develop professionally and in my career.	1	2	3
2. My manager spends time with me discussing how to perform to my highest abilities.	1	2	3
3. My manager observes me and targets any skills or behaviors for further development.	1	2	3
4. When giving feedback to me, my manager prefers to guard my feelings by softening the feedback.	3	2	1
5. When meeting with me, my manager ensures privacy and uninterrupted time.	1	2	3
6. In a developmental meeting, my manager encourages me to tell him or her as much as I can about the issue.	1	2	3
7. My manager revises development plans that have previously been agreed upon with me as needed, and provides further coaching.	1	2	3
8. My manager resists losing his or her best employees to other opportunities within the company.	3	2	1
9. During a formal performance appraisal or employee progress review, my manager devotes time to discussing plans to further improve my performance.	1	2	3
10. My manager identifies and communicates the consequence of my not developing to my potential.	1	2	3
11. In a performance or development discussion, my manager describes to me specifically what the ideal performance or behavior is.	1	2	3
12. In a developmental or performance discussion, my manager concentrates on his or her own perspective rather than on mine.	3	2	1
13. My manager encourages a two-way discussion by asking me for my perspective on areas for development or improvement.	1	2	3

PART I: COACHING INVENTORY (Employee) (CONT.)

	Rarely or Seldom	Occasionally or Sometimes	Frequently
14. My manager periodically reviews with me my progress toward established development goals.	1	2	3
15. My manager sets time aside throughout the year, outside of performance appraisal and other formal processes, to discuss my professional development and advancement.	1	2	3
16. My manager creates a work environment that allows me to change and improve my performance over time.	1	2	3
17. When my manager identifies a development need for me, he or she just discusses it with me without worrying about any formal advance planning for the meeting.	3	2	1
18. My manager provides specific feedback to me on performance and development and suggests changes for improvement.	1	2	3
19. In a development or performance discussion, my manager pays attention to and considers my perspective.	1	2	3
20. In a meeting with me, my manager tends to concentrate so much on what he or she wants to say that he or she doesn't always hear what I am saying.	3	2	1
21. My manager evaluates my development and reinforces any increase in competence.	1	2	3
22. During a formal performance appraisal or employee progress review, my manager devotes time to discussing development and career advancement aspirations.	1	2	3
23. My manager leaves performance discussions to performance appraisal meetings only.	3	2	1
24. Before actually conducting a developmental meeting with me, my manager determines specifically what he or she wants me to do differently and why.	1	2	3
25. In a developmental meeting, my manager helps me to identify barriers to future development and ways to overcome them.	1	2	3

PART I: COACHING INVENTORY (Employee) (CONT.)

	Rarely or Seldom	Occasionally or Sometimes	Frequently
26. When meeting with me, my manager shows that he or she is interested and attentive through nonverbal behaviors, such as facing me directly, making eye contact, etc.	1	2	3
27. My manager makes sure he or she has understood everything I have said through behaviors such as concentrating, paraphrasing, and checking for understanding.	1	2	3
28. In implementing development plans, my manager leaves employees on their own for the most part.	3	2	1
29. My manager helps me to better understand the expectations of our organizational culture and environment, and how they can impact my professional aspirations.	1	2	3
30. My manager actively identifies performance improvement opportunities for individual employees.	1	2	3
31. If and when my manager notes a development need or opportunity for me, he or she takes time to analyze the situation and to determine the root causes and barriers to improvement.	1	2	3
32. My manager gives honest feedback that helps me to better understand how my behaviors and performance are perceived within the organization.	1	2	3
33. My manager conveys a positive attitude throughout a coaching session that communicates his or her belief in my ability to reach agreed-upon goals.	1	2	3
34. My manager probes for further information from me through behaviors such as concentrating and paraphrasing and checking for understanding.	1	2	3
35. My manager monitors my use of a skill or behavior that was targeted for improvement on the job.	1	2	3

PART II: SCORING (<u>Employee</u>)

Directions: Transfer the numerical values (1, 2, 3) you have given to each item to the spaces in the columns below. (Please record each individual number carefully, as some of the numerical values change within each column or category.) Add the numbers in each column for a total score for each category, then return the inventory to your coach or manager.

Commitment toward Professional Development	Commitment toward Performance Development	Assessment, Diagnosis, and Planning
1.	2.	3.
8.	9.	10.
15.	16.	17.
22.	23.	24.
29.	30.	31.
Total:	Total:	Total:

Meeting Face-to-Face and Giving Feedback	Attending	Listening and Responding	Implementation and Follow-Up
4.	5.	6.	7.
11.	12.	13.	14.
18.	19.	20.	21.
25.	26.	27.	28.
32.	33.	34.	35.
Total:	Total:	Total:	Total:

INTERPRETATION (For the Coach/Manager)

Look at your scores in each category as one indication of the degree to which you use or are committed to this coaching philosophy, behavior, or skill.

Scores in the 12- to 15-point range indicate use of or commitment to these coaching areas.

Scores in the 5- to 8-point range indicate areas of coaching on which you may want to focus more attention.

PLOTING EMPLOYEE SCORES

To create a profile of your coaching strengths and highlight opportunities for improvement, as seen by your employees, plot the scores from each of the seven categories on the graph below. Create a plot line by connecting the circled numbers.

	Commitment toward Professional Development	Commitment toward Performance Development	Assessment, Diagnosis, Planning	Meeting Face-to-Face and Giving Feedback	Attending	Listening, Responding	Implementation, Follow-Up
MOST	15	15	15	15	15	15	15
	14	14	14	14	14	14	14
	13	13	13	13	13	13	13
	12	12	12	12	12	12	12
	11	11	11	11	11	11	11
	10	10	10	10	10	10	10
	9	9	9	9	9	9	9
LEAST	8	8	8	8	8	8	8
	7	7	7	7	7	7	7
	6	6	6	6	6	6	6
	5	5	5	5	5	5	5

You may want to plot these scores on your Self profile graph as well.

PERSONAL LEARNING JOURNAL: COACHING INSIGHTS

Use this section to analyze the results of the Coaching Inventories to identify the coaching areas in which you want to improve.

1. Look at the Coaching Inventory (<u>Self</u>) scores as well as the Coaching Inventory (<u>Employee</u>) scores. What do the score values (Self and Employee) and profile graph tell you about each category below? Also compare your self-score to your employees' scores and reflect on the possible reasons for any differences.

   a. **Commitment toward Professional Development:** This category refers to your commitment to coaching employees for career advancement and growth within the organization.

   b. **Commitment toward Performance Development:** This category refers to your commitment to coaching employees to achieving even higher job performance.

   c. **Assessment, Diagnosis, and Planning:** This category refers to your skill at assessing and diagnosing the need for coaching for each employee, as well as planning for an upcoming coaching meeting.

   d. **Meeting Face-to-Face and Giving Feedback:** This category refers to engaging in actual face-to-face coaching meetings with employees and your skill in giving them relevant and direct feedback.

   e. **Attending:** This category refers to your skill in attending to the employee's perspective, needs, and self-esteem during the coaching meeting.

   f. **Listening and Responding:** This category refers to your own skill at listening carefully to the employee and responding appropriately during the coaching meeting.

   g. **Implementation and Follow-Up:** This category refers to working with the employee to establish, implement, and monitor a development plan as a result of the meeting.

2. Look over the relative scores and plotted points from your inventories. Which categories appear to be most in need of your further attention?

11

HOW DO YOU COMPARE WITH THE PEOPLE YOU FIND DIFFICULT?

Mel Silberman and Freda Hansburg

Overview We all work with people we find difficult. It may be that their behavior is downright annoying to us, or just puzzling. In either event, we have an unsettling perception that we "just don't get" them.

One of the best ways to understand others, especially when their behavior is difficult for us, is to compare ourselves to them. Each of us looks through the world with his or her own set of glasses. Some of us wear rosy glasses and see the world mostly in positive terms, while others wear darker lenses and see things in negative terms. Some of us look through glasses that make things appear very close, so that we always feel pressured: "Wow, that presentation is only a week away! I'd better get busy preparing!" Others' glasses make things look further away: "That presentation isn't for another week. I've got plenty of time to get ready." The more we can recognize the glasses others see the world through, the better we can understand their perspectives and behavior.

This instrument is a tool to compare ourselves in these categories to other people we might find difficult. Often, it can shed light on the tension in the relationship by revealing one of two possibilities:

1. We are very different from the other person and need to "walk in their shoes."
2. We are very similar to the other person and don't like what we see.

Use the instrument to shed light on the challenging employees you manage. Or, have your team use it to explore their relationships with others.

Contact Information: Mel Silberman, Active Training, 303 Sayre Drive, Princeton, NJ 08540, 609-987-8157, mel@activetraining.com, www.activetraining.com

COMPARING STYLE, GENDER, AGE, AND CULTURE

Directions: Circle the point on each continuum that fits the way you see a person you find to be difficult. Put a square on the point that fits the way you see yourself. Note: If you are of the same gender, age, or cultural group as the other person, complete the section anyway since you may still be very different in how you participate in that group. Are there differences in gender, age, culture, and style that might explain the difficulties between you? Are there similarities that might also account for the difficulties?

Style Differences

spontaneous . . . . deliberate

   •   •   •   •   •

social . . . . private

   •   •   •   •   •

emotional . . . . logical

   •   •   •   •   •

take-charge . . . . responsive

   •   •   •   •   •

Gender Differences

seek to fix things . . . . seek to discuss things

   •   •   •   •   •

competitive . . . . collaborative

   •   •   •   •   •

seek independence . . . . seek relationship

   •   •   •   •   •

give opinions . . . . ask questions

   •   •   •   •   •

COMPARING STYLE, GENDER, AGE, AND CULTURE (CONT.)

Generational Differences

intense . . . . easy-going

•   •   •   •   •

need to focus . . . . able to multitask

•   •   •   •   •

loyal . . . . uncommitted

•   •   •   •   •

need to control others . . . . need to control self

•   •   •   •   •

Cultural Differences

confronting . . . . avoiding

•   •   •   •   •

self-oriented . . . . group-oriented

•   •   •   •   •

respect for talent . . . . respect for authority

•   •   •   •   •

loose . . . . rule-oriented

•   •   •   •   •

INTERPRETING THE RESULTS

Look over the circles and squares. Do you notice many differences? Think about how your differences in style, gender, age, or cultural characteristics affect your relationship with that person. Do you notice many similarities? Think about how those similarities in style, gender, age, or culture contribute to your relationship with that person.

Which of these differences or similarities may be interfering with your effectiveness with this person? Try to imagine yourself as this person, seeing the world through his or her eyes. How do you feel? How do things seem different to you?

12

ARE YOU A LOVE 'EM OR LOSE 'EM MANAGER?

Beverly Kaye and Sharon Jordan-Evans

Overview   Want to keep your stars? From the best-seller, *Love 'Em or Lose 'Em* (Berrett-Koehler, 1999), this instrument will help you determine if you are the type of manager who creates an environment that encourages employees to stay, or one who sends them running, or somewhere in between.

Contact Information: Beverly Kaye, Career Systems International, Inc., 3545 Alana Dr., Sherman Oaks, CA 91403, 818-995-6454; Beverly.Kaye@csibka.com, www.keepem.com

Sharon Jordan-Evans, The Jordan Evans Group, 565 Cheswick Way, Cambria, CA 93428, 818-347-6565, sjordevans@aol.com, www.keepem.com

ARE YOU A LOVE 'EM OR LOSE 'EM MANAGER?

Instructions: Read each of the 26 statements below and check those that are most true for you. Be completely honest. Your score will tell you where you stand and what to do next.

1. _____ I inquire about how to make work more satisfying for my employees.

2. _____ I realize that I am mainly responsible for retaining the talent on my team.

3. _____ I know my employees' career ambitions.

4. _____ I demonstrate respect for the different backgrounds, values, and needs of my employees.

5. _____ I take steps to ensure that my employees are continually challenged by their work.

6. _____ I respect the work–life balance issues that my employees face.

7. _____ I make my employees aware of the different ways in which they can develop and advance their careers.

8. _____ When hiring, I look for more than a match of skills.

9. _____ I share with my employees most, if not all, of the information to which I'm privy.

10. _____ I apologize when I think I have hurt one of my employee's feelings.

11. _____ I encourage humor at work.

12. _____ I introduce my employees to others within my internal and external network.

13. _____ I encourage my employees to stretch in their own development.

14. _____ I am committed to my employees and value their contributions.

15. _____ I watch for internal opportunities for my employees.

16. _____ I support the work-related interests of my employees.

17. _____ I question and bend the rules to support my employees.

18. _____ I recognize and reward the accomplishments of my employees in a variety of ways.

ARE YOU A LOVE 'EM OR LOSE 'EM MANAGER? (CONT.)

19. _____ I provide my employees with as much choice as possible on how their work gets done.

20. _____ I tell my employees where they stand and what they need to do to improve.

21. _____ I take time to listen to and understand my employees.

22. _____ I take the initiative to learn what my employees value.

23. _____ I recognize signs of stress or overwork in my employees.

24. _____ I am tuned in to the special wants and needs of the GenX-ers on my team.

25. _____ I give power and decision-making authority to my employees.

26. _____ I continually try to improve upon my own managerial and retention strategies.

SCORING

Give yourself one point for each statement you marked as true. Then check here to see where you stand.

0-6: Alert. You are at risk of losing your best people. Start by asking what it is they want. Then immediately move to three to five of the ideas from this quiz and put them into action.

7-13: Caution. You've got work to do to keep your best people. Begin now to ask them, as well as your trusted colleagues, what's working and what's not.

14+: Kudos. You're on the right track to keeping your best people, but don't stop now. Choose other ideas to work on and give yourself the praise you deserve.

13

DO YOU SUPPORT STAR PERFORMANCE?

Frederick Miller and Corey Jamison

Overview　　How many "stars" work for you? How many of your people burst with energy and innovation? How many of your people experience constant growth, always thinking forward and developing new ideas, new products, and new strategies?

What if you had more? What if *all* of your people were stars?

Many organizations focus on attracting talent from the outside. Yet there is often a great deal of unutilized or underutilized talent within an organization. What we know about how energetic, innovative people operate can be used to tap into that talent, to transform an organization from the inside.

So-called natural leaders have learned to be comfortable expressing their full range of ideas and abilities. They feel supported by their managers in doing so and that sense of support enables them to keep stretching their range. One way to encourage star performance within an organization, therefore, is to create an environment in which *all* people feel both support for expressing ideas and an expectation of constant growth.

Benefits to providing that environment include:

1. New leaders can come forth from unexpected places. Helping existing members of the organization learn to perform higher-level roles is less expensive than hiring new high-level people.

2. Organizations that invest in their workforce this way often recover their investment many times over, because they have "leaders at all levels"—people who produce a constant stream of new ideas, innovative products, and improved processes.

Contact Information: Frederick A. Miller, The Kaleel Jamison Consulting Group, Inc., 279 River Street, Suite 401, Troy, NY 12180, 518-271-7000, familler@kjcg.com, www.kjcg.com

Corey L. Jamison, The Kaleel Jamison Consulting Group, Inc., 29 North Main Street, Upton, MA 01568, 508-529-2338, coreyjamison@kjcg.com, www.kjcg.com

3. Organizations that foster both support and challenge quickly develop reputations as worthy, which helps them retain their key people and also attract new, talented people.

Giving the instrument that follows to your employees yields results such as the following:

1. Data on the extent to which your people:
   a. feel supported in putting forth their ideas and abilities;
   b. offer support to other members of the organization for doing so; and
   c. are oriented toward growth and challenge.

2. Expression in action of your expectation that your employees will continue to grow, both professionally and personally, and will support others' efforts to do the same.

3. Increased commitment from employees to fostering a supportive environment. Asking for people's ideas and opening the discussion that emerges from the questions in Section 4 fosters buy-in by connecting people to the ideas of support and challenge; additionally, it may point to some areas in which you can make simple changes that translate to "quick wins" in the overall environment.

ASSESSING PROFESSIONAL AND PERSONAL EXPRESSION AND GROWTH AT THE WORKPLACE

_____(company name) expects you to bring the full range of your abilities to your job and to work with others to help them do the same. In order to succeed as an organization, we need everyone's talent. The information you provide here and in the discussion to follow will help us understand what we are doing well in supporting you and your growth and what we can do better.

Directions: On a scale of 1 (low) to 5 (high), assess yourself within your work environment.

1. How much of yourself do you express at work?

To what extent:

_____ Do you feel energized and empowered at work?

_____ Do you feel comfortable presenting new ideas at work?

_____ Do you feel welcomed as yourself by other members of the organization?

_____ Do you actively appreciate yourself for who you are?

_____ Does your workplace present difficulty or challenge as an opportunity for growth?

_____ Is your workplace free of demeaning and disrespectful language and behavior?

2. How much support do you offer to others in expressing themselves?

To what extent:

_____ Do you actively appreciate others for the way they are?

_____ Do you listen, listen, and listen before responding?

_____ Do you actively use direct and clear communication with others?

_____ Do you see and acknowledge others' growth?

_____ Do you consciously avoid using put-downs or demeaning behaviors at work?

_____ Do you present challenges or difficulties with colleagues as opportunities for both of you to grow?

3. How willing are you to explore new territory?

To what extent:

_____ Do you challenge yourself to take risks?

_____ Are you committed to your own growth?

_____ Are you willing to persevere through an uncomfortable challenge?

ASSESSING PROFESSIONAL AND PERSONAL EXPRESSION AND GROWTH AT THE WORKPLACE (CONT.)

_____ Are you comfortable with people not liking you at times?

_____ Do you find other energized, empowered people to learn from and grow with?

_____ Are you committed to working through and learning from conflict?

4. What would make it easier for people to show and develop their full selves in your workplace?

What are some ways to create an environment in which you'd be able to thrive and grow?

Identify two other people you want to support in being their best selves.

What will you do to support them?

What are some ways to eliminate demeaning words and disrespectful behaviors in the workplace?

SCORING

Directions: Add your ratings for each section and note the totals in the column labeled "My Score." Add your totals for all three sections to determine your "Grand Total."

Section	Possible Score	My Score
1. Self-Expression	30	
2. Support for Expression	30	
3. Orientation to Growth	30	
Grand Total	**90**	

POSTSURVEY DISCUSSION

The subtotals for each section indicate: 1) how safe people feel being themselves at work; 2) how much support they feel they offer others in expressing themselves; and 3) to what extent people feel they're growing. In addition to having people determine their individual areas of strength and need, summing the totals of a team or other group of people may point to areas of strength or need for the organization as a whole.

The questions in the fourth section of the survey present departure points for a discussion of what individuals and organizations can do to eliminate words and behaviors that demean others and to help create a safe environment that fosters growth for all members of the organization. The discussion can identify organizational strengths and point to areas for development, as well as encouraging buy-in to the initiative.

FOLLOW-UP PROCESS

1. Report back on the findings of the survey as soon as possible, including initial steps for responding to any perceived lack of support for individuals and their growth.

2. Celebrate areas of success. In responding to areas of need, seek multilevel involvement to plan and implement changes to policies, practices, and procedures.

3. Measure the effectiveness of any changes. Continue to ask for feedback and to communicate ongoing results.

References:

Jamison, Kaleel. *The Nibble Theory and the Kernel of Power: A Book about Leadership, Self-Empowerment, and Personal Growth.* Paulist Press: Mahwah, NJ, 1985.

14

MOVING FROM BOSS TO COACH

Barbara Pate Glacel

Overview   Leadership in organizations of the twenty-first century requires more than the basic skills of business, vision, and interpersonal relationships. The successful leader in today's organization must not only master the basics, but must also be able to operate at the speed of change while bringing others along in this fast-paced process. Leadership requires followership, and it is the coach who makes this happen. The leader as coach demonstrates consistency and excellence in action, behavior, modeling, and teaching.

This guide explains the necessity of the coach's role in today's business environment, and provides ten tips for starting your own process of moving from boss to coach.

DEMANDS FOR LEADERSHIP IN THE HYPERGROWTH ENVIRONMENT

Particularly in high-technology and knowledge industries where hypergrowth is the order of the day, there is less evidence of good leadership than in traditional business models. Organizations are hiring the best of the best with regard to technical skills. These individuals can often get away with having poor leadership and interpersonal skills, because their technical skills are in such high demand.

At some point, however, the undeveloped leadership and interpersonal skills cause the organizational progress to derail. The organization must deal with leadership development in order to survive over the long haul. The hypergrowth environment does not always allow for traditional classroom teaching models, so it becomes incumbent on all leaders to set the example and teach others about what is acceptable organizational behavior. In other words, leaders must become coaches to develop other leaders.

Contact Information: Barbara Pate Glacel, Glacel Development Group, 12103 Richland Lane, Oak Hill, VA 20171, 703-262-9120, BPGlacel@aol.com, www.glacel.com

The job of the traditional boss is to perform management activities, such as planning, organizing, hiring and firing, providing direction, tracking metrics and preparing reports, and creating and adhering to a budget. These activities all focus on the present. The coach, on the other hand, focuses on the future. The coach determines the organization's success through people-development activities, such as relationships, motivation, trust, communication, vision, decision making, and interpersonal skills.

The traditional model of the hierarchical organization portrays people at the top making decisions, while those lower in the organization receive direction and implement the decisions of others. This old-school model no longer applies in the hypergrowth environment. The current implementers must be able to make rapid decisions. Point-of-service workers must understand the organization and the vision to the extent that they can make immediate decisions to serve the customer. The implementers, regardless of their level in the organization, must be coached continuously and in real time, in order to translate organizational strategy into practice and guarantee continued organizational success.

FORCES OF CHANGE IN THE HYPERGROWTH ENVIRONMENT

In the hypergrowth environment, information as power diminishes, and the relationship between the manager and the employee changes. Often the employee has more information than the manager because of proximity to the operation. Electronic communication has provided immediate access to information, allowing employees, suppliers, and customers to become more knowledgeable. Far from having all the answers, the manager may have less detail than others. Therefore, the manager must become a mentor and coach more than a problem solver and controller.

The global market requires more strategic and systems-thinking skills and an appreciation of foreign cultures, complexity, and virtual decision making. This is true even in small organizations operating within the regional confines of one area, because of the cultural and demographic mix of personnel. Often bosses and employees are not physically in the same place, and it is more difficult to get to know one another. Bosses must be able to relate on others' terms in order to motivate and build trust.

Demographics are changing, particularly with the onslaught of Generation X and Y employees in the workforce. Organizations face challenges in attracting and retaining talent. The younger workforce places a higher priority on lifestyle issues of balance and interpersonal relationships. The hierarchy does not immediately command respect, and there is diminished loyalty to institutions. The boss who directs without compassion is soon left without a workforce to direct.

To compete successfully, organizations must demonstrate more efficiencies in their practices. The greatest inefficiencies, however, are in the realm of human interactions. People simply do not change as quickly as technology and organizational structures change. While people must work together to produce the knowledge, service, or product of the organization, the levels of emotional literacy and personal responsibility may conspire to produce inefficiency. Leaders then must be able to intervene to improve human interaction skills, by demonstrating those skills themselves and coaching continuous behavioral development.

REQUIREMENTS FOR SUCCESSFUL COACHES

The leader's transition from boss to coach does not mean that inherent business skills are left behind. Organizational success still requires the management activities that focus on the present operation and success at meeting the organizational mission. However, the focus expands to a triple bottom-line issue of finances, employees, and customers, requiring the leader to manage much more complexity. The leader must be able to think strategically and operationally at the same time, and to balance both analytical and intuitive skills. A systems orientation allows the leader to "connect the dots" of disparate pieces of information and relationships. The leader must be able to articulate where the organization is going and what kind of organization it will be. The coach must be able to translate that direction for the people of the organization.

The leader as coach must have increased skill at managing continuous, large-scale, and transformational change. Change is a constant process, not an event that is completed and institutionalized. The current environment makes change the everyday norm, so that policies, procedures, and relationships must be currently evaluated and modified to meet new and different situations. The coach must be able to help others operate in this change dimension so that good decisions are made.

In doing all this, the leader as coach must demonstrate other skills to assure future success through the performance of the organization's most important asset—its people. The coaching relationship calls for communication skills of listening, speaking, forming interpersonal connections, and sincerely caring for people. A pro forma relationship between boss and employee does not allow for the coaching and learning that allows trust, loyalty, and high performance to develop in organizations. Personal issues of family, lifestyle, and balance must be part of the communication and caring in order for the coach's lessons to be fruitful.

A coach must have a deep understanding of his or her own personal strengths, weaknesses, passions, drivers, and needs, as well as personal and professional goals for growth. Coaches who do not understand themselves cannot demonstrate the truth of what is being said. The old notion of "walk the talk" takes on deeper meaning when the coach is trying to influence the behavior of others. Knowledge of self is a prerequisite for working with others, particularly others of different ages, cultures, and ethnicities.

The leader as coach must demonstrate both hard and soft skills. The hard skills of decision making, business knowledge, financial knowledge, strategic planning, and market analysis are important content lessons that must be passed on to leaders at all levels in the organization. The soft skills of self-knowledge, interpersonal communication, trust-building, information sharing, and building of followership among diverse personalities and cultures are vehicles for assuring the organization's success through continuous learning and adaptation in the environment of hypergrowth.

HOW TO BECOME A SUCCESSFUL COACH

1. *Spend time articulating to yourself what you believe in, what the company strategy is, and what values you want demonstrated.*

   The more you think about these issues and put words into meaning, the more clarity you may gain for your own thoughts and the message you deliver. Meaning is often not discovered in a vacuum; talk to others about your ideas and theirs. Make this a continuous and evolving discussion so that the strategy evolves in relationship to the changing environment, but also in conjunction with your deeply held values and beliefs.

2. *Take every opportunity to tell others about your beliefs, your strategy, and your values.*

   In every action of individuals and the organization, there is a lesson to be learned. Take the time to relate the lesson to your beliefs, your deeply held values, and the strategy of the organization. This teaching opportunity allows others to apply the basics to individual events and improves their own potential for good decision making when new situations confront them.

3. *Tell stories about the history of the organization, the profession, and the principles you want demonstrated.*

   Often, lessons are learned in the stories that allow others to understand behaviorally the values and culture of the organization. Learn from the "old-timers" about how the organization was at its origins and how it evolved over time. Trace the strands of success and the lessons learned from mistakes.

4. *Meet in small groups with colleagues and employees to discuss the business and where it is headed.*

   Plan brown-bag lunches or end-of-the-week reviews to reflect on what is happening in the rush of events surrounding the work you do. Have cascading meetings down through the hierarchy so that communications are passed down in a consistent manner and all employees have a chance to be heard as they discuss the operations and changes taking place.

5. *Spread knowledge by every means available: written, spoken, and behavioral.*

   Construct a communications plan that takes advantage of every possible medium. Daily voice mail messages, frequent e-mail messages, a company newsletter or bulletin board, speeches, and video broadcasts are important ways to provide a consistent message. Even more important is that the message is consistent over time, consistent among all leaders in the organization, and consistent with all leadership actions throughout the organization.

6. *Explain "why" as well as "what."*

   Employees want more than the final answer. Explain the decision-making process and the factors and options considered. Be able to articulate how an action fits with the company's vision and how it will impact individual employees. In the face of any change, employees will always experience it first in terms of impact on themselves. To improve the chances of success, consider the individual first when you communicate any change or decision.

7. *Lead by example so your behavior becomes the teacher.*

   More lessons are learned by watching others than by listening to their rhetoric. Take a moment to consider whether the example is the behavior others should follow. Expecting people to "do as I say, not as I do" is a proven formula for disaster.

8. *Use activities outside the organization, such as community service, as the classroom for teaching values and principles.*

   The volunteer arena is an excellent training ground to develop leadership and coaching skills. Community activities provide a valuable training ground for one to practice these behaviors in a "safer" setting than when one's job, the bottom line, or the success of others' performance and livelihood may be at stake.

9. *Never miss the opportunity to turn an interaction into a teachable moment.*

Despite the speed of change in the environment in which organizations and individuals operate, taking a moment for reflection in the present is always time well spent. It saves time later when mistakes might be repeated, when events must be recreated for analysis, or when a plan has gone awry and must be salvaged.

10. *Be a coach and have a coach.*

Coaches are valuable for leaders and employees at all levels of the organization. A coach provides a resource for reflection, learning, and thinking outside the box. The coach does not have all the answers of "how to," but offers the opportunity to improve processes and decisions that will in turn improve productivity and efficiency in the organization.

WHEN ALL IS SAID AND DONE, WHAT MUST COACHES DO?

- Explain and reinforce the vision.
- Exemplify organizational values routinely.
- Keep appraisal, measurement, and reward systems in line with goals and priorities.
- Ensure that channels for communication remain open as advertised.
- Encourage risk-taking and empowerment while focusing on quality output.
- Develop future key people.

15

IMPROVING MORALE AND ENHANCING PRODUCTIVITY

Barbara Glanz

Overview Study after study has shown that what workers want from their jobs is not merely better benefits or more money. Rather, it is the small things that make workers feel committed to an organization. One study indicates that the top three things workers want are interesting work, full appreciation for the work they do, and a feeling of being in on things. Baxter Labs recently conducted a study in which they asked their employees worldwide what they could do to make things better for them. The resounding answer was that the employees wanted to be "respected as whole human beings with a life outside of work."

What seems critical, then, in workplaces today is for leaders to respond to workers as human beings and to foster an atmosphere that is inclusive, caring, creative, appreciative, and joyful. People are looking for a deeper sense of meaning and purpose in their work; above all, they want to be respected and valued.

This guide describes 25 ideas that you can adapt and introduce in your organization to make an immediate difference in spirit. Common sense as well as current research tell us that happy employees are more productive employees. Implementing even a few of these ideas will not only boost morale, but will also impact productivity and profit.

Contact Information: Barbara Glanz, 4047 Howard Ave., Western Springs, IL 60558, 708-246-8594, Fax 708-246-5123, bglanz@barbaraglanz.com, www.barbaraglanz.com

25 IDEAS TO IMPROVE MORALE AND ENHANCE PRODUCTIVITY

1. *Does everyone in your organization have business cards?* If not, providing them is one of the fastest ways to boost morale. They can be designed on a computer for little or no cost. What a meaningful way to tell an employee how valued and important he or she is! If you already have a business card, look at it for a moment. We use business cards to network and create relationships. However, most business cards are boring, say nothing memorable about the individual, and are blank on the back! Ask yourself these questions about your business card: Is there anything distinctive about it? Is there anything that represents you as a unique human being? If not, turn it over and add something on the human level, such as a quotation, a personal motto, or a graphic or picture of something you love. Not only will you make a distinctive impression, but people will have a way to connect with you on a deeper level when they learn something important about you, the human being. That is the beginning of a relationship.

2. *Hold a contest for employees:* "If my company or department were a T-shirt, it would say...." Have employees actually design the shirt, either on a real T-shirt or on paper. Photograph, post, or videotape the results. You will learn amazing things about the way people feel about your organization; you will encourage people to get their creative juices going; and you will have fun in the process. Company legends are created from experiences like these.

3. *Collect drawings from employees' children or grandchildren* of "What my Mom [Dad, Grandma, Grandpa, Aunt, Uncle] does at work all day." Compile the drawings into a company booklet or display them for customers to enjoy. That helps to blend work and family by involving workers' family members, and it creates memories. If possible, display the drawings where employees can bring their children in to view them as well. That will add a sense of involvement and pride in the organization for the whole family.

4. *Send a handwritten note to at least one employee a week.* They can be as simple as small Post-It notes or even a printed card with your added handwritten sentence at the end. Doing this will not only impress your employee, it will build loyalty internally. We are all desperate to be appreciated. To help you remember to write the notes, pick one day of the week and do not leave the office on that day until you have completed your notes.

5. *Keep a bulletin board in your office of pictures of direct reports.* This will not only help build relationships as you post the pictures, but it will remind everyone visually of their importance to you. Send birthday cards to them on their special day and congratulations cards when they achieve a personal or business success. Set up another board where you post pictures of employees' families, weddings, graduations, vacations, new grandchildren, and other successes. Thus, you will celebrate their loyalty as well.

---

25 IDEAS TO IMPROVE MORALE AND ENHANCE PRODUCTIVITY (CONT.)

6. When your people first turn on their computers, *greet them with a message of the day*, such as a quote on customer service or personal growth, something humorous, or even the birthdays of employees during that week. Beginning the day with inspiration helps lift the level of interaction in your workplace. If you start doing this, be prepared to continue; it will be a negative experience if employees expect this encouragement and on some days it isn't there.

7. After any accomplishment of note, *put a specially wrapped package* of candy, flowers, or other tokens of appreciation on your employee's desk.

8. For an all-company or team celebration, *have small groups creatively dramatize significant events* from the year or from the company's history, or even a company legend. The presentations can be either live or videotaped. This experience will bring out talent and creativity that you didn't even know existed, and it will be a team-building experience for everyone. The pride that comes from celebrating one's organization is long-lasting and creates a special kind of employee loyalty.

9. *Collect company legends and success stories on video or audiotape.* If possible, interview the employee or the customer involved. These tapes become a source of pride for current employees and a wonderful addition to orientation sessions for new hires. Record and celebrate the moments of peak performance in your organizational culture.

10. Once a month, *encourage senior management to do something creative* for all employees or for employees in their divisions: Cook them breakfast, bring around an ice cream cart, serve them doughnuts and coffee, wash the windshields of their cars as they arrive at work, or even take them all to lunch. These small acts of appreciation will be remembered and talked about for weeks.

11. *Add a personal signature to your memos* to differentiate yourself from all the others who do the same work as you.

12. *Have a company or team poster party* for all frustrated or aspiring artists to create signs and posters that demonstrate the company's values. Use quotations, graphics, and bright colors. Display them in clear plastic frames throughout the building and move them once a week so that everyone can see all of them. Not only will you find talent you did not know existed; you will also create an atmosphere of inspiration and delight. Tom Peters says that if your hallways are boring, chances are everything in your organization is boring.

---

13. *Purchase a Red Plate for your organization or department* that says "You are special today." This can be passed around to anyone in the company as an affirmation. It is amazing how such a small thing can make a huge difference in morale. You may want to keep a record of who gets the plate and why—another way to celebrate one another.

14. *Add a quotation, graphic, cartoon, or seasonal reminder to memos and fax cover sheets.* Make them fun and interesting. Most fax cover sheets are boring, and the organization has missed a wonderful opportunity to make an impression, differentiate itself, and communicate its ideas and values.

15. As an organization, *give out buttons* that say "Kindness Is Contagious—Catch It!" or something similar when someone does a kind deed for you. Then ask the person to pass the button on to someone else.

16. *Create a company mascot* that goes along with the spirit of the company. For example, Rosenbluth Travel uses a salmon because they're always "swimming upstream." They give their clients stuffed salmon and chocolate salmon, and a salmon pin is their highest internal award. Another company has a marketing department mascot, a green frog. The company has had lots of fun with other departments "kidnapping" the frog and then sending ransom notes.

17. *Have a Laugh a Day bulletin board* where you display appropriate cartoons and humorous writings. You may also want to keep a fishbowl of cartoons and jokes in the reception area so that visitors, too, can enjoy a smile while they are waiting. Research has shown that the most productive workplaces include about 10 minutes of laughter each hour. Is your workplace one where people are enjoying themselves?

18. *Designate one room as the company Whine Cellar*, the place for anyone to go who is having a bad day or wants to gripe. Put a sign on the door and have fun decorating it (in black?). Bring in stress toys, stuffed animals, cartoon books, and perhaps even treats. When someone is crabby, suggest spending some time there. It will probably become everyone's favorite place to go.

19. *Take a look at your office*; what does it say about your human level? Always display one or two reminders of things you really love in your office. Not only will it be more comfortable for you because it reminds you of the really important things in your life, but it will also help others to connect with you more quickly.

25 IDEAS TO IMPROVE MORALE AND ENHANCE PRODUCTIVITY (CONT.)

20. *Create a service guarantee for your work unit.* For example, a suburban hospital says, "If you're not seen by a professional in our emergency room in 15 minutes, your visit is free!" An accounting department says, "If you find an error in our work, lunch is on us." This guarantee will differentiate you to your clients and will help build teamwork and pride, as every employee commits to personally upholding the guarantee.

21. *Have a Four A's jar* (acknowledge, appreciate, affirm, assure). Keep it filled with wonderful, uplifting thoughts for anyone who needs one. You may also give these jars as gifts to your employees with one positive thought for every day of the year.

22. *Purchase pieces of clear acrylic to use as blotters on each employee's desk.* Have the employee create a collage under the blotter that contains creative reminders and examples of the company's values, such as photos, quotations, cartoons, mission statements, customer service models, slogans, or signs. This encourages creativity, creates anchors to remember what is important, and provides a delightful way to share as employees spend time looking at what others have done.

23. *Post "street" signs to name hallways in your building.* Choose names that communicate your company's mission or values or relate to your core business. Or name hallways after valued employees. If you make your values visible daily, employees will constantly be reminded of the organization's reason for being.

24. *Plan a "Bring your family to work day" for your organization.* Be sure to include activities for different age groups. Younger children will love sending a fax to someone, helping to stuff envelopes, copying things, and running errands. Older children will want to learn more about the actual business of the organization. You can even let them role play their parent's job to help them gain more empathy for what a parent or relative does all day. Use pieces from your new hire orientation, tours, and even special treats in the cafeteria to help make families feel a part of the organization. Make this day a fun celebration for everyone. Employees who have the full support of their families, especially during high-stress times at work, are more productive on the job.

25. *Think of something creative you could offer your employees as a free sample.* Everyone loves giveaways, and they can become powerful tools of appreciation.

Remember that it is truly the little things that really count. You might decide to try one new idea a month; or form a Spirit Committee and have them design a plan to incorporate some of these ideas into your culture; or simply use these ideas as is to get your own creative juices going.

16

DESIGNING AND IMPLEMENTING AN EFFECTIVE PERFORMANCE MANAGEMENT PROGRAM

Kammy Haynes and Warren Bobrow

Overview Despite its bad reputation, performance management can be one of the most powerful interventions an organization can implement. When designed and implemented correctly, the potential for a return on investment exists because:

- Performance standards that are related to organizational success are implemented throughout the company.
- High-performers can be more easily retained.
- A mechanism exists for correcting substandard performance.

This guide presents a framework for implementing a performance management program that will increase the likelihood of meeting your organization's objectives and gaining support from your employees.

INTRODUCTION

The mere mention of performance management (PM) elicits negative responses from all parties involved. Managers dread giving negative feedback and dealing with disgruntled employees. Employees often feel attacked and unappreciated, and are concerned about whether or not they are being treated fairly.

Contact Information: Kammy Haynes, The Context Group, 2073 Lake Shore Drive, Suite A, Chino Hills, CA 91709, 909-591-2848, kammyh@contextgroup.com, www.contextgroup.com

Warren Bobrow, The Context Group, 5812 W. 76th Street, Los Angeles, CA 90045, 310-670-4175, warrenb@contextgroup.com, www.contextgroup.com

Given all the pain associated with this process, why do the vast majority of organizations continue to put their staffs through it? The answer is simple: Without performance management, there is little accountability for performing at acceptable levels. Documentation and consistency would be nonexistent and most employees would never get any feedback about their performance, positive or negative. Handled correctly, though, an effective PM program can increase productivity and morale in your organization and help you retain valued high-performers.

Productivity will increase because you'll have standards and metrics to evaluate employee performance against. Morale can increase because employees are differentially rewarded for their performance based on objective criteria rather than on favoritism. In addition, high-performers eventually get tired of carrying the weight for low-performers and want the poor performers to be dealt with. A well-executed PM program can provide the tools to make that happen.

In contrast to performance appraisals, performance management is a process, not an event. In order to be effective, observing and documenting performance must be a continuous, ongoing activity. Because feedback is most effective when it occurs immediately after a behavior or action, managers should attempt to respond to their employees' actions promptly. You need to acknowledge positive behavior when you see it or hear about it and take immediate corrective action when you see or hear about negative behavior. If you wait too long, the power of the reward or discipline is diminished.

For example, you could thank an employee for a job well done ("Thanks for staying late to get that report out on time. I appreciate your dedication.") or issue a reprimand ("Sara, I overheard your conversation with Pete. It is not appropriate to discuss confidential information with people outside our department. Do you understand that you have violated a company policy?"). In either case, the key is to respond quickly. The longer the delay between the behavior and the feedback, the less likely you are to see a change in the employee's behavior. That's why appraisal meetings held once a year have little impact on overall performance.

When developing your PM program, consider three phases:

1. the preparation before the appraisal meeting;
2. conducting the appraisal meeting; and
3. the follow-up after the meeting.

A breakdown in any one of these areas will decrease the effectiveness of your PM. Within each phase, a variety of steps can be taken to improve your PM system and employee reactions.

Before the Appraisal Meeting

In order to design an effective PM program, you need a strong foundation. Considerable thought must be given to the corporate strategy, job analysis, the format of the appraisal tool, documenting performance, goal setting, and the communication plan. If you take these factors into consideration during your design, your PM program will be viewed more favorably by your employees and will be more likely to achieve the desired productivity results.

Strategy. The strategy will help you determine what skills, abilities, and behaviors you require of your employees currently, as well as what will be needed in the near future. It is important that you clearly link the strategy to the performance goals for each employee. Here is an illustrative scenario:

Carol is a phone representative in a customer call center. She needs to understand that the reason you are asking her to increase her troubleshooting skills is so that she spends less time on the phone with each customer. Spending less time with each customer means that Carol answers more calls and customers spend less time on hold. Cutting the time on hold for customers means their satisfaction ratings go up. Increasing customer satisfaction by 15 percent is a corporate goal. Meeting the goal will result in a larger pool of money available for raises. Carol is able to see how she contributes to the corporate goal and benefits from meeting that objective.

The strategy also keeps employees focused on the actions that will make the company successful. If a primary goal of the organization is to increase customer satisfaction, decisions need to be driven by whether a particular action will result in an increase in satisfaction. If the goal is to decrease costs, decisions should be evaluated based on cost–benefit ratios.

Job analysis. A job analysis (whether formal or informal) will help you determine what tasks are being performed and should be performed in the future as business conditions change (e.g., automation is introduced, staffing levels are reduced, functions are outsourced). The job analysis also provides the important links between key job behaviors and the organization's strategy. It is critical to understand the purpose and processes associated with each position in order to determine how the performance will be measured and evaluated. This understanding also helps you clarify where each employee's accountability begins and ends, so you can establish appropriate goals.

Format. The format of the appraisal tool is of primary concern to the management staff who complete them. The forms should be:

- simple to understand, with clear instructions and definitions of rating scale points (e.g., unacceptable, meets standard, exceeds standard);
- easy to use, such as a template to fill in that does not require complicated formatting, flows logically (e.g., mark the scale from 1 to 5), and provides a place for some narrative explanation.

Technology (on-line forms) can make the forms more convenient to complete.

Documentation. As is the case with many personnel-related issues, documentation is critical. By recording specific behaviors, dates, and consequences, you will be able to provide the employee with an objective assessment of his or her performance. Using objective data helps you avoid judgmental terms that are prone to upset employees or put them on the defensive. For example, rather than telling Mark that he is lazy or irresponsible, you can tell him that he has missed three critical deadlines in the last five months (projects x, y, and z). He would be insulted by the use of the term lazy, but it will be difficult to deny the fact that he missed the deadlines. This type of dialogue based on fact cannot occur unless you have documented performance on a regular, ongoing basis.

Managers often make the mistake of completing appraisals immediately before the meeting. As a result, their evaluations are often clouded by recent events (positive or negative) and do not reflect the employee's overall level of performance. This points out the importance of documenting performance over time, so that we develop a more balanced picture of the employee's capabilities and areas for improvement.

Goal setting. Goal setting is a key component of an effective PM program. If they are not given careful thought, goals can have a negative impact on productivity. In some cases, goals aimed at creating positive change have the opposite effect. Here is an example:

Greg works in the shipping department of a manufacturing company. At a meeting last month, management told everyone that quick turnaround times were the most important measure of success. From now on, raises and bonuses would be based on how many orders each employee was able to process each day. Within two weeks, the number of orders processed increased by 35 percent.

On the surface, this appeared to be a positive outcome. Unfortunately, the number of complaints from customers who received the wrong or damaged merchandise increased by 20 percent. Upon investigation, the warehouse manager found that employees were rushing through the orders and not packing them properly.

By focusing on one part of the job (quantity) without considering the impact on other parts of the system (quality), the goal produced negative results that made the gains in turnaround time moot. In many cases, managers can benefit from some goal-setting training (preferably using the new PM format and tools). In order to promote consistency, they should be given some direction in two critical areas:

1. *Rewarding the right behavior:* Employees will focus on what you measure (and reward). Be sure that you are rewarding the behaviors that will help your organization meets its objectives in the long term and the short term.

2. *Establishing clear goals and expectations:* If employees don't understand what they are supposed to do, as well as the quality or quantity they are expected to produce, the results are left to chance. If you give instructions that are open to interpretation, you may not get the results you want. For example, if you tell Jim (who arrives late at least two days per week) to "improve his attendance" and he is late only once a week thereafter, he has satisfied your request. However, this level of improvement is probably not what you had in mind.

Communication plan. It is important to communicate the changes in the PM program and to share the new process with all employees. Do not rely on the grapevine to disseminate the information. Given the level of distrust surrounding PM, it is best to address the issue head-on. Allow for some venting of past grievances and be prepared to explain how the new system addresses those issues. This communication effort is the first step in changing the culture and will impact the success of your implementation effort.

Communication should focus on the benefits of the new system for all parties. Collect information about your organization's concerns so you can incorporate those issues into your PM program design and into subsequent communication efforts.

During the Appraisal Meeting

An appraisal meeting is stressful for all parties involved. The manager is often uncomfortable about confronting poor performers and avoids the pain by giving acceptable ratings or making vague comments about the need for the employee to improve his or her performance. Some managers also avoid giving positive feedback, which eventually undermines the high-performers' motivation. At the same time, employees are nervous about being judged and dealing with the consequences of their managers' opinions. In many cases, both parties rush through the meeting, wanting it to be over rather than using the time in a constructive manner to review past performance and make plans for the future. Here are some suggestions to help you make the meeting more productive and less stressful.

Have an agenda. To reduce the stress for both parties, establish an agenda for the meeting, in advance, so both of you know what to expect. A typical agenda might include:

- reviewing the performance appraisal form and the ratings or comments,

- seeking input from the employee on the ratings or comments, and

- identifying areas for improvement, training needs, and career advancement opportunities.

Focus on the behavior, not the person. By describing events or behaviors rather than personal traits, you are focusing on the behavior that you want to reward or change. As we've already discussed, avoid labels such as "lazy," "irresponsible," and "careless." These words put employees on the defensive. However, if you present the behaviors that would make you attach those labels, it is easy to identify corrective actions. For example, rather than saying, "Tim, your carelessness cost us the Harris account," you might say, "Tim, because you didn't deduct the volume discounts associated with the Harris account, we submitted a bid much higher than our competitor's and we lost the account."

Provide constructive feedback. Focus on behaviors that can change and offer suggestions about how to make those changes. It is also important to solicit input from the employees about how to make the desired changes. Continuing with Tim's story, there are several options for making sure the problem doesn't happen again. If Tim seldom makes mistakes, the manager may ask him to double-check his work or to put a checklist together that would remind him to look for volume discounts. On the other hand, if Tim has made several mistakes in the past, the manager may send Tim to a training course on developing bids or require that someone look at his work before he submits it to the customer. Tim needs to be included in the problem-solving dialogue and allowed to make suggestions about how to avoid the problem in the future.

Set expectations. Don't make vague comments about the need to improve. Be specific about how much improvement you expect and how much time the employee has to make corrective actions. For example, rather than telling Tim that he needs to be more careful or pay more attention, the manager could say that she will monitor Tim's work for the next 30 days and that there should be no mistakes—all estimates must be correctly calculated, all volume discounts must be accurately applied, and the bids must be submitted on time. The manager has made the expectations clear and defined them so that both she and Tim will know if they have been met.

Identify consequences, both positive and negative. Employees take action to achieve results. In some cases, they want to gain something (praise, promotions, or a trip to a conference). In other cases, they want to avoid something (termination, embarrassment, or attention). It is important that employees understand what they have to gain or lose by meeting or not meeting your expectations. Tim needs to understand that if he completes his work for 30 days without any errors, he won't have to have someone check his work (positive). If he makes another error, he will receive a written warning that will go in his personnel file as part of the corporate disciplinary process (negative). Subsequent mistakes could result in his termination. By making these consequences explicit, you put Tim in control of his situation and allow him to make decisions accordingly.

Develop an action plan with input from the employee. While you are responsible for setting the goals and expectations, employees need to participate in developing their action plans for how to achieve those goals. By gaining their support and buy-in, you greatly increase the chances that they will reach those goals. If they aren't given an opportunity to participate in deciding how to do their work, employees are often resentful and may sabotage the project, either willfully or by doing exactly what you say and no more.

Schedule follow-up meetings. Use these meetings to evaluate the employee's progress on his or her action plan. Identify areas where you can offer assistance or support to help the employee continue to progress. If you do not follow up on the action plan, the likelihood of its being completed is greatly reduced.

After the Appraisal Meeting

Performance management is a continuous, ongoing process; it is important to provide additional coaching, which entails three steps:

Monitor performance. Monitoring can occur at follow-up meetings or by observing the employee on the job. You can also solicit feedback from the employee's customers, supervisor, or peers, as appropriate. If you do not follow through on this step, the employee will soon recognize that you are not serious about making the behavioral change and will slip back into his or her previous patterns.

Provide feedback. Acknowledge positive behavior when you see it or hear about it and take immediate corrective action when you see or hear about negative behavior. Don't assume that your employee "knows" how she or he is doing.

Offer support. Support can take many forms: training classes, mentoring, extra resources (money, staffing, equipment), or recognition as milestones are reached. The key is to let the employees know that you are willing to help them succeed.

Key points to remember when designing and implementing your performance management program:

- Performance management is a continuous process, not an event.

- Communicate the purpose, intentions, and process of the new PM program.

- Establish goals that are:
  - ✦ Specific, not vague
  - ✦ Directly linked to the corporate strategy
  - ✦ Observable
  - ✦ Measurable
  - ✦ Linked to specific time frames
  - ✦ Tied to consequences

- Feedback (positive and negative) is most effective when it immediately follows the behavior.

- Be specific in your documentation and during the meeting. Give concrete examples of behaviors. Avoid judgmental terms.

- Provide constructive feedback that includes suggestions for improvement.

- Seek and consider input from the employee regarding action plans.

- Use a format that is easy to use and makes sense to the users.

- Coaching will help employees make their desired behavioral changes.

CONCLUSION

By taking the time to consider the preparation, implementation, and follow-up phases of your PM program, you can increase the effectiveness and acceptance of the program. As you shift from appraisal events to continuous performance management, you will see significant changes in the organization. Once the process is communicated and understood by the organization, there will be less stress associated with appraisals. Employees will see the relationships between their performance and organizational success. High-performers will be reinforced for their efforts and low-performers will know how they can reap the same benefits. Management will then be in a position to reward behaviors that enable the business to thrive.

17

DEVELOPING ACTIVE LISTENING SKILLS AMONG YOUR EMPLOYEES

Sharon Bowman

Overview Here is a way you can have your team observe and practice specific active listening skills designed to enhance effective communication. Through a high-energy, reverse role play, they experience the effects of poor listening and then evaluate their own listening skills based upon the positive and negative practice and group discussion.

✓ This activity is useful in promoting communication in your team.

✓ The activity itself is experiential in nature, with participants working in pairs most of the time. Participants observe, experience, and discuss the insights they reach as a result of this activity.

✓ The processing questions are crucial to the success of the activity.

Suggested Time 30 minutes, depending upon the size of the group and the amount of processing time after each step

Materials Needed ✓ Chart stand and tablet (set up in the front of the room, visible to all)

✓ Broad-tip felt pen (for charting)

✓ Form A (Active Listening Notes)

✓ Form B (Reverse Role Play Scripts, two sets); each participant will get one script from each set during the activity

✓ Koosh™ ball or other soft, throwable object

Contact Information: Sharon Bowman, P.O. Box 464, Glenbrook, NV 89413, 775-749-5247, Sbowperson@aol.com, www.bowperson.com

The activity is divided into three steps:

Step One: Active Listening Modeling and Processing

Step Two: Partner Practice and Processing

Step Three: Reverse Role Play and Processing

Step One: Active Listening Modeling and Processing (10 minutes)

1. Introduction: Tell the group they will be observing you role play one of the most crucial skills in communication. More misunderstandings have occurred because of the lack of this skill than for any other reason. Ask the group to guess the skill (someone will eventually say "listening").

2. Modeling: Ask for a volunteer to role play with you. Explain to the volunteer that he will stand beside you and spend one minute telling you about a problem he's having at work. Because you will be modeling some active listening elements, ask him to speak a little slowly and to pause every now and then so that you can interject a comment. You and the volunteer will be doing the role play in front of the whole group. If the group is large, remain standing. If it's small, you can sit facing each other but in full view, so the whole group can observe the listening skills.

   Tell the whole group that you want them to watch for two things: what you're doing (body language) and what you're saying (words, sentences, and voice tone). Because you're modeling active listening skills, you'll need to exaggerate the following elements a bit so that the whole group can observe them:

   - open body language (body turned to partner, leaning forward, no legs or arms crossed)
   - facial expressions (nodding head, eye contact, smiles)
   - asking clarifying questions ("Is this what you mean? And then what happened?")
   - paraphrasing ("So what you said happened was this. I heard you say that...")
   - mirroring emotions ("You seem angry about that. I can tell this really upset you.")

   After about a minute, stop the role play and have the group give the volunteer a big round of applause as he returns to his seat.

3. Processing: Ask for another volunteer to record group responses on the chart paper during the following discussion. Pass out Form A (Active Listening Notes) and direct the participants to take

notes also. First ask the group what they observed you doing (your body language) during the role play. They will list the elements mentioned in step 2. You can add to the list anything they might have missed. Then ask them what they observed you saying. Again they'll list many, if not all, of the elements listed in step 2. If their responses are not concrete enough (example: "You showed respect" or "You were sympathetic"), ask, "How did I do that? What specific things did you see me do or say that indicated I did that?"

4. Processing, continued: Tell them the most important thing to remember in active listening is not so much what to do, but what not to do. Ask the group what you didn't do or say. They'll respond with answers like: "You didn't give advice, lecture, make suggestions, tell your own story, solve the problem for him, put him down, interrupt, turn away," etc. Have the volunteer chart these responses also. Tell them there is a place in a conversation to do some of that (like giving advice or telling your own story). That place is just not during the active listening part of the conversation.

5. Koosh™ Throw: Direct them to turn to a neighbor (someone sitting next to them) and tell that person three things to remember about active listening. Then do a short Koosh™ throw: Randomly throw a soft object to various participants who have to explain one element of active listening before passing or throwing the object to someone else.

Step Two: Partner Practice and Processing (10 minutes)

1. Introduction: Direct participants to find a partner and move their chairs so that they sit facing their partners. If there is an odd number, you can step in to form the last pair, or you can ask one pair to form a triad. Tell them to decide who is the talker and who is the listener.

2. Partner Practice: Explain that the talker will have about 2 minutes to discuss a work-related problem. The listener's job is to practice the active listening skills that were modeled. After they do this, call time and direct them to switch roles. Repeat the pair practice.

3. Processing: At the end of the practice time, have them give their partners high fives. Then ask the whole group the following processing questions: "As the talker, how did it feel to be listened to in this manner? As the listener, how did it feel to listen this way? What was easy or difficult about listening like this? How often do you listen to others or have others listen to you in this manner? Is

there a time when active listening would not be appropriate? Any other insights or comments?"

Step Three: Reverse Role Play and Processing (10 minutes)

1. Introduction: Tell participants to thank their partners and find a new partner. Once again, they sit facing a new partner. They decide who is the talker and who is the listener. Tell them they will be practicing listening skills again, only this time they will have a script to follow.

2. Reverse Role Play and Processing: Pass out the first set of reverse role play scripts (have someone help you do this). Give Talker #1 script to the talker in each pair and Listener #1 script to the listener. Explain that they will have a few seconds to read their scripts silently. They are not to share their scripts with their partners. When you say "Go," they will have about 45 seconds to act out their respective scripts. When you call time, ask them what happened. After a few comments, continue to process: "What did the listener do and how did it make you, the talker, feel? Have you ever had someone in real life listen to you in this manner? Have you ever done any of the things the listener did to you? What could you do, either as a talker or as a listener, to prevent this from happening or to improve a situation like this?"

3. Reverse Role Play and Processing, continued: Tell participants they will have one more listening practice activity, switching roles this time. Pass out the second set of reverse role play scripts. The new talker in each pair will get the Talker #2 script and the new listener will get the Listener #2 script. The same rules apply. Allow about 30 to 45 seconds (no more) for this part of the role play. Call time and allow for some venting of feelings, as the whole group will be quite active, energetic, and vocal. Then process: "What happened this time? How did you feel, as either the talker or listener? Has this ever happened to you in real life? Have you ever done this to anyone in real life? How could you prevent this from happening or improve the situation?" Direct them to thank their partners, give them a high-five or handshake, and return to their original seats.

4. Processing: Toss a Koosh™ ball (or other soft object) around the room again and elicit answers to the following question: "From the active listening skills practice and the reverse role plays, what did you learn about yourself and your own listening skills?"

5. Lecturette: Explain that the reverse role plays were reminders that often we think we're listening when, in fact, our bodies or voices are giving a completely different message. We need to make our messages congruent so that we don't send mixed messages. We need to be aware of *how* we're listening—what we're saying and doing at the time. If we don't have the time to listen, we need to let the talker know that so our body language isn't misinterpreted. Practicing active listening is not as simple as it appears. It takes time and effort to do it well.

6. Commitment to Action: Invite them to jot down on their Active Listening Notes one element of active listening they will make a commitment to practice for the next few days. Have them share this with a neighbor. End with a round of applause.

ACTIVE LISTENING NOTES
(FORM A)

✳ **Body language:**

✳ **Voice:**

✳ **What not to do:**

✳ **One element of active listening I will practice this week is:**

✳ **Other insights:**

REVERSE ROLE PLAY SCRIPTS (FORM B)

Directions: Photocopy this page. (You will need copies equal to half the number of participants.) Cut the copies into four separate role play strips. See activity directions for script use.

Reverse Role Play Scripts, Set One

Talker #1: You are having a very difficult day at work. You've just had an encounter with an angry customer, you've had some technical difficulties with equipment, and a coworker has been very rude to you. Everything that you think could possibly go wrong does. You turn to a colleague for a listening ear and sympathy. You just want to talk it all out for a few minutes. You tell your colleague about your day and how badly you feel.

Listener #1: One of your coworkers comes to you with some job-related problems. You would like to help this colleague but you really feel that his or her problems are minor compared to yours, so you are quick to negate what the coworker is feeling and offer fast solutions. You say things like: "You're making a mountain out of a molehill." "Why get so upset?" "Here's what you need to do." "That's nothing. When that happened to me, this is what I did." "Oh, don't worry so much about it." Remember to interrupt this colleague to give him or her your reactions and advice.

Reverse Role Play Scripts, Set Two

Talker #2: You've had great news! You just won the Publisher's Clearinghouse Sweepstakes! You are so excited that when you get to work you seek out a coworker to share your excitement with. You tell your colleague what you plan to do with the money, how it's going to change your life, and how excited you are. Be sure to demonstrate your excitement as well.

Listener #2: One of your colleagues comes to you with good news. You are very busy right now and really don't have the time to listen, so you give this coworker indirect signs that now is not a good time for a chat. You begin to shuffle papers, clean off your desk, and gather your things together. You may nod but you don't make eye contact. You finally stand up and walk away, muttering about being late for a meeting. Everything you do indicates you don't have the time to listen.

18

SEEING THROUGH ANOTHER'S EYES

Dave Arch

Overview Often we disagree not because of anything that's right or wrong, but rather because of a difference in perspectives. Seeing the issue through the eyes of another can bring us to the understanding necessary to value the other person's opinion. Here is a simple exercise to demonstrate this point to your employees.

Suggested Time 10 minutes

Materials Needed ✓ Form A (What Is It?) *Note:* Make two duplicates, enlarging them both so that everyone in your group can see them. However, during the enlargement process, please make sure that you keep them both as squares. If you plan to use this activity frequently, you might also wish to laminate them both.

Procedure 1. Invite two volunteers from your group to come to the front of the room and sit in two chairs. For maximum impact, have the two chairs quite a distance from each other.

2. Show the person on your left one of the pictures (so that only he or she can see it). Have the picture turned so that it looks like a picture of a duck. Ask the person to remember what the animal in the picture was, then place the picture face down in the person's lap.

3. Take the other picture to the other person and have the picture turned so that it looks like a rabbit. Ask the person to remember what animal was in the picture, and place the picture face down in the person's lap.

Contact Information: Dave Arch, The Bob Pike Group, 7620 West 78th Street, Minneapolis, MN 55439, 800-383-9210, DaveArch@bobpikegroup.com, www.bobpike group.com

4. Now ask both people to reveal the animals in their pictures. Of course, one will say the picture was a duck and one will say that it was a rabbit. Boldly declare that you will now cause the pictures to change places. Clap your hands, go to the person on the left, and lift the picture to show it to the person (again, so others can't see) in such a way that it now shows a rabbit. Ask what picture is now seen, and the person will indicate a rabbit. Go to the other person and show the picture turned so that it looks like a duck. The person will indicate that the picture is now of a duck.

5. Bow to the thunderous applause...and then turn both pictures around to show the audience the secret to this miracle.

6. Ask participants what can be learned from the "magic of perspectives." This is a wonderful opening activity any time you want people to share their opinions honestly in a meeting. Everyone needs to realize that we will not all agree on what we are seeing. However, others' perspectives are as valid and valuable as our own!

WHAT IS IT? (FORM A)

19

MANAGING REAL TIME

Steve Sugar and Bob Preziosi

Overview Time scheduling is never done in a vacuum. Even the most meticulously planned days are subject to changes to accommodate the unforeseen. This exercise demonstrates the real time and flexibility that are required in planning the next workday and some personal time.

Using Real Time, you can:

✓ Demonstrate the day-to-day demands that require direct reports to be flexible and to focus on the most important priorities.

✓ Demonstrate the need to establish a set of priorities along with a daily plan to guide activity through their workday.

✓ Identify ways that people can be flexible when handling the changing demands of the workday.

Suggested Time 75 to 120 minutes

Materials Needed
✓ Overhead projector
✓ Newsprint or flip chart and felt-tipped markers
✓ One piece of newsprint or flip chart paper per team
✓ Form A (Case Study), one for each participant
✓ Form B (Schedule), one for each participant
✓ Form C (Day Log), two for each participant
✓ Form D (Messages), one for each participant
✓ Set of telephone messages, one for each team

Contact Information: Steve Sugar, The Game Group, 10320 Kettledrum Court, Ellicott City, MD 21042, 410-418-4930, info@thegamesgroup.com

Bob Preziosi, School of Business and Entrepreneurship, Nova Southeastern University, 3301 College Avenue, Fort Lauderdale, FL 33314, 954-262-5111, preziosi@sbe.nova.edu, www.sbe.nova.edu

    ✓   Masking tape

    ✓   Whistle, bell, or other noise-making device

    ✓   Stopwatch or timekeeping device

Procedure

1. Distribute one set of Forms A, B, and C to each participant.

Round 1: Individual Assignments

2. Define the task for round 1: "This is a planning exercise. It is the last half-hour of your Tuesday workday. You are planning for Wednesday, your next workday. You have 15 minutes to review Form A: Case Study and Form B: Schedule, then prepare your Day Log on Form C for the next day."

3. Begin play for round 1

4. After 15 minutes, stop the exercise.

5. Have participants form teams of 3 to 5. Give each team one blank Day Log (Form C).

Round 2: Team Assignments

6. Define the task for round 2: "It is still the night before your next workday. Each team must prepare one Day Log that represents input from the entire team. You have 25 minutes to prepare a new log. At the end of the allotted time, one member of your team will present your log to the rest of the participants."

7. Begin round 2.

8. After 3 minutes, stop play and announce: "It is now Wednesday morning. Continue scheduling your day." (*Note:* Changing the time from Tuesday evening to Wednesday morning allows you to use telephone message interventions.)

9. Eight minutes into the exercise, distribute one copy of telephone message 1 to each team.

    To: Time Management Team

    From: Dr. Berringer

    Message: The staff meeting has been rescheduled for 2 p.m.

10. Thirteen minutes into the exercise, distribute one copy of telephone message 2 to each team.

    To: Time Management Team

    From: Spouse

    Message: Car broke down. Had to put car in repair shop. Please pick me up on the way home.

(*Note:* Driving to spouse's office causes a 15-minute detour.)

11. After another 5 minutes, hand out one copy of telephone message 3 to each team.

To: Time Management Team

From: Property Management Office

Message: There has been a water leak in the cafeteria. The cafeteria will be closed until next Monday.

12. After 25 minutes, call time to end round 2.

Round 3: Team Presentations

13. Define the task for round 3: "Each team must present its plan for the next day to the rest of the group. Select a team member to make a 3-minute presentation and prepare a sheet of newsprint or flip chart paper with your team's plan on it. You have 15 minutes."

14. Distribute one sheet of newsprint or flip chart paper, strips of masking tape, and several felt-tipped markers to each team.

15. After 15 minutes, call time.

16. Have each team present its plan to the group. Time limit for each presentation is 3 minutes.

17. Debrief the exercise using the suggested questions.

Debriefing Questions

This is the time to help players reflect on their experiences during the exercise and ask them what they learned from the experience and how they can apply it.

What did you experience?

- How did you feel when you first received the information?
- What was the hardest part of getting started? What made it easy?
- What happened when your team first met?
- What was helpful or not helpful in your team meetings? Why?
- Who played what roles in helping the team complete the Day Log (i.e., information provider, negotiator, etc.)?

What learning took place?

- What one major concept or idea did you learn?
- What did you learn from your individual work?
- What did you learn from your team work?
- Did you hear things you've heard before but have not started doing yet? Why?

What applications can be made to real life and the workplace?

- From your experiences here, what behaviors would you take back to your own personal scheduling? Your interactions at the office? Your interactions at home?

- What are the challenges in planning and sticking to a daily routine back on the job? How can you make those challenges work positively for you?

- What are your best suggestions for balancing your own work needs with the needs of others?

Variations

1. Expand the times for each round and for team presentations.

2. Create your own telephone messages to substitute for the ones used in the exercise. Add additional telephone messages, as needed.

3. Change days to match the actual day of workshop. For a Thursday workshop you could change the scenario to Wednesday evening and Thursday morning.

4. Have each team record its Day Log on a piece of newsprint or flip chart paper. Allow all teams to review all other teams' Day Logs. Then have each team hold another meeting to revise its Day Log, as necessary.

5. Use this exercise with a cyber team, using computerized scheduling and e-mail messages.

6. Eliminate the personal items in the evening.

CASE STUDY (FORM A)

It is Tuesday afternoon and you are now planning your next workday.

You work at Stone Container Corporation (SCC) as a Project Manager. The work site is 20 to 25 minutes from your home (only 15 minutes in early traffic). Your normal workday is from 8:30 a.m. to 5 p.m. Your normal routine has you awaken at 6 a.m., do 30 minutes of exercises, shower, dress, read the morning paper, have coffee at home, and get to work around 8:20 a.m. You usually check in at your desk and then catch a quick breakfast in the cafeteria.

(*Personal note:* Your best biorhythm times are from 8:30 to 11:30 a.m. and from 3:30 to 6 p.m. Your worst biorhythm time is from 1 to 3 p.m.)

You have several important tasks waiting for your attention on Wednesday. The most important (A1) is the Rosensweig Mineral Easement (RME) project due on Dr. Berringer's desk by 10 a.m. on Thursday. It is heavy work that requires clear thinking, good planning, and attention to detail. You will need at least one hour of solid, uninterrupted time. You may need another 30 minutes of busy work to coordinate the details of the project. A review of the work may require another 30 minutes before you submit the project to Dr. Berringer.

You have a batch of phone calls to attend to. Most of the calls can be handled by your assistant, Kim Kostoroski. But the Rosensweig Mineral Easement (RME) may require your attention for 30 minutes of uninterrupted telephone time to map out a strategy for your resource plan.

Your office is a little too convenient to pedestrian traffic. The Conference Center has booked rooms for meetings all day, starting at 9:30 a.m. The Conference Center is available from 8 a.m.

SCHEDULE (FORM B)

Remembering that minor crises are always surfacing, this is how your schedule looks for tomorrow.

8:00–9:45 Informal meeting with Marie Dillon (extension 472). You are helping Marie write a Project Proposal. Although it is Marie's proposal, you promised your help. The proposal is due next week but Marie needs time to line up clerical support. Marie always gets into the office before 8 a.m.

10:00–11:35 Staff meeting scheduled for conference room B. You have a resource presentation prepared (overheads and handouts are in your desk). You need 15 minutes to brush up on your presentation. You will be allowed to leave after you have finished the presentation. You are scheduled to present from 10:30 to 10:45.

12:00–1:00 Lunch meeting in the cafeteria with Jason David (extension 603) of Production Management. Jason wants to get your feedback on a new product line.

1:30–2:30 Client meeting with Matthew Glyder (475-6047) of Marina Services. Matt's company, a marginal customer, is interested in the new roller container line, a small profit-making item that can lead to sales of other products. Your meeting is scheduled for conference room A.

3:15–4:00 Informal meeting with Bert Randolph (337-9001) of Sports 'R Fun, a client who can always be counted on for a medium-size order. Bert's meetings are always a great deal of fun but usually run past their scheduled closure. Your meeting is scheduled for conference room A.

5:30 Pick up kids (spouse will go directly home to prepare dinner).

6:30 Finish up dinner.

7:15 Attend school play: Wizard of Oz. Your daughter Clarisse plays the Wicked Witch of the East. Your son Michael plays a Munchkin.

DAY LOG (FORM C)

Things to Do Today

Date

Item	Priority	Time Needed	Done
			☐
			☐
			☐
			☐
			☐
			☐
			☐
			☐
			☐
			☐
			☐
			☐
			☐
			☐
			☐
			☐
			☐
			☐
			☐
			☐
			☐
			☐
			☐
			☐
			☐
			☐
			☐
			☐
			☐
			☐

Scheduled Events

7:00	
7:15	
7:30	
7:45	
8:00	
8:15	
8:30	
8:45	
9:00	
9:15	
9:30	
9:45	
10:00	
10:15	
10:30	
10:45	
11:00	
11:15	
11:30	
11:45	
12:00	
12:15	
12:30	
12:45	
1:00	
1:15	
1:30	
1:45	
2:00	
2:15	
2:30	
2:45	
3:00	
3:15	
3:30	
3:45	
4:00	
4:15	
4:30	
4:45	
5:00	
5:15	
5:30	
5:45	
6:00	
EVENING	

Notes

© Time Management Center

Printed in U S A

Nightingale-Conant reorder no 880-I

MESSAGES (FORM D)

Message 1

To **Time Management Team** ☑ **URGENT**

Date _____ Time **8:15** (A.M.) P.M.

WHILE YOU WERE OUT

From **Dr. Berringer**

of **Special Projects**

Phone _____
Area Code | Number | Ext.

Fax _____
Area Code | Number

Telephoned	☒	Please call	
Came to see you		Wants to see you	
Returned your call		Will call again	

Message **The staff meeting has been rescheduled for 2 p.m.**

Signed **SES**

Perfect print®

Message 2

To **Time Management Team** ☑ **URGENT**

Date _____ Time **8:20** (A.M.) P.M.

WHILE YOU WERE OUT

From **Spouse**

of _____

Phone _____
Area Code | Number | Ext.

Fax _____
Area Code | Number

Telephoned	☒	Please call	
Came to see you		Wants to see you	
Returned your call		Will call again	

Message **Car broke down. Had to put car in repair shop. Please pick up on way home.**

(Note: Driving to spouse's office causes 15-minute detour.)

Signed **SES**

Perfect print®

Message 3

To **Time Management Team** ☑ **URGENT**

Date _____ Time **8:25** (A.M.) P.M.

WHILE YOU WERE OUT

From **Property Management Office**

of _____

Phone _____
Area Code | Number | Ext.

Fax _____
Area Code | Number

Telephoned	☒	Please call	
Came to see you		Wants to see you	
Returned your call		Will call again	

Message **There has been a water leak in the cafeteria. The cafeteria will be closed until next Monday.**

Signed **SES**

Perfect print®

Message 4

To _____ ☐ **URGENT**

Date _____ Time _____ A.M. P.M.

WHILE YOU WERE OUT

From _____

of _____

Phone _____
Area Code | Number | Ext.

Fax _____
Area Code | Number

Telephoned		Please call	
Came to see you		Wants to see you	
Returned your call		Will call again	

Message _____

Signed _____

Perfect print®

PART

REPRODUCIBLE TOOLS FOR BUILDING COLLABORATION AND TEAMWORK

20

WHAT DOES YOUR TEAM NEED TO IMPROVE?

Kevin Lohan

Overview   Before teams undertake the challenging task of collaborating on a temporary or permanent project, they need to ascertain whether they are all reading from the same metaphoric sheet of music. This assessment instrument enables teams to determine whether they have reached the readiness point at which optimal performance takes place. The instrument affords insights into the specific aspects of their collective functioning that may require fine-tuning, by addressing four dimensions of team effectiveness: Goals, Roles, Interpersonal Relationships, and Procedures.

Contact Information: Kevin Lohan, 2 Windsor Rd., Wamberal, NSW 2260, Australia, +64-2-4385-2049, endeavr@terrigal.net.au, www.endeavour.net.au

GETTING A GRIP ON YOUR TEAM'S EFFECTIVENESS

GOAL-SETTING CHECKLIST

Directions: The ten items that follow are associated with establishing and maintaining goals for your team. Consider the two statements in each item and then encircle a number between the two options to indicate how closely your team fits one or the other description.

I never discuss objectives with others in the team.	0 1 2 3 4 5						I always discuss objectives thoroughly with others in the team.
Our goal-setting sessions are a year or more apart.	0 1 2 3 4 5						Sessions to update our goals are held at least every 3 months.
We have fewer than 3 or more than 6 major goals this year.	0 1 2 3 4 5						We have a manageable 3 to 6 major goals this year.
We rarely clarify how we will measure our success.	0 1 2 3 4 5						We have tangible measures of our success or otherwise.
We rarely meet to discuss performance.	0 1 2 3 4 5						Performance is either part of our regular agenda or discussed often.
Once set, our goals rarely change as circumstances change.	0 1 2 3 4 5						When unexpected situations arise, our goals are open to renegotiation.
Only staff (and not the manager) have clear accountabilities.	0 1 2 3 4 5						Everyone has clear accountabilities (including the manager).
Unachievable goals are often set for the team.	0 1 2 3 4 5						When we set goals they are almost always achievable.
We rarely check the organizational relevance of our goals.	0 1 2 3 4 5						Individual goals are checked to ensure they are relevant to the organization.
No steps are taken to ensure that people share information about their goals.	0 1 2 3 4 5						We ensure that people share information about their goals.

Total of 10 circled numbers: _____

GETTING A GRIP ON YOUR TEAM'S EFFECTIVENESS (CONT.)

ROLES CHECKLIST

Directions: The ten items that follow are associated with roles within the team. Consider the two statements in each item and then encircle a number between the two options to indicate how closely your team fits one or the other description.

There are no clear, written job descriptions for team members.	0	1	2	3	4	5	Written job descriptions exist for each role.
Lines of responsibility are unclear and people often question their parts of a task.	0	1	2	3	4	5	People know their responsibilities very well and rarely question them.
It is difficult to assign work without making waves.	0	1	2	3	4	5	Assigning work is easy. Team members know their roles and accept them.
When one person is absent, other people are uncertain about how to fill in.	0	1	2	3	4	5	When one person is absent, important things still get done.
No one is being groomed to learn a new role.	0	1	2	3	4	5	People are always being groomed for the next position.
There is no program for addressing staff weaknesses.	0	1	2	3	4	5	Staff development is addressed continuously.
We do not openly discuss our roles.	0	1	2	3	4	5	We openly discuss our roles.
There is very little respect for each other's part in the process.	0	1	2	3	4	5	Everyone respects the part played by every other team member.
Informal roles are often adopted that take over from formal roles.	0	1	2	3	4	5	The formal roles are followed by everyone and attempts to adopt informal roles are not made.
Leadership of the team is unclear.	0	1	2	3	4	5	Team leadership is clearly understood.

Total of 10 circled numbers: _____

INTERPERSONAL RELATIONS CHECKLIST

Directions: The ten items that follow are associated with interpersonal relations among team members. Consider the two statements in each item and then encircle a number between the two options to indicate how closely your team fits one or the other description.

Some people in the team treat others as inferiors.	0	1	2	3	4	5	Everyone treats others as equals and there is clear evidence of empathy.
There is no evidence that people on the team trust each other.	0	1	2	3	4	5	There is plenty of evidence that people on the team trust one another.
If people have problems, they keep them to themselves.	0	1	2	3	4	5	If people have problems, they discuss them with each other.
There is no feedback among the team about each other's work.	0	1	2	3	4	5	Everyone happily accepts feedback and gives it appropriately.
I do not find out about problems I have created until it is too late.	0	1	2	3	4	5	Problems I create are promptly brought to my attention so that corrective action can be taken.
Anger and frustration are displayed as violent outbursts.	0	1	2	3	4	5	Anger and frustration are resolved rationally.
I do not treat others on the team as friends but as coworkers.	0	1	2	3	4	5	Friendships among the team are common and do not cause problems.
During conflicts, one person usually wins at the expense of others.	0	1	2	3	4	5	Conflicts are resolved to the satisfaction of everyone concerned.
Participation in decision making and at meetings is unequal and some people dominate.	0	1	2	3	4	5	Participation in decision making and at meetings is equally shared.
Perceptions held by team members about our relationships are not the same as those of people outside the team.	0	1	2	3	4	5	Our perceptions about the way we get along are the same as the perceptions of those outside the team.

Total of 10 circled numbers: _____

GETTING A GRIP ON YOUR TEAM'S EFFECTIVENESS (CONT.)

PROCEDURES CHECKLIST

Directions: The ten items that follow are associated with the procedures the team follows. Consider the two statements in each item and then encircle a number between the two options to indicate how closely your team fits one or the other description.

There are few, if any, clearly communicated policies and procedures.	0	1	2	3	4	5	Clearly written policies and procedures are readily available for our use.
We have trouble agreeing on tough team decisions.	0	1	2	3	4	5	We have agreed-on procedures for reaching tough team decisions.
We have no procedure for resolving conflict.	0	1	2	3	4	5	We have an agreed-on procedure for resolving conflict when it arises.
Communication is confused and comes and goes in many directions.	0	1	2	3	4	5	Communication is appropriate and we know how and from whom we get information.
Formal rules are rarely followed.	0	1	2	3	4	5	Formal rules are almost always complied with.
Our organization does not welcome ideas for change.	0	1	2	3	4	5	Our organization encourages innovation.
Our operating procedures are out of date.	0	1	2	3	4	5	Our operating procedures are regularly updated to reflect current methods and technology.
Our meetings are usually a waste of time.	0	1	2	3	4	5	Our meetings are productive and well run.
Policies favor labor-intensive, time-consuming procedures that cover all the bases.	0	1	2	3	4	5	Policies favor getting things done rather than guarding against error.
Policies appear inconsistent for different parts of the organization.	0	1	2	3	4	5	Policies are the same for everyone, with a few necessary exceptions.

Total of 10 circled numbers: _____

131

SCORING AND INTERPRETATION

There is no best or worst total score. Your own interpretation of what each of the statements means, together with the variables that exist in a numerical rating system, would make such a diagnosis worthless. The instrument is intended to help you diagnose what you perceive as the strengths and weaknesses of the team as related to a range of team activities and behaviors. Thus, the diagnosis is achieved by comparing your responses within the team, rather than making an assessment against the scores of other teams.

Each response is rated from zero to five points, as shown in the rating scale. The total maximum score for each of the four team dimensions is 50 points. By comparing the score for each dimension against the other three, you can determine which area has the greater need for development. Similarly, within each of the dimensions you can determine the issues that need the most urgent attention by comparing the scores for each of the ten items with others in that dimension.

REFERENCE

Mark Plovnick, Ronald Fry, and Irwin Rubin, "New Development in OD Technology: Programmed Team Development." *Training and Development Journal*, 29, 4, April 1975.

21
WHO'S ON YOUR TEAM?

Bill Stieber

Overview Variety is truly the "spice" of teams, keeping members' interactions lively, creative ideas flowing, and progression steady and on course. Capitalizing on the differences among team members may require some change of mind-sets and a number of very deliberate actions, including these:

- Accept that differences exist and are healthy.
- Discover, understand, accept, and inventory the differences that exist among your team members.
- Affirm the value of team members' differences.
- Make it a habit to build others' self-worth.
- Make it a habit to listen to others for better understanding.

The Team Leader and Team Member Uniqueness Assessment not only helps teams understand some of their differences, but it can also serve as a validation of an individual team leader's or team member's self-perception.

Contact Information: Bill Stieber, InterPro Development, Inc., PMB 388, 2865 South Eagle Road, Newtown, PA 18940, 215-860-6098, Bill.S@Stieber.com, www.stieber.com

TEAM LEADER AND TEAM MEMBER UNIQUENESS ASSESSMENT

Team Leader Name: _____   **Team Member Name:** _____

Part 1 Directions: Read the list of motivators and examples of character traits. Place a check in the column adjacent to the motivators that most closely represent your nature.

Motivator	Team Leader Name:	Team Member Name:
1. Accomplishment I like setting and working toward goals. I take pride in my work. It is important to me that our team accomplish its goals.		
2. Attention I like others in the organization to see my work. I don't mind being the center of attention. Recognition from others means a lot to me.		
3. Autonomy I enjoy the freedom to decide how to do my work. I don't mind being the center of attention. I rarely feel the need for supervision or instructions.		
4. Challenge The more challenging the work, the more I like it. I like to take on the tough jobs or assignments. I need to feel that the work I do is important.		
5. Clarity I do my best work when I know what is expected. I work better when procedures are well-defined. I work best when instructions are provided.		

TEAM LEADER AND TEAM MEMBER UNIQUENESS ASSESSMENT (CONT.)

Team Leader Name:	Team Member Name:	Motivator
		6. Camaraderie Being part of a team is important to me. I like working closely with teammates and other teams. Relationships are very important to me.
		7. Competence I welcome opportunities to sharpen my skills. I get satisfaction from training other people. I look for ways to change and improve myself.
		8. Encouragement I prefer working with a coach or instructor. I appreciate encouragement from other team members. I perform best when there is not too much pressure.
		9. Expertise I like to be known as an expert by my peers. I appreciate being recognized for my skills and abilities. I welcome people asking me for my advice. I welcome opportunities to learn new things. I enjoy making decisions.
		10. Harmony I try to accommodate the opinions and desires of others. It is important that team members agree as much as possible. I do what I can to smooth things over and maintain good working relationships.

TEAM LEADER AND TEAM MEMBER UNIQUENESS ASSESSMENT (CONT.)

Team Leader Name:	Team Member Name:	Motivator
		11. Order I like having a system to accomplish tasks. I work better when routines are stable. I work best when there are no sudden problems.
		12. Stability I don't like a job that has too much variety. I need time to adjust to change. I perform best with few changes to accommodate.
		13. Supportive I am open to advice and suggestions from others. I try to meet the expectations of my team members. I am willing to follow the leadership of others.
		14. Variety I like to have a wide range of responsibilities. I like to perform different jobs and rotate assignments. I welcome changes in priorities or procedures.

TEAM LEADER AND TEAM MEMBER UNIQUENESS ASSESSMENT (CONT.)

Part 2 **Directions:** Review the capabilities assessment and rate yourself on the capabilities listed, using the following scale:

1 = significant improvement needed
2 = improvement needed
3 = average
4 = strong
5 = very strong

	CAPABILITIES	RATING (1-5)
Social Capabilities:	Leading Groups	
	Selling proposals and influencing others	
	Communicating	
	Resolving conflicts	
	Obtaining support and cooperation	
	Humor	
	Working with others	
	Supporting others	
Administrative Capabilities:	Planning and scheduling	
	Solving problems	
	Understanding complex concepts	
	Coordinating	
	Presenting	
	Organizing	
	Creative thinking	
	Collecting information	
	Writing reports, memos, proposals	
	Analyzing information	
Technical Capabilities:	Training others	
	Learning new things (job knowledge)	
	Learning new jobs	
	Following instructions and procedures	

SCORING

Part 1: Motivators

Using the table below, mark the motivators that were identified by each team member (TM) and team leader (TL). List the total for each motivator in the Total column. Review the totals, paying attention to the balance or imbalance between the individual motivators. Reinforce the motivators needed by the team members.

Motivator	TL	TM 1	TM 2	TM 3	TM 4	Total
1. Accomplishment						
2. Attention						
3. Autonomy						
4. Challenge						
5. Clarity						
6. Camaraderie						
7. Competence						
8. Encouragement						
9. Expertise						
10. Harmony						
11. Order						
12. Stability						
13. Supportive						
14. Variety						

Part 2: Capabilities

Place the ratings given by each team member or team leader to the individual capabilities in the respective columns. Total the ratings for each capability.

CAPABILITIES	Ratings	Ratings	Ratings	Ratings	Ratings	Ratings
Social Capabilities:	TL	TM 1	TM 2	TM 3	TM 4	Total
Leading groups						
Selling proposals and influencing others						
Communicating						
Resolving conflicts						
Obtaining support and cooperation						
Humor						
Working with others						
Supporting others						

CAPABILITIES	Ratings	Ratings	Ratings	Ratings	Ratings	Ratings
Administrative Capabilities:	TL	TM 1	TM 2	TM 3	TM 4	*Total*
Planning and scheduling						
Solving problems						
Understanding complex concepts						
Coordinating						
Presenting						
Organizing						
Creative thinking						
Collecting information						
Writing reports, memos, proposals						
Analyzing information						
Technical Capabilities:						
Training others						
Learning new things (job knowledge)						
Learning new jobs						
Following instructions and procedures						

Review the totals, looking for strengths and weaknesses within the team. List those strengths and weaknesses below. Develop an action plan to capitalize on the strengths of the team and improve areas of weakness.

Areas of strength within our team are:

_____

Areas of weakness within our team are:

_____

To capitalize on our strengths we will:

_____

To develop our areas of weakness we will:

_____

22

IS YOUR TEAM FUNCTIONING ON ALL CYLINDERS?

Valerie MacLeod

Overview The Highly Functioning Team Assessment Tool allows teams to determine how well they are functioning against 12 criteria. These criteria form the basis for a highly functioning team unit. The instrument was developed to provide teams with feedback on possible areas for improvement, as well as provide an opportunity for team members to share in the creation and monitoring of plans to increase their functioning as a team.

The Highly Functioning Team Assessment Tool is valuable for both new and experienced teams. When a team is initially formed, it can use the Highly Functioning Team Assessment Tool to determine where they should invest time in order to become a highly functioning team as soon as possible. Experienced teams can use the Highly Functioning Team Assessment Tool to fine-tune their functioning.

All teams should strive to function at a more productive level. Even high-performing teams can achieve some level of improvement in one of the 12 assessment areas. As a result of using the Highly Functioning Team Assessment Tool, teams will:

- Identify one to three criteria for a highly functioning team in which they desire to improve.

- Create action plans for improving the team behaviors in the selected criteria.

- Monitor their improvement in the selected criteria for a highly functioning team.

Contact Information: Valerie MacLeod, Centre for Strategic Management, 28 Riverwood Manor SE, Calgary, Alberta, Canada T2C 4B1, 403-236-3928, Vmacleod@teleplanet.net, www.csmintl.com

HIGHLY FUNCTIONING TEAM ASSESSMENT TOOL

Directions: The Highly Functioning Team Assessment Tool is a behaviorally anchored rating instrument. For each highly functioning team criteria, the ratings 1, 3, and 5 have a behavior description attached to them. Anchoring a behavior to three of the ratings allows more consistency among the ratings.

The instrument shows how individuals perceive the team is functioning in the 12 areas. Differences in ratings are neither right nor wrong; instead, they provide an opportunity for the team to discuss differences in team functioning perceptions.

Individually rate how you perceive the team is functioning in each area, using the descriptions associated with ratings 1, 3, and 5 as a guide. For example, if you understand team goals and some of the links to organization strategy, then you perceive yourself as better than a 3, "understand team goals," but not quite up to a 5, "understand link between team goals and organization strategy." Therefore, you would rate Team Goals as 4.

Highly Functioning Team Criteria	1	2	3	4	5
Team Goals	Unclear on team goals		Understand team goals		Understand link between team goals and organization strategy
Roles	Not clear on my role on team		Know my role		Understand roles of all team members
Ground Rules and Norms	We don't have or don't use Ground Rules and Norms		Have Ground Rules and Norms and use them occasionally, mostly at team meetings		Always follow Ground Rules and Norms in all of our interactions
Tools, Resources, and Physical Setting	Tools, resources, and physical setting hinder or do not contribute to our work		Tools, resources, and physical setting allow us to meet most team goals		Tools, resources, and physical setting assist us in meeting and exceeding team goals
Team Meetings	A waste of time		Regular meetings are generally useful		Excellent forum for sharing information and solving issues
Conflict	Conflict is ignored		Some conflict managed by leader		All team members proactive and skilled at managing conflict
Trust	Prefer to work alone; when we work together we check others' work		Do some work together by choice; occasionally check up on others		Prefer to work together; trust others to do their part

HIGHLY FUNCTIONING TEAM ASSESSMENT TOOL (CONT.)

Highly Functioning Team Criteria	1	2	3	4	5
Valuing Differences	Differences ignored or not valued		Starting to understand and work with differences		Capitalize on differences to create better solutions
Training and Development	Little or unplanned training and development		Some training and development but not part of overall plan		Training and development for current and future jobs as part of regularly reviewed team training plan
Improvement	Too busy working to make improvements		Some improvements implemented		Constantly striving for better ways of doing things
Feedback	Do not receive much feedback		Hear from leader on mistakes and errors only		Receive regular positive and negative feedback from all team members
Follow-Through	Action items and delegated duties generally ignored		Some follow-up completed after work is done		Action items and delegated duties completed as part of my work

SCORING INTERPRETATION AND DISCUSSION

Add the scores of each team member for each criterion and divide by the number of scores submitted to create an average score for each of the 12 highly functioning team criteria. For example, if six team members gave the team scores of 1, 4, 3, 4, 3, and 4 for Team Meetings, then the average score for Team Meetings is 3.2.

During the discussion following the scoring, do not allow the averages alone to guide the discussion. In the example of Team Meetings, the average is 3.2, which seems to be acceptable. However, one individual rated the Team Meetings as 1, "a waste of time." A discussion on each of the 12 items is appropriate.

After a review of the averages for the 12 criteria, as well as a discussion of how team members perceive the team is functioning for each criterion, the team should choose the top one to three criteria to work on. These questions can help the team decide where to invest their time:

1. Which of the 12 criteria for a highly functioning team had the lowest averages?

2. Which criterion caused the most discussion regarding the perceptions of our performance?

3. What criterion would our customers like us to improve?

4. Which of the criteria do our other stakeholders want to see improvement in?

5. What criterion causes us the most problems, heartburn, or conflict?

6. Where would we get the most improvement from our investment of time?

ACTION PLANNING

For each of the criteria that you have chosen to work upon, create a measurable, specific action plan with times to start and end, name of who is responsible, and list of resources required. The following chart shows one format that is useful in creating and tracking action plans.

Highly Functioning Team Action Plan					
Criterion: **Valuing Differences**					
Specific Action	Who Is Responsible	Start Date	Completion Date	Resources Required	Status

The team should agree upon how often the actions will be monitored. Checking up on actions daily is too frequent, but waiting until the end of the year is unadvisable. The team should decide whether weekly, biweekly, or monthly checking is appropriate.

NEXT STEPS

Many teams create action plans and then ignore them. A highly functioning team follows through on its action plans.

When the Highly Functioning Team Assessment Tool scores were discussed and action plans were created, the team agreed upon the frequency of reviewing the action plan. Therefore, at the appropriate team meetings, the Highly Functioning Team Action Plan should be reviewed. The review should be quick. If the actions are on schedule, then the discussion is kept to a minimum. Only when there are issues or problems in achieving the plan should there be much discussion by team members.

The Highly Functioning Team Assessment Tool can be used as a measurement to gauge progress. Remember that the numbers reflect only how team members perceive the way we function. The discussion of each criterion is what is important and what should drive any changes or updates to the Highly Functioning Team Action Plan.

23

ALIGNING YOUR TEAM

Cynthia Solomon

Overview   This guide provides a description of the process and benefits of conducting a team alignment tailored to the unique needs of any team, as well as helpful hints for the skilled facilitator. The guide will also be helpful to a team coach or manager who is looking for a process by which a team can take full advantage of the formation phase to lay a foundation for the team as it moves into more mature phases of working together.

WHAT IS A TEAM ALIGNMENT?

A team is a group of people who share purpose, process, involvement, communication, commitment, and trust. Not all groups function as teams; in fact, not all groups are successful when they function as a team. But when the team culture is appropriate, it is most helpful for the team to engage in a purposeful team formation process by which they come to know how they will function together. The process, called the team alignment, is facilitated by a skilled facilitator who understands and supports the need of individuals to contribute to the formation of the team early in their work together. The team alignment results in team discussions and decisions that carry the group through the team storming, norming, and performing phases.

A team alignment is a planned process by which a skilled facilitator helps a group of individuals define themselves, their purpose, and the conditions and processes under which they will function as a team. Individuals leave the session as a newly formed team.

Contact Information: Cynthia Solomon, 114 Walosi Way, Loudon, TN 37774, 865-408-1520, nomolos55@msn.com

WHY WOULD A TEAM COACH USE
THE TEAM ALIGNMENT PROCESS?

The advantages inherent in using the team alignment process are based on the idea that teams live through phases—forming, storming, norming, and performing. (Descriptions of these phases and guidance on helping teams understand and work through these phases are included in previous editions of the *Team and Organizational Development Sourcebook,* edited by M. Silberman, McGraw-Hill.)

The forming phase is characterized by the individual members of the team—each bringing diverse talents, skills, experiences, and preferences—engaging in initial meetings in which they understand what they must do, but are trying to determine how they will work together. Without giving attention to a sound team formation phase, the team is at risk of moving into the storming, norming, and performing phases without having identified, reconciled, and negotiated the group's processes and needs.

The team alignment process involves an investment of time to get the team off to a strong start, and to provide a foundation that will support them through their challenges. Because of the time involved, conducting an alignment is beneficial for a team that will have an extended lifetime or will work on a difficult or complicated activity. Short-term or simple projects can be performed by a team without an alignment; conducting a complete team alignment may not be worth the time invested for those teams.

The advantages of engaging a team in a team alignment are:

1. The team members have an opportunity to acknowledge what they individually have to bring to the overall activity of the team, and to understand what others have to bring.

2. The team members have an opportunity to express their own expectations and needs so they feel that they can participate in the team most effectively.

3. The team anticipates any barriers to their success, and plans approaches in advance to help them avoid or overcome those barriers. Preparation for a contingency allows the team to think clearly while they have time, rather than to react quickly, rashly, or emotionally.

4. The team develops its process for meetings, communication, sharing of information, integration of individual efforts, delineation of roles and responsibilities, identification of clients or customers, and understanding of the client's or customer's expectations for success.

5. The team has an opportunity to talk about and decide on conflict, problem-solving, and decision-making processes and expectations before they must use them. These processes are team tools; having tools in place before you need them is a good business practice and a good team practice.

6. The team takes time to know one other as individual members of the team, and to develop an appreciation for the unique needs, abilities, and preferences of others.

KEY PRINCIPLES OF A TEAM ALIGNMENT

The team alignment process is based on four key principles:

1. The participants share a sense of purpose, process, commitment, communication, involvement, and trust to a sufficient degree that they desire to develop as a team.

2. The participants desire and agree to strengthen the ties that bind them as a team. A team alignment that is imposed upon an unwilling team who do not understand its benefits may create an environment of mistrust or caution and inhibit openness, creativity, and risk taking.

3. The participants have the right to define themselves as a team and determine how they will function, to some known degree. The team must understand the givens (that is, the rules and conditions under which they must operate) so they can focus on the elements of process and environment of their team that they can define.

4. The alignment process is predicated on a sense of trust among the team members. That is, they each feel they can trust one another to be accepted for what they have to contribute, without being judged personally. There is a sufficient confidence level among the participants that the process is not perceived as threatening.

GENERAL RULES FOR CONDUCTING AN ALIGNMENT

Preparing for the Alignment

The facilitator begins by obtaining background information about the team from the client. The background information is most likely obtained from the team coach, or the person who asked the facilitator to conduct the alignment. Conducting brief, individual interviews of some or all team members prior to the alignment also helps the facilitator understand the nature of the team and its work, and become sensitive to individual needs and issues that should either be supported and addressed during the team alignment or approached cautiously.

Questions for the Team Coach (or Team Alignment Requestor)

1. Who are the individual members of the team?
2. Why were they selected? Did they volunteer to be on the team?
3. What is the intended purpose of the team?
4. What is the team expected to do? What is the product or service they are to produce?
5. For what amount of time is the team expected to be together?
6. What constraints are now known that the team will work under?
7. What are some anticipated barriers that might interfere with the team's success?
8. What are some of the strengths of this team that will enhance its success?

Questions for Individual Team Members

1. What is the overall purpose of the team?
2. What do you contribute to the team?
3. What do you think others will contribute to the team?
4. Who is your client (or customer), and what does the client expect of your team?
5. What barriers do you foresee that might interfere with the team's success?
6. What do you personally need from this team in order for you to be a successful member and contributor?

Preparing the Alignment Agenda

Preparation for the alignment is critical for the success of the alignment. Each alignment is tailored to the needs of the team. Preparation means giving careful consideration to the background information that has been gathered and preparing the discussion topics the team will use during the alignment session.

Prepare a list of discussion topics for the team. Begin with simple, nonthreatening ideas about what the team is. Then guide the team into developmental issues that require more open, trusting discussion.

Here is a suggested sequence of topics for discussion, ranging from the simplest to the most challenging for the team:

A. Introductions of individual members of the team.

B. Understanding the team's client, the client's expectations and requirements; understanding the purpose of the team.

C. The diversity and uniqueness of the members—what each member brings to the team.

D. Strengths of the team to achieve its purpose.

E. Potential barriers to success.

F. Team process issues: roles and responsibilities, meeting process, problem solving, conflict resolution methods, lines of communication, delineation and integration of roles.

G. Wrap-up—conclude and summarize what happened.

Based upon your proposal, determine how much time will be needed to conduct the alignment. You may have to redesign your alignment agenda to fit your team's time constraints. It is not unusual for a team alignment to require four to eight hours. Alignments for technical teams, such as an engineering project that involves subcontractors or many regulatory requirements, may take longer. To be effective, a team alignment should not be rushed; but the facilitator should attend to moving the planned agenda along to avoid an unnecessarily extended and tiring session. Imposing time limits helps to expedite discussion and bring it to closure.

Prepare an agenda for the session that includes the major discussion topics. Distribute the agenda to team participants in advance of the session, if possible, so they arrive with some understanding of what they will be doing that day. On the agenda, list the names of the individuals who will participate, and include a brief statement of the purpose of the meeting, such as: "This team alignment will include a series of discussions and decisions to help the team members define how they want to approach their work in a manner that is satisfying to the team and respects the diversity of the group."

Characteristics and Practices for the Alignment Facilitator

Ideally, the alignment facilitator should not be a member of the team. Sufficient knowledge of the team, its purpose, and its work is required to be helpful as a facilitator, but the facilitator should not influence or judge the input from the team members during the session. Neither should the team members be expected to educate the facilitator during the alignment session; that education should occur during the preparation time.

The team alignment is not a training session. Any team training or development need that is identified as a result of the team alignment should be planned and conducted at another session. For example, it might be tempting for a facilitator to provide some instruction on decision-making methods during the alignment. But if that instruction is needed, then the conclusion of the alignment is that the team needs to take the time, later, to learn some decision-making methods and become equipped to use them appropriately.

The alignment facilitator should have assembled flip charts, markers, tape, Post-It notes, and any other aids that would be useful. Arrange the room so that team members feel they are equal contributors to the process. A round table or arrangement of chairs in a circle works best. Seat the team leader or coach in the middle, not at the head of the table.

Based on the discussion topics or questions that were selected, prepare flip chart pages with key questions or topics already listed to facilitate the recording of responses. The facilitator may also serve as the recorder, but if the team is very active and expected to contribute many ideas, a second person should serve as recorder so the facilitator can support the discussion.

The facilitator should collect all flip charts or other session records to prepare an alignment report for the team to review and use. It is helpful to give an electronic copy of this final report to the team in case they want to modify their alignment decisions at a later date.

Some Tips for Working with the Team Coach or Leader

Prior to conducting the alignment, the facilitator should discuss and clarify the purpose of the alignment and the manner by which it will be conducted with the team coach or leader. For this activity to be successful, the team coach or leader should be aware of and agree to several concepts about the team alignment:

1. The team alignment requires full participation of the team members, in an environment in which their contributions are given freely, honestly, and creatively, without fear of judgment from the coach or leader.

2. The team coach or leader should give a few words of support for the activity and stress its importance to helping the team become more effective. The basic operating principle is that the team is as strong and effective as the individual, integrated efforts of the people who comprise the team.

3. The team coach or leader should participate in the session, but in a minor role so that the work of the team is done by the team. Advise the team coach or leader to avoid making decisions for the team during the session, and to refrain from assuming the facilitator role.

4. The team coach or leader should show appreciation and value for the participation of the team members. This appreciation will help establish trust among them.

Conducting the Alignment

The facilitator begins by explaining the purpose of the alignment: for all members of the group to share their concepts of what the team will become and how the team will function to accomplish its mission.

The facilitator must be able to foster a climate of open, fair, constructive, and nonthreatening discussion. There must be a climate of trust and nonjudgmental sharing. Establish team ground rules, if that is appropriate for the team.

Everyone in the group should be encouraged to contribute to each element of the discussion. One person should record the discussion items on a flip chart and collect the pages to prepare the summary report. The summary report can be discussed at a later date and negotiated or modified if needed.

SUGGESTED DISCUSSIONS AND DECISIONS FOR A TEAM ALIGNMENT

Sixteen discussion questions are provided as guidance for a skilled facilitator to tailor the team alignment process to meet the specific needs, cultures, and time constraints of the team. Select and adapt the discussion questions that would be most helpful to the team. Inclusion of too many discussion topics results in a tiring session, and several are so closely aligned that the discussion would be redundant. Each question should be adapted to the particular nature of the team and the culture in which it exists. To give you ideas, the examples included come from team alignments from different team cultures such as churches, businesses, a nursing home, and a college.

1. *What is our purpose?*
Facilitate a mission, vision, or values statement with the team if members think that these statements would help them to clarify their purpose.

2. *What are we trying to accomplish?*

List the products or services you provide to yourselves or others; for example, a religious education program for a church, skill development for nurses' aides in a nursing home, the construction of a new building for a construction company, a marketing approach for a new line of products.

During this discussion, it is often helpful for the facilitator to have the team not only list what they are trying to accomplish in terms of product or service, but also identify desired characteristics of that product or service. Some teams also like to discuss what they are trying to accomplish for themselves; for example, a team formed to develop a public relations plan for the company might also want to accomplish the development of a friendly work relationship among the team members. The team might also want to conduct cross-training among members to broaden their individual skills.

3. *Who are our customers or clients, and what do they want, expect, and need from us?*

Take time to help the team identify a good customer list. For example, the college faculty of a Health Careers Department initially listed students as their customers. With the help of their facilitator, they established a more inclusive customer list: students, employers of their graduates, other professionals who care about the integrity and reputation of their profession, patients who are cared for by their graduates, insurance companies, residents who are concerned about the quality of health care in their community.

Each identified customer could have separate, unique lists of expectations. Determine whether knowing this is valuable to the successful planning and operation of the team. Using the Health Career Department example, students want the best education that will be affordable and one they can complete successfully. Taxpayers want efficient, not wasteful, use of tax money. Employers want graduates who are competent in applying current skills.

4. *How will we know that we are successful at what we are doing?*

List some standards or criteria that indicate success. Here are some examples from various types of team alignments:

- A church that wants to expand religion education will be successful if more people are able to participate in various programs and indicate that they are satisfied with them.

- A nursing home that wants to retain nurse aides will be successful if the rate of attrition declines.

- A college admissions office team that wants to increase enrollment will be successful if they increase overall enrollment by 5 percent over the previous year.
- An engineering company that does design work for its clients will be successful if it reduces the number of design changes by 25 percent.
- A construction crew will be successful if they have no accidents or injuries.

5. *What does each of us bring to the team effort?*

This discussion opens the team to hear about the diverse skills and experiences of individual members of the team. Facilitators often use a skill identification instrument that is less threatening than an open discussion. At an alignment of a product marketing team, individuals offered these various skills and experience: art design, copy writing, advertising contacts, technical editing, marketing psychology, finance and budgeting support, and marketing management.

An interesting adjunct to this discussion is to lead the team in determining what additional skills and experiences (and perhaps resources) it needs to be successful, but does not currently have among the members. How will they obtain what they need, or must they adjust and operate without?

6. *What does each participant need from others in the team in order to be a welcomed, effective, and participating member of the team?*

Some potential answers are: need time to make community contacts; need technical information in advance so that a report can be completed; need some patience from other team members because this is new territory for me; need to know what other decisions have been made by individuals so that we provide current information to the public; need quick turnaround time when we need to respond to a news release; need flexibility in meeting times because of my personal schedule.

7. *Under what conditions would participation on this team be most satisfying for each member of the team?*

This is a discussion of the environment in which the team works. Some teams need a meeting room, others like to meet in a living or dining room or at the kitchen table. Some want an informal process, while others need formal procedure. Some teams need independence of the individuals to operate, while others need team members to collaborate on many discussions and decisions.

8. **What conditions would create dissatisfaction or alienation for each member of the team?**

This discussion must be presented in an environment of trust. This is an opportunity for individuals to openly state their frustrations and how they can mitigate them. Knowing the conditions for satisfaction or dissatisfaction helps the team create the environment that is most supportive and least dissatisfying in the future, when they are storming, norming, and performing.

9. **At this point, what are the differences (our diversity) that we have identified among the participants, and how can we use those differences for the growth of the team?**

This discussion is based on acceptance that the team is composed of individuals who share the team, but are different in abilities, skills, preferences, experiences, and personalities. Encourage teams to discuss ways to use their diversity to grow and become stronger as a team, rather than focus on how the diversity might cause division among them. Highly effective teams appreciate their diversity and find ways to make it work for them.

10. **What are the processes we need to establish in order to be effective in accomplishing our mission and creating a satisfying experience for each member of the team?**

Examples are formality or informality of meetings; working with an agenda or having an open meeting; having a meeting facilitator; sharing facilitation; time, day, and place of meetings; who will keep records or make decisions.

Team members should not assume that each member comes to the team with the same experiences or preferences in team process. At this point, the team may have discovered that some members are open and informal, and others are structured and prefer to follow an agenda or procedure.

11. **How will team members communicate with one another?**

The facilitator approaches this subject from the perspective of who needs to communicate with whom, at what frequency, and using what preferred method. How will the individual members of the team inform one another, obtain input from outside the team, and obtain permission for what they do? Getting these ground rules established early in the formation process helps avoid potential problems that are common to all teams.

12. **What are the individual tasks or roles that the team has to accomplish to achieve its mission? Who will assume lead roles for each of these tasks?**

This is the roles and responsibilities element of the alignment. The facilitator might ask the team to list the types of roles the team needs, and then guide them in determining who will fill these roles. The team might also benefit from a team roles and responsibilities survey to more objectively determine which "hat" or position each person wears on the team. The purpose of this discussion is to ensure that the work of the team is done without stepping on each other's toes, and that lines of communication are opened as they need to be.

13. **How will the team deal with making decisions?**
    With conflict?
    With the need for effective communication?

At the alignment stage, an experienced team might already have some sense of how they want to deal with these elements, but a newly formed team may feel awkward. During the alignment, the team might conclude that it needs another session to learn team decision-making and conflict resolution processes.

14. **In order to achieve our mission, what are the key areas we need to focus on?**

The answers to this question form the basis for a planning session. Key areas could include team process development, key activities for the team to move into the performing stage, and continued development of the team plan.

Basic planning includes documenting and agreeing to a list of activities, and determining for each activity who will have main responsibility, the schedule or calendar for the activity, and the needed resources.

15. **What methods will the team use periodically to check its progress toward accomplishing its mission? To check whether being on the team is a satisfying experience for each member? To identify process problems that need to be raised, discussed, and resolved? To identify changes it must make to get back on track, correct errors, grow, or revise as needed?**

This is a good time for the facilitator to recommend that the team use the alignment report, team process analysis, or other method to periodically self-assess its progress. The alignment session itself should not be used as a training session for these evaluations; but a session should be scheduled later to familiarize team members with the evaluation methods available.

> **16. What additional team activities should the team perform as a result of what they learned about themselves during this alignment?**
> This is an opportunity for the facilitator to help the team to creatively plan its own continued development.

AFTER THE ALIGNMENT

1. Type all the recorded discussion results for each question and give a copy of the report to each team member. This alignment report is not a charter or a formal document. The report should avoid any faciltator's organizational analysis. It is a team formation document meant to change, if needed, and to guide the team through some discussion of ideas as it goes through the storming phase, moves into the norming phase comfortably, and arrives at the performing phase quickly.

   The report is not intended to be meeting minutes or a detailed record of all that happened during the session. The report is a summary of the major discussions and decisions the team agreed to. It should come from the flip charts that were created during the session. Brief, simple bulleted lists are preferred over lengthy narrative text.

   A recommended outline for the report is:

   A. Name of the team; date, time, and location of the session.

   B. Names of team members who participated in the alignment.

   C. Bulleted lists of ideas contributed or decided at the session for each discussion topic.

2. Review the draft with the team coach or with the entire team.

3. Encourage the team to use the alignment document to periodically assess itself in terms of what it defined for itself. This is an opportunity to coach the team on a method of process analysis or team self-evaluation as an additional team development activity. As an additional service, use the alignment report to create a self-assessment instrument for the team to use periodically.

4. Raise and discuss other team development agenda items that will help the team become what it wants to be. Suggest other team development approaches that would be helpful.

24

CLARIFYING TEAM ROLES AND RESPONSIBILITIES

Edwina Haring

Overview   The purpose of this guide is to provide the user with justification and methods for designing clarification activities for roles and responsibilities for your team. There are three options for using this guide: 1) Follow the performance tool supplied at the end of the guide to create custom activities; 2) modify one of the example activities provided in the text; or 3) use one of the example designs as articulated.

The guide provides the logic, tools, and examples needed to design novel approaches to team role clarification so that users can create custom activities for the teams they support. A discussion of the need for team member role and responsibilities clarification is followed by some signals interventionists may derive from analysis that suggest roles may be overlapping or unclear. Next, we examine the considerations to be attended to in approaching team member roles and responsibilities clarification exercises and why a novel approach may be warranted for the target team. Examples are provided from the author's consulting experience in designing and facilitating successful, innovative clarification activities for various teams. Step-by-step instructions for designing, facilitating, and debriefing the various methods of achieving role clarification are outlined. Finally, a performance tool to guide the design strategy is included.

INTRODUCTION

Successful team development and execution of responsibilities depend on many factors. Some of those factors are organizational structure and support; having a clear, agreed team purpose; and having the right people in the right positions. One of the key areas for successful teamwork is reaching an understanding of the roles and responsibilities of

Contact Information: Edwina Haring, 7 Kris Court, Newark, DE 19702, 302-455-1727, Erharing@magpage.com

each team member. This not only assists individual team members in seating themselves within the team, but helps prevent overlap or gap in responsibilities. For newly formed teams, clarifying roles and responsibilities is fundamental to building trust and openness. Troubled teams suffering from missed deadlines, inefficient work processes, and the like may also benefit from engaging in a role clarification exercise. Post-activity feedback from participating team members is very positive, indicating that although these teams almost always request team member role clarification, it is rarely provided.

WHY CLARIFY ROLES AND RESPONSIBILITIES IN TEAMS?

In *Team Building: Blueprints for Productivity and Satisfaction* (W. Brendan Reddy and Kaleel Jamison, eds., 1988), the Team Performance Model™ (© 1987 Drexler/Sibbet) portrays a thorough picture of the stages of team development. The first two stages, referred to as "sets of concerns team members face as they work together," are Orientation (Why am I here?) and Trust Building (Who are you?). Resolution of these concerns is critical for the team's opportunity to achieve high performance; concerns left unresolved produce disorientation, fear, mistrust, and façade.

Project teams consisting of members with similar backgrounds or from the same departments within a company may be better versed about each team member's role. However, cross-functional teams, sometimes global in nature or the result of merged companies (and company cultures), often do not have a clear understanding of the roles of other team members. In addition, cross-functional project teams within the same company may operate very differently, rendering a team member's previous cross-functional team experience less effective in addressing the expectations of another project team.

Clarification of team member roles and responsibilities in cross-functional teams also provides opportunities for the team to identify gaps in functional role coverage. Identification of these gaps allows the team to strategize countermeasures or preventative measures to ensure that team goals are met. Moreover, with a clear understanding of team member roles, the team is equipped to capitalize on hidden talents and experience that may not otherwise be evident, thus providing more options to ensure accomplishment of team goals. Developing the bonds between team members is another positive outcome of roles and responsibilities clarification, as team members discover commonalities. Bonding with others, sharing some of our "selves" with others is how people begin to form trusting relationships. Finally, clarifying team

159

member roles sets the expectations for performance and identifies the areas of contribution and responsibility for each team member.

WHEN TO PROVIDE ROLES AND RESPONSIBILITIES CLARIFICATION ACTIVITIES

It is expected that a credible analysis of the current situation within a team will be completed prior to engaging in this or any other intervention activity. There are a number of reasons why particular feedback from the target audience (and other stakeholders) may indicate that roles clarification is a viable intervention. Some of the signals that a team may need roles and responsibilities clarification derive from negative acts and experiences; others spring from a more proactive perspective.

For example, roles and responsibilities clarification may be considered an appropriate intervention when a project team is missing its goals (either budget, time, or deliverables). Frequently, confusion exists about who is responsible for key aspects of a project; therefore, no individual team member owns the responsibility. Another situation that may signal the need for a role clarification activity is when team members' prior negative experiences as members of cross-functional teams are brought to the new team (intentionally or unintentionally). These negative experiences build expectations just as positive experiences do, and they frame the way a team member may view the project team process. Other negatively derived reasons for engaging in a role clarification activity include signs that the team is suffering from infighting, turf wars, unresolved conflict, backstabbing, gossiping, and within-team alliances (cliques within the team).

Proactively, a newly formed team will find this exercise very helpful in setting expectations, checking perceptions, and starting their work together with full knowledge of other team member's roles. Roles clarification in new teams has the added benefit of helping team members become better acquainted, thus facilitating their team bonding. When teams are comprised of members inexperienced in cross-functional teamwork, clarifying roles will assist them in understanding the value that cross-functionality can bring to a project. A team member's or team leader's request for roles clarification is also a good reason to provide an exercise, if other confirming evidence supports the request.

When a team's member composition has changed significantly or the team's purpose has changed appreciably, a roles clarification activity may help to incorporate the new members into the team, level the playing field for all members, or set new expectations for differing roles, given the new direction or goal of the team.

Additional signals that clarification of roles and responsibilities may be needed within a cross-functional team include the complexity or novelty of the project assignment, or when cross-functional project teams represent a new work method for the organization.

CONSIDERATIONS FOR DESIGN OF ROLES AND RESPONSIBILITIES CLARIFICATION ACTIVITIES

Typical factors to consider when designing any type of team intervention also apply to roles and responsibilities clarification activities. Customary team and organizational variables to consider are items such as the team's history together, current issues or challenges for the team, organization structure and climate, and individual likes or dislikes. Typical audience analysis factors should not be overlooked, such as age, education, positions held by team members within the organization, length of time in current position, and so on. Logistically, consider items such as time allotted for the activity and physical attributes of the meeting space.

Why Use a Novel Design Approach?

When designing a more novel approach to roles and responsibilities clarification, consider carefully the level of team member sophistication and maturity, as well as their exposure to other, more predictable roles and responsibilities clarification exercises. Determine whether the team needs a more novel approach in order to flush out greater detail about roles, build bonds between team members more quickly, or define responsibility boundaries, or simply as an alternative process, to name a few possibilities. In addition, as the facilitator, you may need the professional challenge of conducting the roles and responsibilities clarification exercise by using a new process—staleness in repertoire is usually evident to the audience.

Depending on the team members' experience with these types of interventions, they may be accustomed to other approaches: "the usual," "the boring," and "the predictable." Some of the more familiar approaches are:

- "What animal (or bird) are you most like and why?"
- "If you could be any tree, which would you be and why?"
- "State your name, title, and responsibilities."

The roles and responsibilities clarification interventions outlined in the remaining text are more robust designs that produce better results than the usual methods because the designs are customized to the team and its particular issues. The design examples encourage perception checking in a no-fault environment and recognize the inherent worth (value) of all team members. They build strength and build on strengths. Preconceived notions about other roles are quickly and accurately addressed. This creates the opportunity for team members to learn more fully about an individual's background and experience, allows for identification of teamwork (interpersonal) skills in addition to functional skills, and differentiates a specific functional role from one team to another (recognizing that the same function may serve varying roles on differing projects). Last, and perhaps most importantly, these intervention designs are active and interactive.

EXAMPLES

This section of the guide illustrates three roles and responsibilities clarification exercises in detail. Each example exercise is prefaced with a short synopsis of pertinent team attributes and the audience analysis (Team Composition). Next, the Goals (derived from the analysis) for the target team's roles and responsibilities clarification exercise are provided, followed by the Design and Process Steps used to create and conduct the exercise. Facilitator Role notes are additions to the customary facilitator responsibilities (such as introducing the activity or ensuring the team has articulated a shared purpose), as are the Activity Debriefing (whole group; close of activity) questions. Freely substitute your own words and questions in debriefing the exercises and elsewhere in the process.

In order to assist the reader in locating the activity most appropriate to the team you are supporting, the activity design examples are organized in the following manner:

> **Team A: Established Team.** The focus of the exercise is on individual team member role and responsibilities clarification in relation to team purpose and to demonstrate appreciation of each other.
>
> **Team B: Newly Formed Team.** The focus of the exercise is perception checking of individual team member roles and responsibilities.
>
> **Team C: Project-Specific Team with Predetermined Termination Date.** The focus of the exercise is on small-group role clarification in relation to deliverables and partnership.

TEAM A: ESTABLISHED TEAM

Team Composition

Multinational (3 countries and 5 cultures); 1 team member ESL (team worked in English); cross-functional; product development team; 10 years old; numerous personnel changes in previous year as people moved on to other projects; experiencing conflict and delays in deliverables; 13 members (3 females, 10 males); male leader; average age 45; senior level; most Ph.D.; private sector; many knew each other (to some extent) from previous teams; most lead functional teams.

Goals

1. Learn more about each other professionally and personally.
2. Show appreciation for each other's talents and skills.
3. Seek common bonds to unify team members.
4. Check misperceptions about team member roles.

Design and Process Steps

1. Instruct each team member to create a concept map on flip chart paper of his or her roles and responsibilities including interpersonal or team skills they bring as assets to the team and any personal information (as desired) to share with fellow team members (Form A). Team members work individually. Provide about 20 minutes; post the maps on walls.

2. Next, instruct the team members to walk around the room reading and reflecting on their teammates' concept maps. Ask team members to write comments on each other's maps, noting personal qualities that they admire in that person, adding roles they assumed were that team member's, and asking questions. Encourage team members to do this silently and to take their time. Ask them to write on the flip charts using a different color marker than the color used by the original team member. Depending on the size of the group, allow about 5 to 8 minutes per team member (for example, expect about an hour for a team of 12 members).

3. Next, ask each team member to return to his or her own concept map and read what others have written. Ask them to check the accuracy of items added and to add any missing items. Provide about 5 to 8 minutes for team members to prepare to introduce themselves.

163

4. On a volunteer basis, one at a time, ask individual team members to stand by the concept maps; introduce themselves, their role and responsibilities and team or interpersonal skills; and comment on what other team members added to their concept maps. Encourage team members to ask questions of the team about their comments and additions, in order to clarify meaning and promote understanding. Encourage the other team members to just listen at this time. Allow about 15 to 20 minutes for each presentation.

Facilitator Role

Explain each step of the activity as it occurs rather than explaining the entire process ahead of time. This may help to circumvent less-than-honest disclosure of perceptions. Debrief each team member presentation by asking the listening team members if they have questions or need clarification on anything the presenting team member has said, before moving on to the next team member's introduction.

Activity Debriefing

The facilitator asks questions such as, "How did this exercise work for you? What did you learn? How do you feel about your role on the team now? What misperceptions have been clarified for you? How will your new knowledge of other team member roles and responsibilities help you in moving forward together as a team to deliver the project?"

ILLUSTRATION OF CONCEPT MAP FOR ROLES AND RESPONSIBILITIES CLARIFICATION ACTIVITIES (FORM A)

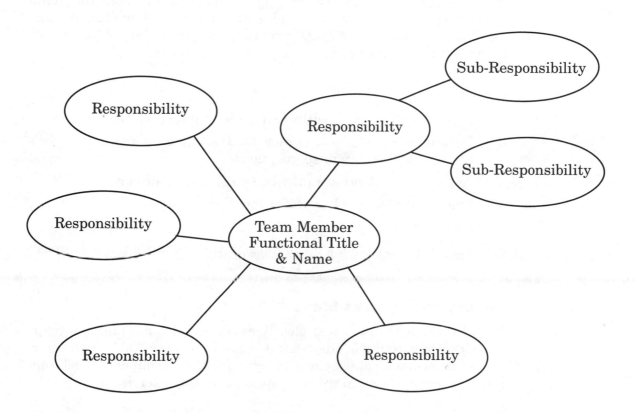

TEAM B: NEWLY FORMED TEAM

Team Composition

Multinational (6 countries and cultures of origin); 4 team members ESL (team worked in English language); cross-functional; product development team; new team; exploratory: single product for market not yet defined; most team members are new to this type of product development team; a few team members had prior unsatisfactory team experiences; 15 members (3 females, 12 males); male leader; average age 45; senior level; most Ph.D.; private sector; most did not know each other; most lead functional teams.

Goals

1. Kick off project team with clear understanding of roles.

2. Determine degree of accuracy held about each team member's function and rectify misperceptions.

3. Appreciate each other's talents, skills, and experience.

4. Learn about each other professionally and personally.

5. Build community.

6. Educate team members unfamiliar with product team composition and cross-functional teamwork.

Design and Process Steps

Initially, the facilitator must clearly establish an atmosphere of tolerance for perceptual misjudgment. It is important to establish an error-forgiving, no-blame atmosphere in order for team members to feel comfortable participating in this perception checking exercise.

1. Write the functional title of each team member on a separate slip of paper, fold so as not to reveal the title, and place in a hat or fishbowl. Ask each team member to draw one slip of paper. (If they draw their own functional title, have them draw another and then put the paper with their own title back into the container.)

2. Ask each team member to draw a concept map (on flip chart paper) of the functional role and responsibilities to the team for the functional title they drew. Encourage team members to include any and all responsibilities they think belong to the function. Remind team members that this is an opportunity to check the accuracy of their perceptions and that there is no penalty or

fault for mistaken perceptions. Allow about 10 to 15 minutes; post the maps on walls.

3. Next, ask team members to move around the room, visiting each functional concept map except their own. Ask team members to read and reflect on what is written for each functional role. Then, using a contrasting color marker, ask team members to add their perceptions to the roles and responsibilities concept maps and write questions for that team member to address. Depending on the size of the group, allow about 5 to 8 minutes per team member.

4. Ask each team member to go to his or her own chart, read what has been written regarding the role and responsibilities, and make any additions or corrections necessary to display an accurate picture of the role. Allow about 10 minutes.

5. On a volunteer basis, one at a time, ask team members to stand beside the concept map of their function, introduce themselves, review their role and clarify the responsibilities, clearly negating those that are not accurate (perhaps stating what function is responsible for that item), and embellishing on the responsibilities that are part of their function. Encourage the presenting team member to ask questions of the team about their comments and additions in order to clarify meaning and promote understanding. Encourage the other team members to just listen at this time. Allow about 15 to 20 minutes for each presentation.

Facilitator Role

Explain each step of the activity as it occurs rather than explaining the entire process ahead of time. This may help to circumvent less-than-honest disclosure of perceptions. Don't rush this exercise—allow team members to reflect and return with more thoughts. When most are finished, they usually sit down or start chatting in groups about topics unrelated to the activity. Call time at each interval of the exercise. Debrief each team member's presentation by asking other team members if they have questions or need clarification on anything the presenting team member has said, before moving on to the next team member's introduction.

Activity Debriefing

The facilitator asks questions such as, "How did this exercise work for you? What did you learn? How do you feel about your role on the team now? What misperceptions have been clarified for you? How will your new knowledge of other team member roles and responsibilities help you in moving forward together as a team to deliver the project?"

TEAM C: PROJECT-SPECIFIC TEAM
PREDETERMINED TERMINATION DATE

Team Composition

Project-specific team with finite project deliverable and end; 3 organizational partners to the contract—one executes, one manages and contracts, one is the ultimate client; organizations had worked together previously, though not necessarily all the same individual representatives; previous partnership had some decision-point conflicts; 23 members (1 female, 22 males); 3 male leaders; average age 45; military, military-civilians, and private sector partnership; education levels widely diversified; most lead functional teams.

Goals

1. Clarify the perceptions about the role each party holds in the project.

2. Alleviate, through roles clarification, some of the issues that occurred in the first project.

3. Ensure that all key parties to the project understand who is responsible for what actions.

Design and Process Steps

1. Assign the three individual groups to separate areas of the room. Provide flip chart paper and markers.

2. Ask each group to list how they see themselves as a party to the contract (not job or contractual requirements, but rather what expertise or skills they bring to the contract). Provide 10 minutes; post the lists on wall out of view of the other groups.

3. Next, ask each group to list how they see one of the other groups. Provide 5 minutes.

4. Next, ask each group to list how they see the third group. Provide 5 minutes.

5. Instruct groups to exchange their perception lists with the other groups. (Each group retains its list of how they see themselves, but exchanges the other lists with the appropriate teams. Now, each group should have its own list of how they see themselves, and a list from each of the other groups describing how the other groups see them.) Instruct groups to post the lists from the other groups next to their own lists. *Warning: Do not use this written exchange of perceptions in very hostile or very nonconfrontational groups.*

This exercise is good for moderately healthy groups. If you sense hostility or an unwillingness to confront others, either allow the groups to explain what they have written about the other groups or, better still, choose another exercise.

6. Ask groups to compare their perceptions of their group to the other group's perceptions of them and to identify where there is agreement and where mismatches in perception occur. Provide 10 minutes; post the responses on separate flip chart paper.

7. Instruct groups to brainstorm the cause(s) of the misperceptions. Provide 10 minutes; post the responses on same flip chart paper as in step 6.

8. Next, instruct groups to identify ways they can correct what they identify as misperceptions. Provide 15 minutes; post the responses on the flip chart paper used in steps 6 and 7.

9. Ask a spokesperson from each group to explain the group's discussion, what perceptions they agree with and which they feel are misperceptions, what they think causes the misperception, and what they plan to do to correct that misperception. Allow 10 to 15 minutes per group.

Facilitator Role

Introduce the activity by stating that perception is reality for many people and, as humans, we act and react based on our perceptions. In any team, misperceptions often lead to miscommunications and unfulfilled (or unwarranted) expectations.

While conducting the exercise, keep groups on track and keep this exercise moving. Do not let the groups dwell too long on any one step in the activity. Encourage groups to be as honest as they are comfortable with in describing how they see the other groups. Explain each step of the activity as it occurs rather than explaining the entire process ahead of time. This may help to circumvent less-than-honest disclosure of perceptions.

Debrief each group when they are done presenting their findings. Ask questions such as, "Were you surprised to learn what others thought of your group? How accurate were the perceptions? How did your group choose which misperceptions to focus on changing? How did your group decide what action to take to change the misperception(s)?"

Activity Debriefing

The facilitator should check in with team members to ensure that everyone is okay and that there are no lingering issues or resentments.

Debrief the activity by asking questions such as, "What worked well in this exercise? What was difficult? Why do you think the exercise was designed this way? What benefits have you received from this exercise? How do you think this exercise can be improved?"

SUMMARY

Conflict and miscommunication in teams can often be attributed to mismatched perceptions: Team members do not share the same perceptions about their own roles on the team as do other team members. These mismatched perceptions are not only the source of much conflict and miscommunication, but they also set inaccurate expectations that inevitably lead to disappointment, missed opportunities, overlapping work, or work gaps. Failure to address basic team member needs such as helping them identify their roles within the team or assisting team members in building trusting relationships has detrimental effects on team accomplishments and efficiencies over the long term.

A carefully constructed and meaningful clarification exercise returns not only immediate benefits, but long-term benefits as well. Participating team members will readily experience the correction of misperceptions and clarification of responsibilities for each team member. Another immediate benefit is learning about the additional skills, experience, or talents other team members bring to the team experience. In the long run, role clarification activities invite team members to begin self-disclosure—the first step in building relationships and establishing an atmosphere of openness. The process is fundamental to successful team performance.

Feedback from client teams about these exercise designs is very positive. Team members claim the roles and responsibilities clarification exercises are highly effective, relatively easy, fun, novel, keep them moving (active!), and are considered time well invested.

ROLES AND RESPONSIBILITIES CLARIFICATION ACTIVITY DESIGN TOOL

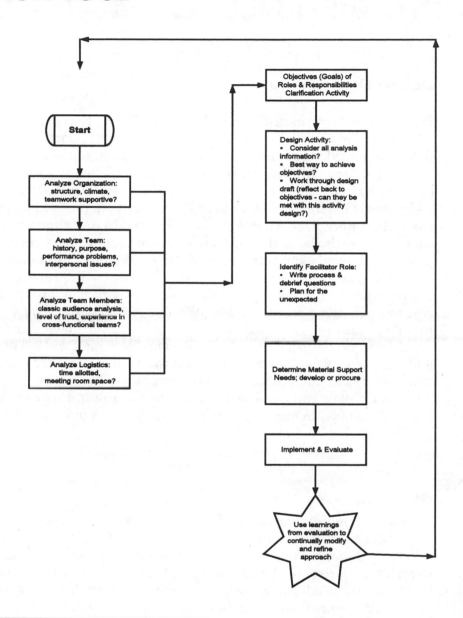

25

BUILDING DISTANCE TEAMS

Debra Dinnocenzo

Overview   Increases in geographically dispersed workforces, telecommuting, and other forms of virtual work have had a significant impact on the establishment and development of distance teams. In spite of geographic separation, time differences, and greater dependence on technology for communication, teams must remain productive while no longer being co-located. This trend is likely to continue, as it pervades and redefines the virtual workplace. Therefore, it is essential to reevaluate work relationships, methods, and communication practices to be certain that productivity goals and worker satisfaction are not compromised.

This guide provides distance team members with practical tools to understand the communication challenges they face and to implement creative solutions for achieving effective results. Regardless of the industry, function, or organization structure, all businesses are experiencing increased exposure to virtual work arrangements. The topics addressed in this guide are timely and the applications are relevant to effectiveness in our evolving virtual workplace. The content and exercises that follow can be incorporated into a training program, used in the context of team meetings, or used as coaching guidelines by a team leader.

OBJECTIVES

An increasingly pervasive workplace reality is the amount of teamwork that must be accomplished virtually. In this age of globalization and transnational business, teams made up from a geographically dispersed workforce are facing the critical challenge of achieving results in an effective and timely manner. Whether a formal team or a loosely organized project team, a virtual team will achieve its goals only if its

Contact Information: Debra Dinnocenzo, ALLearnatives®, 10592 Perry Highway, Suite 201, Wexford, PA 15090, 724-934-9349, ddinnocenzo@allearnatives.com, www.allearnatives.com

members have the key skills necessary to successfully function as virtual team members. Successful virtual team members:

1. Know and nurture their team.
2. Stay in touch with coworkers.
3. Are creatively accessible.
4. Utilize effective interaction skills.
5. Deliver results with distance delegation.
6. Reach agreements that foster commitment and collaboration.
7. Establish a foundation of trust.

EXERCISES

Choose from the following exercises to develop awareness, build skills, strengthen team relationships, and establish guidelines for those who function within or with virtual teams.

1. Know and Nurture Your Team

The relationships and interdependencies within a formal team—those coworkers who work together directly or who focus on the same projects, accounts, or function—are inherent in the structure of organizations and the processes whereby work is accomplished. The relationships require nurturing, and efforts to strengthen them should be ongoing as a team develops and evolves. Virtual teams can achieve superior results in part through effective relationship-building, communication, and interaction skills with colleagues who comprise their formal and informal teams. Therefore, it is essential to also understand and nurture relationships within the entire virtual team.

Exercise: Who's On Your Team?

Purpose: To help team members identify who comprises their formal and informal teams and to help them understand the critical role all team members play in their success.

Process: Team members discuss the following:

- Who are the members of your formal team?
- Beyond your formal team members, who else contributes to your success or provides critical support, resources, and information?

- Identify some of the specific things your informal team members do that allow you and your team to accomplish your objectives.

- Identify action steps you can take to recognize the efforts of your informal team members and to communicate how valuable they are to you and why their contributions are critical to your success.

2. Stay in Touch with Coworkers

With the time virtual team members invest each day in accomplishing work, communicating with clients, partners, and supervisors, and addressing the technological and administrative issues critical to the job, it's very easy to find little or no time to stay connected with coworkers. Certainly communication occurs when it's essential to job requirements, but it's also important to stay in touch with coworkers for non-task purposes. This not only strengthens the foundation of relationships, it assures coworkers that those team members who work remotely are indeed present (albeit in a virtual way!), available, and aware of them and their issues. It also helps to minimize any resentment that nonvirtual coworkers may feel toward those who work at a distance from the traditional workplace.

Exercise: Staying Connected

Purpose: To help team members understand the importance of maintaining communication with coworkers and to explore creative ways to expand communication and networking opportunities.

Process: Team members discuss the following:

- What are some of the ways you can keep in better touch with coworkers?

- Think about your schedule of meetings, travel plans, company meetings, and other natural opportunities you may have to interact with coworkers. How can you better utilize these opportunities for face-to-face interactions with coworkers?

- What are some specific steps you can take to improve your contact with formal and informal team members when working at a distance?

3. Be Creatively Accessible

The demands of a job, pressures of life, and the distances that often separate virtual team members make being accessible a triple challenge. Establishing both the sense and the reality of accessibility, in spite of being geographically separated, is vital to success. No one doubts that live, real-time, face-to-face interactions generally are superior, but opportunities for this type of interaction are increasingly limited. So virtual teams must work together to find creative ways to overcome accessibility barriers and to compensate for time and distance factors.

Exercise: Creative Accessibility

Purpose: To help team members identify effective ways to be accessible and to consider steps to improve their levels of accessibility.

Process: Team members discuss the following:

- Identify the various ways you are accessible to your coworkers, supervisors, customers, support staff, etc.

- Consider whether the level of access others have to you is adequate. Evaluate your level of responsiveness to requests for information and assistance.

- Identify ways you might improve your accessibility. Consider creative ways you might use technology resources, as well as specific actions you can take to be more accessible.

4. Master Effective Interaction Skills

Working within a virtual team will pose some unique challenges for anyone who feels that having face-to-face interactions is the only way to communicate effectively. While no one would dispute that live interactions usually are preferable, these are fast becoming a luxury. Mergers, acquisitions, and global competition have resulted in a geographically dispersed workforce and a growing number of distance workers. As part of this trend, it's critical that virtual team members become expert in the essential communication skills for successful virtual work.

While there is some loss of the communication subtleties gleaned from eye contact, body posture, gestures, and voice tone, virtual interactions can be supplemented in ways that minimize the negative effects of *distance dialogue*. Key communication and interaction skills involve: listening, clarifying, establishing agreements, checking for understanding, two-way conversations, and limiting distractions.

Exercise: Virtual Interaction Skills

Purpose: To assist team members in understanding the obstacles inherent in *distance dialogue* and identifying ways to overcome barriers to effective virtual interactions.

Process: Team members discuss the following:

- What are some of the essential components of effective communication among members of a virtual team?

- How might you ensure that appropriate listening skills are being utilized when interacting with someone who is geographically distant from you?

- What steps can you take during *distance dialogue* to establish a clear understanding of the purpose, desired outcomes, and necessary follow-up?

- What types of distractions have you experienced while participating in a virtual interaction or meeting? How can such distractions be eliminated or minimized?

5. Deliver Results with Distance Delegation

Those who successfully work remotely or as part of a virtual team find themselves benefiting tremendously from the use of appropriate delegation skills. Delegating tasks and responsibilities can be an unnerving proposition for some people, especially those who like to be in control of things or on top of details. Virtual workers have the added dynamic of distance, resulting in the sense of even less control, more frustration, and elevated worrying. Distance delegation, however, doesn't need to be riskier or more haphazard if both the delegation and the follow-up are handled properly. When delegating from afar, it's important to clearly communicate the task to be accomplished, listen carefully for confusion or concerns, discuss issues, clarify agreements and follow-up action, and establish communication points and accessibility guidelines.

Exercise: Distance Delegation

Purpose: To provide team members with a process for effectively handling a delegation discussion and to help them understand the importance of follow-up and monitoring of the delegated assignment.

Process: Team members discuss the following:
Think of a task or responsibility you might delegate to someone on your formal or informal team who does not have a direct reporting rela-

tionship to you. Specifically, identify what you would say to accomplish each of the following steps in the discussion:

1. Describe the task or responsibility you're delegating and explain its importance.

2. Ask for input, concerns, or feedback regarding the delegated assignment.

3. Discuss any issues and verify understanding of the requirements.

4. Agree on follow-up actions, monitoring methods, and ways to communicate if help is needed.

5. Clarify your availability and best ways to reach you for necessary assistance, and offer your appreciation.

6. Reach Agreements That Foster Commitment and Collaboration

Setting clear agreements regarding accountabilities and commitments with coworkers, supervisors, and support staff minimizes a plethora of difficult, unpleasant, and time-consuming problems. Without clear agreements, there is risk of diminished work standards, missed deadlines, delayed shipments, lack of follow-through, disappointed customers, increased stress and frustration, as well as declines in productivity and achievement of goals. Effective virtual teams must establish clear standards for reaching agreements and ensuring the commitment of coworkers to work collaboratively to implement agreements.

Exercise: Reaching Agreements

Purpose: To establish guidelines for team members to use in handling discussions, to reach agreements and resolve conflict, and to create awareness of the importance of utilizing these skills routinely.

Process: Team members discuss the following:

- Are there any areas of confusion, ambiguity, or wavering commitment relative to the support you need from others to achieve your goals? If so, plan and practice a discussion to resolve one of these situations using the following guidelines:

  1. Clearly state the needs and expectations.

  2. Explain why they're important and the consequences of not meeting them.

3. Describe how the agreement will look when it's operating as needed.

4. Ask about issues, concerns, and additional information.

5. Listen, reflect, discuss, and summarize periodically.

6. Mutually agree to parameters, requirements, and resolutions.

7. Document the agreements and distribute to everyone affected.

8. Establish a follow-up time to review progress and revise the agreement as required.

- Are any areas of conflict having an impact on your work or the productivity of the team? If so, it's wise to address these situations quickly. Prior to having a discussion with the people involved in the conflict, think about the solutions you'll propose and concerns or barriers you expect others to raise.

7. Establish a Foundation of Trust

Underlying every successful relationship is trust. Without it, people become suspicious, noncommittal, uncaring, undermining, and jaded—all of which leads to deteriorated and nonproductive relationships. This further leads to unpleasant work environments, disgruntled workers, frustrated customers, dejected leaders, and unprofitable organizations. It is particularly vital that virtual team members establish confidence in relationships with colleagues and supervisors, since distance and the absence of day-to-day interactions can create pressure that will erode trust.

The fundamental ingredients of trust in working relationships critical to the effectiveness of virtual teams include reliability, consistency, and integrity. Knowing how these factors affect trust and how behavior affects perceptions and beliefs is important to the success of virtual teams.

Exercise: Establishing Trust

Purpose: To provide team members with an understanding of the components of trust and the critical role trust plays in relationships, with particular emphasis on its importance among members of a virtual team.

Process: Team members discuss the following:

- Identify ways to establish and strengthen the key ingredients of trust in working relationships:
  ✔ reliability.

- ✔ consistency.
- ✔ integrity.

- Consider steps you can take immediately to be more reliable and consistent.

- Evaluate your work habits, team involvement, and interactions with coworkers. Also recall any feedback you've received regarding concerns about your availability and follow-through on commitments. What actions can you take to improve your effectiveness, responsiveness, and contributions to the team?

26

BECOMING A TEAM PLAYER

Mel Silberman

Overview This guide provides advice that anyone can utilize to collaborate more effectively with others. Share it with any person who is part of your team.

INTRODUCTION

All of us are involved in some kind of teamwork. Being a member of a team really tests us, because we have less personal control over the outcome than in a one-to-one relationship. It's often frustrating, since we have fewer opportunities to get our point across and persuade others when participation has to be shared among many. On the other hand, being part of a team effort, even with its frustrations, can often be exciting and productive.

As a team player, one works more to advance the group's goals rather than one's own. This can be a daunting challenge to all of us who are raised in a culture that values individual rather than group effort. It involves an attitude shift in which we let go of our egos and the desire to advance our own agendas in favor of giving our ideas readily to the group. This shift is vividly demonstrated in a classic team exercise called Broken Squares. Each participant in a group of five is given pieces from five broken squares. Each person's job is to make one of the squares alone. The temptation is to build your own square and let others fend for themselves. However, only by working together, sharing, and helping each other is it possible to complete the five squares. The process can be frustrating. A participant may even have to disassemble a square he or she has formed in order for the group to succeed. However, the outcome is exhilarating. Typically, groups let out a loud cheer when they have completed the task. The counterpart to the exer-

Contact Information: Mel Silberman, Active Training/PeopleSmart, 303 Sayre Dr., Princeton, NJ 08540, 609-987-8157, mel@activetraining.com, www.active training.com

cise in the real world occurs when people have blended their talents to be victorious in a sporting event, to complete a massive project, or just to create a supportive setting for each other.

There are three abilities everyone must cultivate to become a team player:

1. Joining with others: seeking ways to contribute to a joint group effort.
2. Facilitating teamwork: employing techniques to enhance team activity.
3. Building consensus: helping others to make decisions that everyone supports.

Let's look more closely at each of these abilities.

JOINING WITH OTHERS

The 1980s was the *me* decade. The 1990s was the *we* decade. In the first decade of the new millennium, with teams and teamwork nearly everywhere, we are building on the momentum of the 1990s. We no longer look out for number one; we look out for the group.

Each of us comes to a group with his or her own talents. Team players come with something else: the ability to blend their talents with the skills of others around them. We also come with our own ideas and preferences. Team players balance an interest in what they are advocating with interest in what others are saying. Team players see themselves and others as group resources rather than as individual egos. They act as if they are part of the group's pool of knowledge, skills, and ideas and they are successful in getting others to act that way themselves.

Key steps in joining with others are observing what's going on in the group, making contributions where needed, and building a climate of dialogue.

Observe What's Going On in the Group

Many people in group situations are oblivious to what is happening around them. They are focused on themselves and fail to pick up cues about the situations of others. Perhaps someone has been excluded. Perhaps someone has a good idea but it's not expressed well. Perhaps the group is off on a tangent or caught up in debate when it should be brainstorming.

Here is a list of things you might watch for in a group:

- Does everyone have the same understanding of the group's goals? Does everyone support them?

- Do people seem free to express themselves?

- Do people listen to each other?

- Is there equal opportunity for participation?

- Is the group floundering and without energy?

- Are members of the group building on each other's ideas?

- Is conflict accepted and handled?

- Do group members know about each other's needs?

Based on your observations, you will be in a position to be helpful to the group.

Make Contributions Where Needed

Imagine a basketball team in which each player looked exclusively for an opportunity to shoot instead of passing the ball to an open player, setting screens for teammates, or getting into position for the rebound. As we have said before, people who are not attuned to the team concept focus on their own needs and ignore the needs of others. If you have made some accurate observations of the group situation, however, you have uncovered many opportunities to contribute to the total group effort. In basketball terms, you have good court awareness and can sense what you need to do to help the group succeed.

Here is a list of things you might contribute:

- Assist someone else when appropriate.

- Offer to take minutes at a meeting.

- Ask quiet members for their opinions.

- Objectively describe the different viewpoints in the group.

- Bring together members who are in conflict with each other but are using others to air their grievances.

- Express appreciation for the efforts of others.

- Offer to facilitate a discussion.

- Share the credit you receive for a job well done.

- Summarize the group discussion.

- Suggest problem-solving techniques you may know.

- Relieve tension by telling a joke.

- Check decisions you are about to make yourself to determine whether they might affect others.
- Include everybody in the information loop.
- Seek the information and expertise of others.
- Communicate your own activity so that it is public knowledge.
- Tell others what they can do to support your efforts and ask them to do so in kind.

Build a Climate of Dialogue

We use the expression "everyone is entitled to his or her own opinion" when we want to support freedom of speech. However, there are social limits to this right in team situations. Too often, team discussion becomes a debate about my idea versus your idea. People advocate for the causes dear to their hearts, hoping to gain support from others. The climate becomes very politicized. By contrast, when a climate of dialogue exists, team members listen to each other, react to and build upon each other's ideas, and look for and acknowledge real differences of opinion.

Dialogue means "two minds together." The purpose of dialogue is to enlarge ideas, not diminish them. Here are ways you can help to build a climate of dialogue:

- Ask questions to clarify what others are saying. Invite others to seek clarification of your ideas.
- Share what's behind your ideas. Reveal your assumptions and goals. Invite others to do so in kind.
- Ask for others to give you feedback about your ideas.
- Give constructive feedback about the ideas of others.
- Make suggestions that build on the ideas of others.
- Incorporate the ideas of others into your proposals.
- Find common ground among the ideas expressed in the group.
- Encourage others to give additional ideas to those already expressed.

FACILITATING TEAMWORK

Whenever you are in a leadership position in a group, it pays to examine your leadership style. If you are a traditional leader, you may be used to directing, controlling, and monitoring. As a team-oriented leader, your role shifts to coaching, motivating, and empowering. Also, you may be accustomed to developing individual strengths among the members of the group you lead. As a team leader, you need to develop those strengths within the team.

You don't have to be the leader in a group, however, to play a facilitative role. Anyone can offer suggestions that might help the group to work more effectively. Here's an example:

A religious organization applied to a municipality for permission to build a group home for adolescent girls who had come from homes where they were abused. The organization wanted to buy one of a series of mansions that lined the main street of the town. The night the plan was introduced before the town council, a small but outspoken group of neighbors fought the idea feverishly. The neighbors complained that the organization wouldn't have the funds to keep up the property. They said the girls were ill-behaved and might be thieves, would surely be a bad influence on younger children and boys of their own age, might party all night and subsequently destroy the neighborhood. They refused to listen to the religious organization's plans and even booed its representative.

It was apparent to someone in the crowd that the meeting was going nowhere and would not if this continued. He suggested the town council select three people from the minority group and have them meet with the religious organization to iron out some of the problems. Given a little time to cool down, the two groups met, and a deal was struck: The organization got its group home and the neighbors received the safeguards they wanted.

There are three important steps to facilitating teamwork: Promote a common vision, encourage participation, and stimulate creative problem solving.

Promote a Common Vision

When people join a group, there may be no clear goals around which to coalesce. Or the announced goal may be interpreted differently by various members. Also, people may come to a group with their own individual goals that may or may not be supportive of the group goal. Given all these possibilities, most groups don't begin with a common vision. Many remain that way for months or years.

Effective teams are united in purpose. Clear, exciting goals mobilize teamwork. Whatever you can do to facilitate the creation of a common vision is worth its weight in gold. Here are some suggestions:

- If you are the team leader, suggest a few goals that will excite the group and ask for their reactions. Don't settle for business as usual. Teams thrive when business is *unusual*. Perhaps you might raise some specific targets for the coming year, identify some special projects that the team might want to undertake, or announce your commitment to changing work conditions.

- If you are a group member and sense that the group is not unified around clear and exciting goals, ask for permission to set aside time for creating a common vision.

- Whether you are a team leader or merely a member, raise any of these questions for discussion:

    Imagine our meetings were coming to an end. What would you like to see as our accomplishments?

    Imagine coming to work here with your heart beating and your steps skipping. What would be going on here? What would the place look like? What would staff members be doing that is exciting and worthwhile?

    How could you state in a brief sentence or two the end results we might obtain if we work together?

    Here are some sample statements:

    For a customer service unit: "We make customers glad they bought our product."

    For a hospital dialysis unit: "Because of us, patients have more dignity and hope."

    For a manufacturing plant: "Our customers know when they operate one of our machines, they are operating the finest equipment money can buy."

Encourage Participation

Teamwork falls flat if the group is reluctant to participate or if certain persons dominate. A wide range of methods can be used to obtain active team participation. If you use a few of them on a consistent basis, you will avoid the phenomenon of hearing from the same people all the time. Here are several possibilities.

1. *Open discussion:* Ask a question and open it up to the entire group without any further structuring.

Use open discussion when you are certain that several people want to participate. Its voluntary quality is appealing, but don't overuse this method. If you do, you will limit participation to people who are comfortable about raising their hands. If you have a very participative group and are worried that the discussion might be too lengthy, say beforehand: "I'd like to ask four or five people to share...." If you are worried that few people will volunteer, say, "How many of you have an idea...?" versus "Who has an idea...?"

2. *Response cards:* Pass out index cards and request anonymous answers to your questions.

Use response cards to save time, to provide anonymity for personally threatening self-disclosures, or to make it easier for shy people to contribute. The need to state a position concisely on a card is another advantage of this method. Say: "For this discussion, I would like you to write down your thoughts first, before we talk together any further." Have the index cards passed around the group or have them returned to you to be read at a later point. Be careful to make your questions clear and to encourage brief, legible responses.

3. *Subgroup discussion:* Form people into subgroups of three or more to share and record information.

Use subgroup discussion when you have sufficient time to process questions and issues. This is one of the key methods for obtaining everyone's participation. You can assign people to subgroups randomly (e.g., by counting off) or purposively (e.g., by gender). Pose a question for discussion or give them a task or assignment to complete. Often, it is helpful to designate group roles, such as facilitator, timekeeper, recorder, or presenter, and to ask for volunteers or assign members to fill the roles. Make sure that people are in face-to-face contact with each other. Try to separate subgroups so that they do not disturb each other.

4. *Partners:* Form people into pairs and instruct them to work on tasks or discuss key questions.

Use partners when you want to involve everybody but do not have enough time for small-group discussion. Pair up people either by physical proximity or by a design to put certain people together. Often, it is not necessary to move chairs to create pair activity. You can ask pairs to do many things, such as reading and discussing a short written document together, responding to a question, or developing a solution to a problem.

5. *Go-around:* Go around the group and obtain short responses from each person.

   Use this method when you want to hear from each person and equalize participation. Sometimes, sentence stems (e.g., "One thing we could do is...") are useful in conducting go-arounds. Allow people to "pass" when they wish. Avoid repetition, if you want, by asking each person for a new contribution to the process.

6. *Calling on the next speaker:* Ask people to raise their hands when they want to share their views and request that the present speaker in the group call on the next speaker (rather than having the facilitator do that).

   Say: "For this discussion, I would like you to call on each other rather than having me select who to speak next. When you are finished speaking, look around to see whose hands are raised and call on someone." (Do not allow people to call on individuals who have not indicated a desire to participate.) Use calling on the next speaker when you are sure there is a lot of interest in the discussion and you wish to promote person-to-person interaction. When you wish to resume as moderator, inform the group that you are changing back to the regular format.

7. *Fishbowl:* Ask part of the group to form a discussion circle and have the remaining people form a listening circle around them.

   Use a fishbowl to help bring focus to large-group discussions. Although it is time-consuming, this is the best method for combining the virtues of large- and small-group discussion. Bring new groups into the inner circle to continue the discussion. You can do this by obtaining new volunteers or assigning people to be discussants. As a variation to concentric circles, you can have people remain seated at a table and invite different tables or parts of a table to be the discussants as the others listen.

   Bear in mind that you can combine some of these methods of obtaining participation. For example, you might pose a question, form partners to discuss it, and then obtain whole-group reaction through methods such as open discussion or calling on the next speaker. If the partner exchange takes place first, more people will be ready to participate in the full group setting. Or begin with response cards, followed by a go-around or subgroups.

Stimulate Creative Problem Solving

A group's creativity is fostered by thinking outside the box—looking at issues in new ways and developing novel solutions to problems. Brainstorming is a well-known technique to free the imagination to come up with new ideas about goals, projects, solutions, or whatever is needed. Most people assume that brainstorming is a fast process for getting as many ideas as possible in a very short period of time. However, brainstorming can be done at a leisurely pace as well. Here are two alternatives.

1. Fast brainstorming can be compared to making popcorn. Kernels form in people's minds and out pop ideas (some of which may be "corny"). If things go well, you get a lot of ideas and then the process gets exhausted. The process typically involves these guidelines:

   - Participants are urged to go for quantity. The more ideas, the better.

   - Participants are encouraged to think freely. In some cases, the crazier the ideas, the better.

   - Participants are invited to toss out ideas as they occur.

   - Participants are required to hold back any comments about the ideas until the time for brainstorming is up.

As a result of these guidelines, the pace of brainstorming is usually frenzied and uninhibited.

2. Slow brainstorming has a different tempo and feel. Participants are expected to be thoughtful and responsive. As a result, fewer ideas might be developed, but perhaps of better quality. However, there are still rules that qualify it as a form of brainstorming:

   - Participants are asked to wait a few seconds before shouting out their ideas.

   - Participants are sometimes requested to write down ideas first before making them public.

   - Participants are sometimes required to limit themselves to one contribution until everyone else contributes or passes.

   - Participants are urged to ask clarifying questions. When an idea is offered by someone, others are "allowed" to seek more information about the idea, as long as their questions aren't judgmental. For example, you might ask: "How much do you estimate that will cost?" (in a friendly tone of voice), but you would not ask (rhetorically): "Don't you think that's expensive?"

- Participants are encouraged to add to an idea ("Maybe we could also...").

The keys to either type of brainstorming session, fast or slow, are creative imagination and open, nonjudgmental interaction. Of course, after the ideas are produced, whether quickly or slowly, they must be listed, discussed, and evaluated. One way to quickly sort out the participants' reactions to the brainstormed ideas is to group them into these categories:

- keepers (implement immediately);
- maybes (promising enough to warrant serious consideration); or
- hold-offs (put aside for now).

Often, brainstorming new ideas is difficult because the size of the problem taxes the creative imagination of the group. One way to overcome this situation is to break the problem, issue, or goal down into its constituent parts and examine each part separately. Then, participants can brainstorm ideas involving each part. Doing this will help participants to loosen up, and they may produce some truly novel and productive ideas.

As the meeting begins, state the problem, issue, or goal about which you want to have a brainstorming session. Next, ask the participants to think about all the elements or parts of the problem, issue, or goal by breaking it down. [You might do this analysis for them prior to the meeting.]

As an example, consider the planning of a successful fund-raising race. These are some aspects of the project to be considered:

- a slogan,
- the course to be run,
- a length for the race,
- a date for the race (Is Saturday better than Sunday? Rain date or no? Maybe a holiday weekend?),
- prizes,
- a deadline for entries,
- emergency services, and
- publicity before, during, and after the race.

Take each part and think about the alternatives. New ideas in each of the areas could be so powerful that next year's race could be a real winner or it could change into a different kind of event altogether, as a result of the planners looking at the project from a different perspective.

A third strategy to encourage creative problem solving employs a technique called scenario thinking. Participants are asked to set aside present realities and dream up a wide range of new possibilities.

Select an issue, problem, or creative project facing the group. For example, a group might be discussing employee morale, slackening attendance or participation, or customer service. Tell the group that you would like them to set aside their current concerns about "things the way they are" and to think about a range of future possibilities to resolve the issue, problem, or project by engaging in scenario thinking. This is done by asking: "Can we look at it this way...and this way...and this way, and...?"

Display one or more of the following sentence stems and say to participants: "Let's dream a little together. How could we expand our thinking about this?" Encourage participants to share their ideas, beginning with the phrase(s):

> I wonder...
>
> What if...
>
> Maybe, we...
>
> I have a dream that...
>
> If only we...
>
> I wish...
>
> Why can't we...

Allow participants to speak when a thought comes to their minds. Encourage participants to accept silences between contributions. Insist that people listen but not respond to what is shared until several statements are made.

BUILDING CONSENSUS

It's now crunch time. Your group has been exploring ideas and debating its options. Some ideas will have to be discarded for now. Difficult decisions need to be reached and priorities need to be established. Agreement and commitment are the order of the day.

Most experts agree that groups should make important decisions by building consensus as opposed to taking votes. A consensus exists when all participants are willing to support and commit themselves to a specific decision. It may not be everyone's first choice, but everyone can live with the conclusions being reached. When a group builds consensus, there is greater commitment to implement the group's decision. When voting is used to make decisions, a disgruntled minority usually winds up upset and lags in their commitment to the implementation phase.

While many people agree in principle with the value of achieving consensus, they voice practical objections. They may have experienced a group taking a long time to reach consensus, and may have serious doubts that it can be accomplished at all. There are many ways to counteract these concerns.

When building consensus, consider three steps: narrowing ideas down, polling the group, and checking for commitment.

Narrowing Ideas Down

Multivoting is an efficient way to narrow the choices from a long list of decision options. Once the list is narrowed, it is often easier to obtain consensus. The members of the group prepare a list of possible solutions to a complex problem and are permitted to narrow the list themselves by casting a specified number of votes until only a few possibilities remain—those that are acceptable to the majority of the voters. This eliminates the loss of many good ideas, one of the problems created by holding a single vote on a long list of items. This technique is more likely to keep second-tier ideas viable.

On a flip chart, list all possible alternatives that could solve the particular problem, along with their attendant difficulties and advantages. If two or more alternatives are very similar, combine them as long as the group agrees they should be combined. Tell the participants to think carefully about what options they can accept. Pass out ballots and ask the participants to vote for each alternative they find acceptable. They may vote for as many as they want. Inform them, however, that only alternatives receiving one-half of all the possible votes will remain in contention and be placed on a second ballot, to be voted on at the next meeting.

Hold a discussion of the remaining choices. Then, vote again. The alternatives that receive one-half of all the possible votes on the second ballot remain on the list. Determine at this point whether more voting is needed to narrow the choices to begin working on a consensus.

When many solutions to a problem have been suggested, probably the most effective way to select the best ones is to have the group weigh them against specific standards. The process can be as simple or as comprehensive as necessary in order to achieve consensus. It can be used by small groups as well as large ones.

On a large flip chart, prepare a list of all the proposed solutions to the problem on which the group is focusing. Before going any further, propose a set of standards against which the group can evaluate its options. Or ask the group to brainstorm their own standards for judging the choices available to them. Such standards might include cost, feasibility, time needed, impact on results, and so forth. Ask the participants to discuss each option according to the standards you have suggested. Be sure to go through each option, collecting judgments. Don't allow the process to get bogged down in a campaign for a particular option.

Polling for Consensus

Polling for consensus is one good way to get the pulse of the group. When you survey the group, you are better able to pinpoint the degrees of difference in the participants' opposition or support of an idea or action and assess how close the sides really are. Your polling results will tell you whether further discussion is needed or if the opposing groups are ready at this point to seek a serious solution.

Tell the participants that they have reached a point in the meeting when no new ideas are being presented and the participants are merely recycling the same opinions and positions. This is the time to conduct a poll to determine whether a decision is near. Explain to the group that there are a number of different stages of consensus readiness. They can be graded from A through E:

A. I'm willing to accept the plan.

B. I admit the plan is a fair solution, but not one that I can get really excited about.

C. I don't fully agree with the plan, and feel the need to explain why it is not acceptable, but I'm not willing to try to block the idea.

D. I disagree with the decision and feeling strongly enough about it to try to exercise all of my influence to eliminate the plan.

E. I'm concerned that the group is not able to agree on the plan and I want to do more work on the concept before reaching consensus.

Ask the participants to indicate where they stand on the readiness scale. They may indicate this by raising their hands as you call out the grades, or by jotting down the grade on an index card to be collected and tallied. The grades will show you whether more work needs to be done. If there are a lot of As and Bs, then you and the group will determine that consensus has been reached. If the grades are mostly Cs and Ds, and if there are some Es, more discussion time is needed.

Checking for Commitment

When a group is attempting to build consensus, it is important to provide some kind of forum for the minority to speak as well as to collect any splinter ideas they might have that could be extremely important to the project involved. Providing a way for the minority to be heard is a practical tidying-up experience. It can be a healing one as well, in terms of the group's future ability to work together.

As a group is discussing a course of action, ask: "Who is still concerned about this proposal? What problems do you have with it?" Set aside time for the minority to speak. Another possibility is to provide time for the group that is obviously in the minority to make a statement. You might set aside 15 minutes or a half hour at a meeting when consensus seems near. After hearing from the minority, ask the total group if there are suggestions for alleviating the concerns expressed.

If consensus is finally reached, ask participants to think about what they can commit themselves to doing to implement decisions that have been made. If the team effort has required a long series of meetings, consider sending a letter or e-mail message to participants with a summary of the main points covered at the meetings. If they are involved in implementing the course of action decided on at the meeting, encourage them to keep in touch with you and offer your expertise to help them solve any unexpected problems.

PRESCRIPTIONS FOR TEAMWORK

As you attempt to become a team player, expect that the road ahead will be full of personal bumps and detours. As you navigate this road, be aware of those factors that have prevented you from influencing others in the past. Here are the major barriers most of us have to overcome to create lasting change, along with prescriptions to help you to move forward.

I don't think anything can be done to save the group I work with. It's too late.
Rx: Established groups develop habits that are as difficult to break as individual habits. Take the attitude that it's never too late and there is no better time to start than right away. Don't complain that the group is not productive. That message will be resisted by some or accepted

with an air of resignation by others. Instead, ask the group to evaluate itself. Use questions like:

> How well is our group meeting your expectations?
>
> What are you taking away from this group?
>
> How have we worked together? What has been helpful? What has not been helpful?
>
> If we had to start all over again, what, in hindsight, should we do?

I don't have the power to change things.
Rx: Remember that even making one recommendation might turn things around. Look for these opportunities. You also can speak to others with more power and authority than yourself and give them suggestions they can act on.

We are a team but we hardly ever see each other. People travel a lot or have other reasons to be away from the office.
Rx: This phenomenon is becoming prevalent in many companies. Explore ways to increase e-mail communication or use meeting shareware to keep your team in communication with each other.

I'd like to partner with some of my colleagues, but they seem busy doing their own things.
Rx: Develop a small project you would like to work on with someone else. Arrange it so the other person can't reject your invitation to collaborate. Maybe, greater collegiality will grow from there.

I wind up doing all the work.
Rx: The group has gotten used to your rescuing it from disaster. Select the very next opportunity in which you think it's worth the risk to insist that others have to contribute. Stay positive by saying something like: "I would like your help here. When I do the gut work myself, I start to feel resentful. I want to feel good about our working relationship."

27

SOLVING A TEAM PUZZLE

Sivasailam "Thiagi" Thiagarajan

Overview This activity requires teams to solve a logic puzzle. In the process, they learn to trade off among time, money, and information. You can use the activity to focus on many aspects of team dynamics, such as leadership, collaboration, inclusion, and so forth.

Suggested Time 45 minutes

Materials Needed

✔ Form A (Team Conference: A Logic Puzzle)

✔ Form B (A Dozen Questions and Answers)

✔ Form C (Cross-Check Matrix)

✔ Form D (How to Play Time, Money, and Logic)

✔ Form E (Solution Table, for facilitator's use)

✔ An envelope with $20,000 in play money for each team

Procedure

1. Divide participants into teams so that each team has 3 to 7 members.

2. Distribute one set of Forms A, B, and C and an envelope of $20,000 in play money to each team.

3. Explain the rules of the game. Walk participants through the set of instructions on Form D, How to Play Time, Money, and Logic.

4. Begin the game. Announce the time limit and start the timer.

5. At the end of each minute, collect $1,000 from each team.

6. Whenever any team comes with a question, collect the required fee first. Secretly check with the solution table and give a "Yes" or "No" response.

Contact Information: Sivasailam "Thiagi" Thiagarajan, Workshops by Thiagi, Inc., 4423 East Trailridge Road, Bloomington, IN 47408, 800-996-7725, thiagi@thiagi.com, www.thiagi.com

7. If a team comes with a completed solution table, secretly check it against your solution table. If the team's solution is not correct, send them back to work on the correct solution. Do not give any additional feedback. If the team's solution is correct, congratulate them and tell them to keep the rest of the money.

8. Stop the game at the end of 20 minutes or when all teams have correctly solved the problem. Identify the winning team, the one with the most money.

9. Debrief participants by using the *What? So What? Now What?* sequence: Ask participants to share what happened to them during the game. Next, invite participants to ask themselves, "So what?" What does the activity reveal about how they work together in their own teams? Finally, ask participants to consider, "Now what?" and to list steps they can take to apply what they learned from this game.

TEAM CONFERENCE: A LOGIC PUZZLE (FORM A)

Dr. Glen Barker is organizing a conference on high-performance teams. He has invited five prestigious researchers (Dr. Armstrong, Dr. Bennett, Dr. Collins, Dr. Dalton, and Dr. Edwards) from the departments of Business, Anthropology, Sociology, Psychology, and Political Science. These researchers (from MIT, Stanford, Yale, Harvard, and Princeton) are presenting their latest findings in the areas of goal setting, conflict resolution, trust building, decision making, and leveraging diversity among team members.

Review the Dozen Questions and Answers handout. Using the information given on that handout, correctly complete this solution table:

Name	Department	University	Topic
Armstrong			
Bennett			
Collins			
Dalton			
Edwards			

A DOZEN QUESTIONS AND ANSWERS (FORM B)

1. **Question:** Is Dr. Collins making the presentation on conflict resolution?
    Answer: Yes!

2. **Question:** Is Dr. Armstrong from the Political Science department?
    Answer: No!

3. **Question:** Is Dr. Dalton from the Psychology department?
    Answer: Yes!

4. **Question:** Is Dr. Armstrong's presentation about decision making?
    Answer: No!

5. **Question:** Is Dr. Edwards from Yale?
    Answer: Yes!

6. **Question:** Is Dr. Dalton from Stanford?
    Answer: No!

7. **Question:** Is the Anthropology professor making a presentation on decision making?
    Answer: Yes!

8. **Question:** Is Dr. Edwards from the Anthropology department?
    Answer: No!

9. **Question:** Is the Princeton professor from the Sociology department?
    Answer: Yes!

10. **Question:** Is the MIT professor from the Anthropology department?
    Answer: No!

11. **Question:** Is the professor from MIT making a presentation on goal setting?
    Answer: Yes!

12. **Question:** Is the professor from Stanford making a presentation on building trust?
    Answer: Yes!

CROSS-CHECK MATRIX (FORM C)

How to Use This Matrix:

Enter the information from A Dozen Questions and Answers in the appropriate boxes in the matrix. Use an "X" to indicate a definite "No," a dot to indicate a definite "Yes." After placing a dot, place X's in the other four boxes in the same row and in the same column in that section of the matrix.

For your convenience, the information from the first two questions and answers has already been entered in this matrix.

	Conflict	Decision Making	Diversity	Goal Setting	Trust Building	Harvard	MIT	Princeton	Sanford	Yale	Anthropology	Business	Political Science	Psychology	Sociology
Armstrong	X												X		
Bennett	X														
Collins	•	X	X	X	X										
Dalton	X														
Edwards	X														
Anthropology															
Business															
Political Science															
Psychology															
Sociology															
Harvard															
MIT															
Princeton															
Stanford															
Yale															

HOW TO PLAY TIME, MONEY, AND LOGIC (FORM D)

You have:
- a logic puzzle,
- a play period of 20 minutes, and
- funding of $20,000.

At the end of each minute, we will collect $1,000 from you. Whenever you solve the puzzle correctly, you keep the remaining money. For example, if you solve the puzzle in 10 minutes, you keep the unspent $10,000.

The team with the most money at the end of the 20-minute play period (or whenever all teams have solved the puzzle) wins the game.

Notice that it is not that the fastest team wins the game, because you can also spend money to purchase additional information to help you solve the puzzle. For additional information, ask the facilitator a yes or no question similar to the ones on the A Dozen Questions and Answers handout. Your facilitator will give you the correct answer.

Additional information costs money. Here's how much the answer to each question will cost:
- First question: $ 1,000
- Second question: $2,000
- Third question: $3,000
- Fourth and all subsequent questions: $4,000

For example, if you ask a total of four questions, it will cost you $10,000. However, you may be able to solve the puzzle faster.

You may ask questions at any time during the play period, but only if you have the necessary funds. You have to pay in advance for the answer.

SOLUTION TABLE (FORM E)

Solution Table for facilitator's use

Name	Department	University	Topic
Armstrong	Business	Stanford	Trust Building
Bennett	Anthropology	Harvard	Decision Making
Collins	Sociology	Princeton	Conflict Resolution
Dalton	Psychology	MIT	Goal Setting
Edwards	Political Science	Yale	Leveraging Diversity

28

GETTING TO KNOW YOUR TEAMMATES

Gina Vega

Overview

When new teams are formed, many potential problems can be forestalled by investing some time and effort in initial introductions and bonding activities. This exercise encourages groups of three to disclose information, listen closely and provide playback, then comment on accuracy and correct any misinterpretations. The groundwork is thus laid for clear future communication and better understanding of the group members' individual expectations.

Suggested Time

30 minutes

Materials Needed

✔ Form A (Data Collection)

✔ Form B (The Story Behind the Statistics)

✔ Form C (Observer Sheet)

✔ Form D (The Other Side of the Story)

Procedure

1. Setup: Present an explanation of critical incidents (occasions that had a significant impact on the parties involved), the difference between open- and closed-ended questions, and the importance of asking follow-up questions to get a full picture of the incident being described. Use examples such as "the assistant who never returned from lunch," "the lost invoice," "the time the boss hit the ceiling," and so on.

2. Distribute copies of Form A to all participants and encourage a brief general discussion about ways to investigate a story.

Contact Information: Gina Vega, Francis E. Girard School of Business and International Commerce, Merrimack College, 315 Turnpike Street, North Andover, MA 01945, 978-837-5000 ext. 4338, gvega@merrimack.edu

3. Distribute copies of Form B to all participants and explain the concept of rich data—information gathered by reading the context of a story and looking for patterns of behavior within the story, as they may lead to deeper understanding of the individuals' actions.

4. Divide participants into groups of three, and assign each person a role: one Interviewer, one Interviewee, and one Observer. Distribute Form C to Observers.

5. Interview and Small Group Discussion: Interviewers proceed to interview the Interviewees about a critical incident of their choosing. Allow about 5 minutes for the interviews. Point out that interviewees are likely to find it hard to provide detail, and interviewers tend to accept statements without further probing. Encourage the players to use the probes provided on Form A.

6. While the interviews are being conducted, Observers should carefully fill out Form C, noting issues of process as well as issues of fact.

7. At the conclusion of the interviews, Observers share what they have written on Form C, and the triad discusses the implications. Allow 3 to 5 minutes for this part of the activity.

8. Distribute Form D to Interviewees and have them record their responses to the questions while the Interviewers then play back the critical incident to Interviewees. Interviewees share their recorded feedback with Interviewers and correct any incorrect conclusions, assumptions, facts, or feelings.

9. General Discussion: Lead a general discussion about the difficulty or ease of performing the interview, framing questions, following up, and maintaining a healthy process while doing so. Ask questions such as:

   • What kind of feedback did you get?

   • What were the most common problems you experienced?

   • What was the hardest part of the interview?

   • How far wrong did the Interviewers go in telling the story back?

Conclude by emphasizing the value of corroborating facts and feelings and the importance of avoiding unconfirmed assumptions to attain clear communication.

Variation This exercise may be repeated with each group so that each member has an opportunity to play all three roles. This variation will not quite triple the amount of time required, because group members become more adept each time they perform the exercise.

DATA COLLECTION (FORM A)

Getting Started

Design evocative questions:

> *Tell me about a time when you had an important decision to make.*
>
> *Tell me about a time when you had a personnel problem.*
>
> *What kind of inventory system do you have in place here? How is that working out for you?*
>
> *What particular kinds of problems have you experienced when training new operators?*

Sample Probes for Interviewers*

<u>The basic probe</u>—Repeat the initial question. (Use when the interviewee seems to be wandering off the point.)

<u>The explanatory probe</u>—Clarify a vague point:

> *What did you mean by that?*
>
> *What makes you say that?*

<u>The focused probe</u>—Get specific information:

> *What kind of...?*
>
> *When does...?*

<u>The silent probe</u>—Wait for the interviewee to answer. (Use with a reluctant respondent.)

<u>Drawing out</u>—Repeat the last few words the respondent said and look up expectantly. (Use when the interviewee has stopped offering new information.)

<u>Giving ideas or suggestions</u>—Offer the interviewee something to think about:

> *Have you thought about...?*
>
> *Have you tried...?*
>
> *Did you know that...?*

<u>Mirroring or reflecting</u>—Express in your own words what the respondent has said. (This may force the respondent to rethink the answer given.)

> *What you seem to be saying is....*

---

* For more information about probes, please see Mark Easterby-Smith, Richard Thorpe, and Andy Lowe. (1991) *Management Research: An Introduction.* London: Sage Publications, p. 80.

THE STORY BEHIND THE STATISTICS (FORM B)

Rich data collection includes indirect processes as well as asking direct questions. Gathering rich data is more fun than just asking questions—it requires that you try to imagine yourself in the other person's shoes. This process provides the explanations, reasons, factors considered, politics, and preferences or feelings behind a particular action, behavior, or set of statistics.

Reading context in three easy steps:

1. A smile or a grimace? Knowing the difference between the two is not the same as noticing the difference between them and being aware of the impact of the smile or grimace on others.

2. Use all your senses. Notice whether a person seems uncomfortable, awkward, or reticent—those are important cues to understanding the environment and to telling the story. They are data.

3. Hear the meaning while listening to the words. "There is too much work for one person to do" may mean just that: There is too much work for one person to do. It may also mean, "I am so talented and work so hard that I can do the work of two people." Or, "I hate my job. I am overworked and no one cares." Or, "I wish I could get some overtime and clear out some of the accumulated backlog." There are many other interpretations that could be accurate. Listen to the clues and read the body language. Above all, make sure to verify the Interviewee's meaning, rather than overlaying your own interpretation on statements.

Looking for patterns:

- Feel the whole experience—consider the case story holistically.

- Use inductive reasoning—let your understanding arise from the story, rather than demanding that the story fit a familiar perspective.

- Test themes—try them out on the Interviewee and ask if they make sense to him or her. Remember, you and the Interviewee are partners.

OBSERVER SHEET (FORM C)

Please listen to the interview and observe the give and take of Interviewer and Interviewee with a narrowed and critical eye. Jot your impressions down on this form. Remember, the focus is on process: Which questions generated the needed information? What kinds of questions were they? Were there any questions that generated confusion? What were those questions? What did the Interviewer do that was particularly helpful?

_____

_____

_____

_____

_____

_____

_____

_____

_____

_____

THE OTHER SIDE OF THE STORY (FORM D)

Interpretation and corroboration by the Interviewee help to clarify where the Interviewer has misinterpreted, gone off the track, placed personal perspectives on the story, or not been true to the intent of the Interviewee. Please listen with a critical ear as the Interviewer tells your story, then record your responses to the questions on this form.

What facts did he or she get wrong? What facts ought to be added to make the story more accurate?

_____

_____

_____

_____

Did the feelings expressed by the Interviewer represent your own feelings accurately? What did he or she get wrong?

_____

_____

_____

Were you portrayed the way you see yourself? Was there enough background in the telling of the story?

_____

_____

_____

_____

What should the Interviewer have asked?

_____

_____

_____

_____

29

A GAME OF TEAM TRUST

Ed Rose

Overview   This game is one of many versions of the classic zero-sum games, such as Prisoner's Dilemma, in which collaboration wins out over competition. Participants are separated into four teams of any size, designated red, blue, yellow, and green. Each team's goal is to generate as much cash as possible through a series of bidding transactions.

The objectives of the activity are:

- to provide a real-life demonstration of group dynamics;
- to provide a learning experience of working together as two separate business units; and
- to have teams establish relationships based on trust.

Suggested Time   90 minutes (60 minutes for the exercise and 30 minutes for the debriefing session)

Materials Needed
- ✔ Form A (Bidding Wars: Yellow and Green Teams)
- ✔ Form B (Bidding Wars: Red and Blue Teams)
- ✔ Form C (Worldwide Bidding Process)
- ✔ Forms D and E (Bid Cards)
- ✔ Form F (Scorecard)
- ✔ Form G (Team Tracking Form)

Procedure
1. Establish four teams of any size.
2. Hand out labels identifying the groups as the Red, Blue, Yellow, or Green team.

Contact Information: Ed Rose, AET, Inc., 1900 S. Harbor City Blvd., Suite 115, Melbourne, FL 32901, edrose@cfl.rr.com, 321-223-9640

3. Give Forms A and B to the respective teams (forms are the same except for the color names of the teams at the top). Give one form to each team. Some teams may choose not to work together. Don't force that issue; discuss it during debriefing if it comes up. Provide each team with a copy of Form C, which explains the bidding process.

4. Announce the rules of the game:
   - Teams are not to confer with other teams unless given specific permission to do so.
   - Each team must agree on a single bid for each round.

   Assure each team that no other team will find out its bid until after it is entered.

5. Give copies of Forms D and E (the bid cards) to each team, placing them face down.

6. Use Form F as the official scorecard for the game. You can make it into a transparency or reproduce it on a flip chart. Provide Form G to each team for tracking the team's bids. Again, instruct participants not to show their cards to anyone.

7. The Blue and Red teams should be close to one another, and the Yellow and Green teams should be close to each other. The idea here is not to stress competition. The setup and the rules should imply competition. However, the key is that the four teams can *all* win (i.e., achieve their goals) if they work together. Let them discover that for themselves.

8. Have each team select a person who will be the team's representative. That person will be the point of contact for the team—the only one who can communicate with the facilitator or negotiate any business outside the team.

9. Representatives must confer with their team members so teams make joint decisions. In rounds 5 and 8, the representatives will have the opportunity to get $1.00 each and the low bid loses $3.00. Have teams track their results on Form G.

10. For each round, ask the representative from each team to deliver the bid to you and display the results. Use Form C to calculate the profit from the bidding process: Count up the number of high bids and low bids. Then follow the bid results column. If all four are high, then the teams lose $1.00 each, according to the table on Form C. If there are three high bids and one low bid, the high bids get $1.00 each and the low bid loses $3.00. Have teams track their results on Form G.

11. Go through to round 4.

12. During round 5, inform the teams that the team representative will be able to negotiate with the other teams (companies) for 2 minutes. This meeting should take place in a hallway or another room away from the other team members. The representatives will then have 1 minute to confer with their teams before the next bid is called for.

13. Before you ask for the bids, summarize the results of the exercise so far. Identify each team and how many points each team has. Be sure to say each team's color, Red, Blue, Yellow, and Green. You are trying to influence them to think they need to win at all costs. However, you should never say that directly; just imply it.

14. Ask for their bids.

15. Proceed through rounds 6 and 7 to round 8, another bonus round. Allow the team representatives to communicate with the other teams, again for 2 minutes. You will find that if any of the team representatives have not lived up to their agreements, not much will happen here. They will not talk to each other. While the negotiators are in this meeting, keep reminding them about the time constraint. Rush them.

16. During the bonus rounds, remember to stress the fact that there are extra profits for this round that pay off three times the result in round 5, five times the result in round 8, and ten times the result in round 10. It is also a good idea to review the scores of each team again and read them aloud as Red, Blue, Yellow, and Green to create a sense of competition.

17. Ask for the new bids.

18. Proceed to the final round. Remind everyone that this round is a major bonus round. In round 10, all participants may initiate conversation with any person or team in the room. You may find that there is very little discussion if there was any lying during the previous negotiation sessions. The role of trust and how it affects relationships becomes apparent in this situation.

19. Allow the teams 2 minutes to communicate.

20. Ask for their bids.

21. Add the bids up and total them all together on Form F.

22. Reveal the final scores. The payout is decided by a collective formula with the total amount divided among the teams (Blue/Red and Yellow/Green). (The participants should notice that you have combined all the scores to reach the one final score. This will not be what they expected.)

23. Conduct the debriefing session. The main theme in this exercise is that if the teams worked together, they would all have been successful in the end. If one or two of the team members violated their agreements, the dynamics that resulted from those actions provided a tremendous learning experience. Here are some questions for discussion that help to make these points. Refer to your notes for additional questions and possible comments regarding what you observed happening during group discussions.

- The best possible score is $10,000 with four teams. How much did each team earn? Did the teams try to work together?
- What problems did you experience with other team members?
- What role did trust play in this exercise?
- If trust was broken, how hard was it to repair? Could it be repaired?
- How did your team define success? Did your definition affect the outcome?
- Did your team representative keep his or her word? What effects did that have on your team?
- Looking back on the exercise, what would you have done differently?
- What did you learn from this experience?
- Based on your experience, how important is trust in, and to, a business?
- How does this relate to the real world? How did you interpret the instruction to generate as much cash as possible?
- Did your team have clear goals?
- Is it important to eliminate some of the team behaviors you experienced in this exercise? Why?

BIDDING WARS: YELLOW AND GREEN TEAMS (FORM A)

Background Information

You are a member of either the Yellow or Green team formed to generate as much cash as you can. The world has changed and business is not what it used to be. Your team members have come from different business disciplines but have one goal in common—**survival**. Survival is translated in this exercise to mean the generation of as much cash as possible. In this new worldwide economy, we must learn new ways to conduct our business.

Bidding Process

You will be selling your services in a world market. Your goal is to generate as much cash as you can. The consultation services that you provide are only offered by the Red, Blue, Green, and Yellow teams around the world. The bidding process will be facilitated by secret bids, and the process will be handled by an outside, neutral body (the facilitator).

The bidding process is relatively simple: You either bid high or low. Due to the structure of the process, the market will decide based on the results of a profit schedule contained on Form C.

At this point, the generation of cash is vital to your success in the future (of this exercise). Bids will be decided on a consensus basis and should not be shown to anyone until the bid is called for on the open market. The bid must be a consensus decision by your team. The strategy you use in this process should be given consideration. Remember, the goal is to **generate as much cash as you can**.

BIDDING WARS: RED AND BLUE TEAMS (FORM B)

Background Information

You are a member of either the Red or Blue team formed to generate as much cash as you can. The world has changed and business is not what it used to be. Your team members have come from different business disciplines but have one goal in common—**survival**. Survival is translated in this exercise to mean the generation of as much cash as possible. In this new worldwide economy, we must learn new ways to conduct our business.

Bidding Process

You will be selling your services in a world market. Your goal is to generate as much cash as you can. The consultation services that you provide are only offered by the Red, Blue, Green, and Yellow teams around the world. The bidding process will be facilitated by secret bids, and the process will be handled by an outside, neutral body (the facilitator).

The bidding process is relatively simple: You either bid high or low. Due to the structure of the process, the market will decide based on the results of a profit schedule contained on Form C.

At this point, the generation of cash is vital to your success in the future (of this exercise). Bids will be decided on a consensus basis and should not be shown to anyone until the bid is called for on the open market. The bid must be a consensus decision by your team. The strategy you use in this process should be given consideration. Remember, the goal is to **generate as much cash as you can**.

WORLDWIDE BIDDING PROCESS (FORM C)

Instructions

For ten successive rounds, you and your team members will choose either a "high" or a "low" bid. Each round's payoff (profit) depends on the pattern of choices made in your group.

Bid Results	Profit
4 high	Lose $1.00 each
3 high	Win $1.00 each
1 low	Lose $3.00
2 high	Lose $1.00 each
2 low	Lose $2.00 each
1 high	Win $3.00
3 low	Lose $1.00 each
4 low	Win $1.00 each

You are to confer with your team members in each round and make a joint decision. In rounds 5, 8, and 10, you and your team members may first confer with the others in the bidding process before making your joint decision.

BID CARD (FORM D)

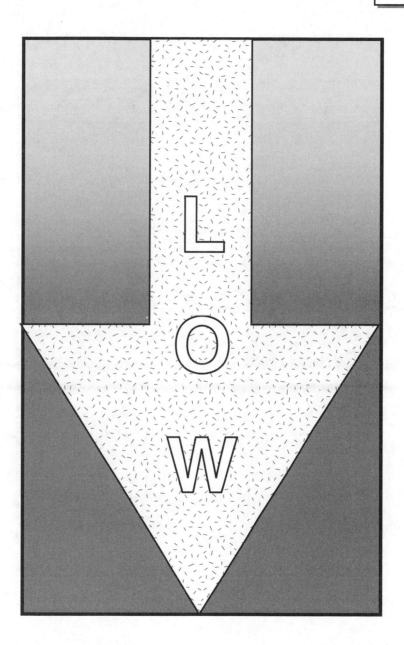

BID CARD (FORM E)

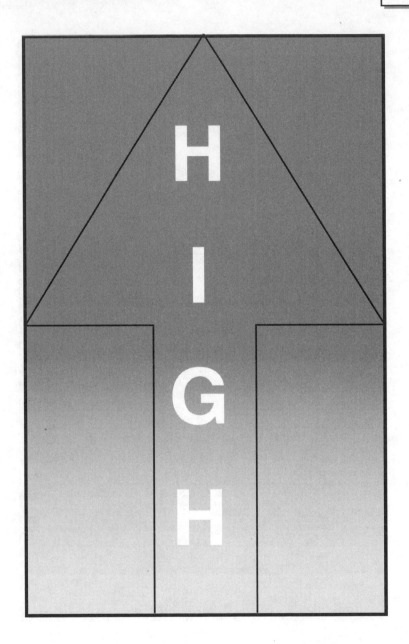

SCORECARD (FORM F)

Round	Bonus	Red	Blue	Green	Yellow
1					
2					
3					
4					
5	(x3)				
6					
7					
8	(x5)				
9					
10	(x10)				
TOTAL					

Worldwide Bidding Process
Generate as much cash as you can!

TEAM TRACKING FORM (FORM G)

	Round	Your bid (circle)	Bidding process choice patterns	Profit balance
	1	H L	[ ]H [ ]L	
	2	H L	[ ]H [ ]L	
	3	H L	[ ]H [ ]L	
	4	H L	[ ]H [ ]L	
Bonus round (payoff x 3)	5	H L	[ ]H [ ]L	
	6	H L	[ ]H [ ]L	
	7	H L	[ ]H [ ]L	
Bonus round (payoff x 5)	8	H L	[ ]H [ ]L	
	9	H L	[ ]H [ ]L	
Bonus round (payoff x 10)	10	H L	[ ]H [ ]L	

Worldwide Bidding Process

IV

REPRODUCIBLE TOOLS FOR FACILITATING PLANNING AND PROBLEM SOLVING

30

HOW CAN YOU MANAGE PROJECTS MORE EFFECTIVELY?

Susan Barksdale and Teri Lund

Overview In today's business world, we are being asked to handle an array of duties, most of which revolve around project management. In looking at your own job, think about the amount of time you spend:

- Managing others who do tasks (even if they do not report to you).
- Ensuring a deliverable is available within a certain time frame that meets specific needs and is within a specific budgeted dollar amount.
- Building and managing relationships with vendors.
- Tracking activities, deliverables, and outcomes to ensure completion within a specific time frame so that other activities, deliverables, and outcomes can be met.

Because so many individuals work to pull together internal and external resources to deliver products, solutions, and services, universities now offer degree programs in project management.

This series of instruments addresses the role risk plays within project management, how it can be managed to maximize performance, and how it can be assessed to determine the activities that are most critical to meet the needed deadline with desired outcomes. The series is intended to be used by individuals or teams to educate them about project risk in general and to identify the risks for a specific project so they can take a proactive stance in managing it.

Contact Information: Susan Barksdale, 25 NW 23rd Place, #6 - 412, Portland, OR 97210, 503-223-7721, sbarksdale@att.net

Teri Lund, 4534 SW Tarlow Ct., Portland, OR 97221, 503-245-9020, tlund_bls@msn.com

WHAT IS "RISK"?

Risk takes many shapes and means different things depending on the situation:

- In contracts or insurance policies, risk is the degree or probability of a loss occurring.

- In safety, it is the risk of being exposed to a hazard or to danger.

- For an individual, it is the risk to one's livelihood, perception of self, or safety.

- In business, it is the risk to capital itself or to the livelihood of the business.

Project risk is a different animal altogether and usually factors in some or all of the above, depending on the project. When you assess project risk, you actually are determining the risk:

1. Is it employee risk? (An individual's safety could be put at risk, or someone's career could be at risk if the outcomes are not met, or it could put others' safety and well-being at risk.)

2. Is it business risk? (An organization's reputation, customer base, or competitive advantage is at risk.)

3. Is it financial risk? (An organization's capital or financial position, or an individual's or group's financial position is at risk.)

4. Is it customer risk? (There is an expectation by shareholders or senior management that certain outcomes will result.)

These are just a few examples of risk. It is important to assess the risks to the project early. By doing so, you're taking a proactive stance rather than the typical reactive stance. The first instrument is an assessment to help you identify where the risks will most likely occur in one of your projects.

RISK ASSESSMENT AND MATRIX

Directions: Individually or in a group, review the 20 statements included in the assessment and rank them using a scale of 3 to 0 (3 = High risk, most likely will happen; 2 = Moderate risk, this may happen; 1 = Low risk, not likely to happen; 0 = Does not apply).

The statements are common responses in final project reviews when project managers are asked to identify the risk that threatened to or did blow the project out of the water. Many are related, and had they been identified early in the project and monitored, they would have had much less impact on overall project compromises.

RISK ASSESSMENT STATEMENT	HIGH RISK	MODERATE RISK	LOW RISK	N/A
1. The project faces a great deal of challenge in the marketplace and it could cost us our competitive advantage.	3	2	1	0
2. The project will push our capacity and we will not have the resource allocations needed to handle the work without compromising quality.	3	2	1	0
3. Our customer will definitely be impacted by the outcomes of this project and if something goes wrong, the customer will be impacted negatively.	3	2	1	0
4. Employee morale is at stake in the way that they view their jobs, the company, and our business.	3	2	1	0
5. There is lack of definition or purpose to the project and the outcomes are unclear.	3	2	1	0
6. There is no clear leadership for the project. Either there is no project manager or it is unclear where in the organization the project belongs.	3	2	1	0
7. Management does not understand the purpose and value of the project's outcomes.	3	2	1	0
8. New technology will be introduced.	3	2	1	0
9. The skills and knowledge to support the project are not present (technology skills are lacking, subject matter experts are lacking, etc.).	3	2	1	0
10. The product we are producing has no defined customer or marketplace.	3	2	1	0
11. There is an expectation of specific outcomes by the shareholders or senior management.	3	2	1	0

RISK ASSESSMENT AND MATRIX (CONT.)

RISK ASSESSMENT STATEMENT	HIGH RISK	MODERATE RISK	LOW RISK	N/A
12. The data for the initial analysis (that resulted in this project's launch) was biased.	3	2	1	0
13. The project has high political visibility.	3	2	1	0
14. Key systems for the organization may be impacted by this project.	3	2	1	0
15. No project methodology is being followed.	3	2	1	0
16. The project team's roles and accountabilities are blurred or undefined.	3	2	1	0
17. The organization's reputation or market presence is dependent on this project.	3	2	1	0
18. Safety could be compromised if this project is not implemented correctly.	3	2	1	0
19. The organization will not be in compliance with federal regulations without successfully implementing this project.	3	2	1	0
20. A similar project was launched in the past and it failed.	3	2	1	0

Once the assessment is complete, identify the statements that were rated 3 and then use the following Risk Matrix to consider their importance.

1.   What tactics would best control each high risk?

2.   What interdependencies or relationships exist between the statements that were rated 3? Typically, the more relationships that exist, the greater the risk (for example, if you rated the statement "a similar project was launched in the past and it failed" as well as the statement "new technology will be introduced" both as 3).

3.   Why did the original project fail and what are the implications for this project?

An example of the completed Risk Matrix is provided below.

RISK (RANKED AS 3)	TACTICS TO CONTROL RISK	INTERDEPENDENCIES OR RELATIONSHIPS TO OTHER RISKS
The project has high political visibility.	Develop a strong (visible) communication plan that is horizontal and vertical.	There is an expectation of specific outcomes by the shareholders or senior management.

IDENTIFYING RISK CONTROLS

An important tactic in risk assessment and management is developing risk controls. Risk controls help minimize damage to the project or disruption when change or problems occur.

Three important risk control techniques are identified and detailed in the following worksheet. Review each technique and describe how you might use it (if appropriate) to minimize the risk to your project.

RISK CONTROL WORKSHEET

RISK CONTROL TECHNIQUES	SPECIFIC TO YOUR RISK CONTROL NEEDS
Communication Horizontal and Vertical 1. Develop a regular communication device that reports project status, risk potential, and other key information and circulate it widely. 2. Develop a separate "alert" communication piece (e-mail or hard copy) so that it is obvious to the distribution list that they should pay special attention to the information included. Use this device when change or chaos occurs. Identify what has happened, the impact on the project, the potential risks, how the risks are being managed, and when or where to expect future information. 3. Have a hotline or war room (a room dedicated to managing the project) available so when risk emerges, questions and answers flow easily. 4. Identify a set of FAQs (frequently asked questions) and send a list to those who must communicate with others about the project. 5. Determine and communicate the critical decision points for the risk. As decisions are made, provide this information in a communication update. 6. Identify communication leaders (especially if the project is worldwide) and have each leader localize and communicate the message to his or her region. 7. Communicate dependent or related risks that may occur as an outcome of the response to this risk. 8. Present communications in a calm, precise, and action-oriented manner. 9. Understand how the organization's culture reflects the way it organizes and disseminates information. 10. Identify the organization's key customers and their key products and services.	
Infrastructure Control 1. Create the team infrastructure so that it is flexible and roles and accountabilities can easily shift if a change in project requires it. 2. Identify the critical knowledge and skills possessed by one or just a few members of the project team and how they can be transferred to others. 3. Determine if different knowledge or skills are needed at different times.	

RISK CONTROL WORKSHEET (CONT.) DOWNLOADABLE

RISK CONTROL TECHNIQUES	SPECIFIC TO YOUR RISK CONTROL NEEDS
Infrastructure Control (Cont.)	
4. Identify what specific knowledge supports the project outcomes and any risks involved.	
5. Identify what procedural knowledge supports the project outcomes and any risks involved.	
6. Identify what relationship knowledge (customer, vendor, across departments) supports the project outcomes and any risks involved.	
7. Identify what specific systems support the project outcomes (computer programs, etc.) and any risks involved.	
8. Identify what specific competencies or expert systems have been identified to manage the project and meet the outcomes, and any risks involved.	
9. Determine if and how rewards can be changed to provide a payoff for meeting the risk and overcoming it through change management.	
10. Determine if there is previous experience with this type of risk within the organization that can be leveraged if needed.	
Backup Planning	
1. Determine what type of support will be needed if backup planning is implemented.	
2. Determine the propensity for avoiding the risk and sacrificing the outcomes and how it can be avoided.	
3. Identify the resources that are available for backup planning.	
4. Educate the project team about the risk and the backup plans that are available and when and how to initiate the backup.	
5. Determine if a specific type of expertise (engineer, financial analyst, specialist) is available to provide information and decision-making criteria if a backup plan is needed.	
6. Determine what impact the back-up plans will have on the outcome and if it is tolerable.	
7. Determine team, management, customer, and other key player response for the implementation of a backup plan.	
8. Determine any resistance to the backup plan and how it can be overcome.	
9. Identify stakeholder support for the backup plan(s).	
10. Determine who would control the project shift if a backup plan were implemented.	

THE 3 "Cs" OF UNANTICIPATED RISK

All savvy project managers know that no matter how much you anticipate risk, there is still an element of surprise. Part of good risk assessment is to be aware of new risks as they emerge and to integrate them into your risk management plan as soon as possible. Unanticipated risk typically occurs for one of three reasons, which we call the 3 "Cs" of Unanticipated Risk:

1. **Change** rears its head the most often. Change creates a need to respond, sometimes in an unknown manner, which exposes you to a higher degree of project risk. That is, because of change you often need to respond in an unplanned or unanticipated way, and this creates higher risk in a project. Change always seems to happen when you can least afford it. You are swamped in the day-to-day details of the project and—bang—change occurs. Change has a huge impact on risk because it usually affects all project monitors (time, milestones, resources, budget, etc.). When dealing with change, you must assess what impact the change will have and what new risks have surfaced (this may be a good time to use the risk assessment again) and how the new risks need to be integrated into your overall backup planning.

   The Managing Change Worksheet can be used to create a dialog with the project team to build an "early warning" change system.

2. **Capability** gap can be a deadly risk if unanticipated. Capability risk is most commonly associated with project personnel, especially when they are expected to have the capability (skills and knowledge) to play specific roles but unfortunately are not proficient or capable. This presents a different but clearly dangerous unanticipated risk. Capability expected from a system or process that is supposed to support the project overall but doesn't is another source of capability risk.

   The Managing Capability Worksheet is provided to help you identify the capability risks that will most likely affect your project, and the unanticipated risks.

MANAGING CHANGE WORKSHEET

Directions: The easiest way to manage change is to create an "early-warning" system to prepare for the inevitable. This worksheet consists of a set of questions to use with the project team to identify potential change and to proactively manage that change. This will limit the risk factors associated with change. A question or probe is provided in the first column for the project team to use to identify potential change factors that will most likely occur in the project. These factors should be noted in the second column. For example, in answer to the first question regarding the trigger for change, the team identified competitor product offering changes, new technological advancements, and economic changes as the change factors. In the third column, a plan for how the project team will proactively manage the change factors is identified. To expand on the previous example, a plan for managing a new technological advancement might be to align with a group that could provide specifications and technical information so you can adjust your plan accordingly.

QUESTION	IDENTIFIED CHANGE FACTOR	PLAN FOR MANAGING CHANGE
1. What is most likely to trigger a change for this project? An internal project change such as a project manager leaving or a major specification change? Or an external change such as a new technological development or a change in the product marketplace?		
2. How can you network with individuals outside of your team on a regular basis to ensure you hear about the changes most likely to have an impact on the project?		
3. What points within the project plan are more open to change and what points are least flexible? How can you manage changes around these within the project plan time frame?		
4. How can your stakeholders assist you in managing change for the project?		
5. What reengineering techniques can you use to minimize the impact of changes on the overall project plan? For example, can you map change? Can you predict side-effects? Can you predict the characteristics of project change?		

MANAGING CAPABILITY WORKSHEET

Directions: The easiest way to manage capability risk is to anticipate it and overcome it. A question or probe is provided in the first column for the project team to use to identify potential capability risk factors. These factors should be noted in the second column. For example, in answer to the first question regarding the most critical capability that is lacking, the team identified technological expertise and product knowledge. In the third column, a plan for how the project team will overcome the capability deficits is identified. To expand on the previous example, the plan might be to add a team member with these capabilities or to provide specific education for the entire team.

QUESTION	IDENTIFIED CAPABILITY FACTOR	PLAN FOR OVERCOMING CAPABILITY DEFICIT
1. What is the most critical capability that is lacking within the team today that puts the project most at risk for failure?		
2. Do the systems, processes, and capital resources provide the needed capability to complete the project?		
3. What points within the project plan are most apt to require a higher level of capability?		
4. How can capability risk be better managed (schedule changes, rationing of resources, etc.) for the project?		
5. What project dependencies rely on capability?		

3. **Capacity** is the last of the 3 "Cs." While capability in this sense is an ability, capacity is the volume or size: Do you have enough resources? Is there enough time? Is there enough money? Is the scope of the project accurate? Managing capacity risk amounts to ensuring that the pipes or silos are large enough not to be clogged—that you have sufficient resources to accomplish the objectives and perform or execute the tasks within the required time frame.

The Managing Capacity Worksheet is provided to help you identify the capacity risks that will most likely affect your project, and the unanticipated risks.

RISK MANAGEMENT PLANNING ACTIVITIES

Identifying and controlling risk is key to managing it. But how can you put together a risk management plan? What activities are critical for managing risk for your projects?

Based on our project and risk management consulting work with organizations in a variety of industries, we have identified five key activities that, when engaged in and used proactively, will result in lowering overall project risk.

Activity 1: Identifying the Most Likely and Most Damaging Risks

In this activity, the team or project manager reviews the key outcomes for the project against the project plan and determines which of the following is mostly likely at risk:

1. Resources
2. Cost
3. Time frame
4. Outcomes

Of these, what is the most damaging risk? How much confidence does the manager (or team) have that the risk can be controlled and the project's outcomes can be realized?

Activity 2: Determining the Risk Control Factors

In the second activity, the approach to controlling risk is established. The team decides how it will determine if the risk is worth taking and how a go/no go decision will be made. They determine what criteria to use to evaluate a risk and what type of analysis (what-ifs, scenarios, etc.) will be used to forecast the "risk to the outcomes of the project."

MANAGING CAPACITY WORKSHEET DOWNLOADABLE

Directions: The easiest way to manage capacity risk is to control it. A question or probe is provided in the first column for the project team to use to identify potential capacity risk factors. These factors should be noted in the second column. For example, in answer to the first question regarding the most critical capacity that is lacking, the team identified a project timetable. In the third column, a plan for how the project team will overcome the capacity deficits is identified. To expand on the previous example, team members might decide to identify where there are potential shortcuts in the project that can be used to "create" time for the more time-consuming tasks.

QUESTION	IDENTIFIED CAPACITY FACTOR	PLAN FOR OVERCOMING CAPACITY DEFICIT
1. What is the most likely capacity challenge facing this project?		
2. How can the resources, scope, and time frame of the project be controlled?		
3. How can capacity issues be communicated before they become critical?		
4. What other dependencies outside the project or the team might contribute to capacity risk?		
5. What would motivate others to control factors that might contribute to capacity risk?		

Activity 3: Analyzing the Risk Control Plan

During activity 3, the team or project manager creates an approach to use to analyze the risk control plan. The risk control plan should be documented, including the resources, costs, and support needed to implement the plan. It is important to identify the pitfalls of taking action at this time or not taking action at all. An important part of this activity is to test the actual outcomes to determine if what it costs to control the risk (or take action as a result of the risk) is equal to or less than doing nothing at all.

Activity 4: Projecting Future Risks

Activity 4 involves analyzing the results from the actions that were taken in activity 3 and projecting any future risks that might result from these actions. The tools previously presented in this guide may be of assistance in this activity.

Activity 5: Learning from Risk Management

During the project's postimplementation review, it is important to assess what can be learned from the way risk was managed during the project. The team, project manager, and evaluation manager should get feedback from those involved in implementing the plan to determine whether the risk management was successful and what, if anything, should be improved in the future.

CONCLUSION

Risk is inevitable—all of us face it every day, whether traveling in our cars or dealing with global competitors. It's natural to try to make order out of chaos, to reassure ourselves that we have mastery over our universe and to reduce risks. The more we understand about the risks we face, the better able we'll be to respond to them rather than react or overreact. Responding appropriately decreases your exposure to further risk, while reaction or overreaction often generates a whole new set of risks.

31

TEN HATS MEETING MEMBERS CAN WEAR

Mel Silberman

Overview   There is a well-known, humorous story of what might happen if each participant is not equally responsible for the success of a team.

A team had four members called Everybody, Somebody, Anybody, and Nobody. There was an important job to be done. Everybody was sure that Somebody would do it. Anybody could have done it, but Nobody did it. Everybody got angry about that because it was Somebody's job. It ended up that Everybody blamed Somebody when Nobody did what Anybody could have done.

Team meetings can be made more effective by giving jobs to several participants to divide up the labor and share responsibility. Here are ten possible "hats" people can wear in your meetings. Consider rotating them to include everyone. Too often, certain individuals get pegged for certain jobs.

Contact Information: Mel Silberman, Active Training, 303 Sayre Drive, Princeton, NJ 08540, 609-987-8157, mel@activetraining.com, www.activetraining.com

TEN HATS MEETING MEMBERS CAN WEAR

1. **Facilitator.** This person leads all or a portion of a meeting, providing structure, giving direction, and stimulating and encouraging participation, problem solving, and consensus.

2. **Timekeeper.** This person tells the team how much time is left for a specific agenda item and alerts the team when time limits are being approached.

3. **Minute Taker.** This person takes notes about the meeting discussion and decisions and disseminates those notes as meeting minutes as soon as possible after the meeting.

4. **Record Keeper.** This person maintains all the records accumulated by the team, such as agendas, minutes, member information, reports, correspondence, data, and other documentation.

5. **Flip Chart Scribe.** This person records team ideas quickly and legibly on a flip chart or other recording surface.

6. **Researcher.** This person researches information of use to the team.

7. **Energizer.** This person conducts activities to energize or relax the meeting participants.

8. **Meeting Planner.** This person organizes and coordinates all the behind-the-scene details of a meeting session.

9. **Point of Contact.** This person acts as a point of contact for participants between meetings. He or she can also be responsible for maintaining contact with outside parties who may be interested in the team's proceedings.

10. **Process Observer.** This person observes the team process and shares those observations with the team when appropriate.

32

HANDLING THE PROCESS DIMENSION OF MEETINGS

Scott Parry

Overview Whenever people meet, their success in achieving the objectives that brought them together is dependent on two dimensions of the interaction: process and content. Content is concerned with what information is to be imparted, what decisions are to be reached, what problems solved, and so on. Process is concerned with how the group will function, how the participants and leader will relate to one another, how the meeting will be conducted, and so on. This guide will outline the types of problems that can arise in meetings, what can be done, and what shouldn't be done.

INTRODUCTION

Members of a group invariably differ in their perceptions of the situation, their purpose for being present, their past experience, and their personality. These four P's—perception, purpose, past, and personality—can disrupt the process dimension of your meeting. Both the leader and the participants share a responsibility for maintaining the quality of both dimensions, process and content.

A characteristic common to many meetings is that participants tend to become absorbed in the content and lose sight of their responsibility to help the leader in maintaining the process. Moreover, they may have expertise or interest in the content, whereas their understanding of the process dimension (i.e., their ability to facilitate group interaction and synthesize the various input of members) may be relatively unsophisticated.

This places a heavy responsibility on the group leader to deal with a broad variety of people problems that can arise during a typical meeting.

Contact Information: Scott Parry, 100 Bear Brook Rd., Princeton, NJ 08540, 609-452-8598, jsparry@erols.com

EXCESSIVE PARTICIPATION

The Situation

A participant is dominating, doing all the talking, answering the leader all the time, and eating up the group time.

The Problem

If the participant has good experience to contribute and the others appreciate this and are benefiting from it, there may not be a problem at all (other than the threat the participant may be posing to the ego of the person up front).

What Can Be Done

There are a number of things you can do to correct the problem. They are listed in sequence according to severity. Try the simpler ones first, moving on to stronger measures if necessary.

✔ After a comment from the dominating participant, ask the rest of the group for their reaction. For example, "How do the rest of you feel about Sue's comment?" Their reaction will tell you and Sue whether there is a problem or not.

✔ Use other means of eliciting responses, ones that preclude Sue's dominating. For example, "I'd like you to discuss this question in three-person groups, you three, you three, etc."

✔ Avoid eye contact with the dominating participant. When you pose a question, look at others for your response. If Sue starts to answer without being recognized by you, interrupt by rephrasing the question or by saying, "I'd like to hear from some others this time, Sue."

✔ Speak to the dominating participant during a break: "Sue, I'm really glad you're here because I know I can always count on you to share your input. But I notice that others in the group are becoming dependent on you and not thinking things through for themselves. So, I'm hoping you'll help me by not answering every issue yourself, thus giving the others a chance to share their input with us. Can I count on you?"

What Not to Do

It's wise not to take on or attack the dominating participant. By doing so, you invite two likely outcomes: 1) She may see it as a tug of war or test of strength, and become even stronger and more dominating; 2) She may retreat, avoid further contributions, become sullen and negative, and so on. Since neither of these outcomes is desirable, it's better to try the other methods.

NONPARTICIPATION

The Situation

One or two people have not spoken or contributed during the past two meetings. The leader has decided to do something about it.

The Problem

All you know is that a couple of people aren't participating. You cannot assume from this that they are lost, bored, confused, disinterested, negative, or anything else. Certain people are reticent to speak up in groups. Thus, the only problem you have is that you aren't getting any responses to let you know how the silent members feel and whether or not they understand.

What Can Be Done

Your objective here is to:

✔ Get a "reading" on the silent ones, and

✔ Ease them into the group interaction without embarrassing them (since this could make them retreat even further).

The safest way to find out whether the silent ones are with you is to pose a question or give a brief assignment, then break the group into subgroups of three to four persons each to work on their responses. As you circulate among the groups, pay particular attention to the silent ones, listening to their comments to see if there are any problems.

Let's say that your two silent people, Tom and Chris, each made good comments in their respective subgroups. After reconvening the full group, you might summarize by calling on several participants whose comments should be shared with the full group, including Tom and Chris. By reinforcing their comments, you have increased the likelihood that they will contribute to the full group in the future.

Another way to bring them into the group is to talk with them during a break to get their opinion on something you're about to discuss. Then, when you've reconvened after the break, you can mention to the full group that, "I was talking about this issue with Tom during the break, whose opinion is perhaps typical. In fact, Tom, why don't you share it with the group...." The silent person now knows in advance that his contribution is welcome, appropriate, and safe.

What Not to Do

Since you don't want to embarrass silent participants into contributing, it's usually better not to call on them by name (unless you're going around the room and calling on everyone by name and in sequence).

Avoid putting any pressure on the silent one. It would not be appropriate, for example, to call on Chris by saying, "How about you on this one, Chris... we haven't heard from you yet?" The wording here implies that Chris hasn't been contributing a fair share and better have a good answer.

SIDE CONVERSATIONS

The Situation

Two or three people who sit together are talking softly among themselves and not paying attention to you, the leader. This has been going on for half a minute. You are becoming annoyed.

The Problem

It's not easy to know if you have a problem here. You are annoyed, but are the talking participants disturbing others? You don't know. Similarly, it would be dangerous to assume that the problem is that several participants aren't paying attention; they might be sharing an insight on how to apply a new idea they just picked up. It would be unfortunate if you were to embarrass them by asking them to rejoin the group, thereby interrupting their insight and punishing the very behavior that you're looking for.

What Can Be Done

If the participants are seated around U-shaped tables or in a circle, you might walk slowly toward the talking participants, while looking at the rest of the group. In other words, the move should not be seen as an attempt to correct them. If their conversation is relevant to the meeting, they will feel no guilt in finishing their comments. However, if they are discussing last night's game on TV, they will probably rejoin the group as you approach.

Other actions might be taken. You might pose a question to the group, then have participants discuss their answers in two- or three-person groups. Put them in groups in such a way as to separate the people who are talking.

Similarly, you might call on the participant who is sitting to the immediate left or right of the talkers. This is likely to get them to return to the group, since it would be rude and disruptive to continue their private conversation while the person next to them is trying to think and respond to your question.

Of course, any participant who is being distracted by the private conversation can also take corrective action, by saying to you, "I'm sorry but I'm having trouble hearing you." This should lead the talkers to realize that they are annoying others. A more direct approach may be appropriate: "Excuse me, but I wonder if you two could rejoin the group. Some of us are having trouble hearing."

What Not to Do

Although you are annoyed by the private conversation, it is important that you avoid resorting to parent–child ways of correcting the talkers. Examples of undesirable ways of taking corrective action:

✔ Scolding them with, "Are you two talking about something you'd care to share with the rest of us, or would you like to rejoin the group?"

✔ Calling on one of the talkers with a question. The likely reply is "Would you repeat the question?" You must then bore (and punish) the others while you repeat the question and reward the talkers with extra attention.

✔ Lowering your voice or stopping your talking so as to catch the talkers, whose voices will stick out above the silence.

These measures are undesirable because they embarrass and "slap the wrists" of the talkers. Whenever participants feel put down or experience a loss of face in front of others, they are likely to withdraw and tune out. Also, other participants will begin to feel uneasy knowing that this could happen to them. They might withdraw and there is some danger that the group may "dry up."

ANTAGONISTIC AND NEGATIVE ATTITUDES

The Situation

Several participants are making their negative feelings known to others—by their side comments, scoffs, folded arms, and uncooperative or antagonistic attitude. This is creating an unhealthy climate and making things unpleasant for others.

The Problem

You don't know the problem. Perhaps the antagonists are attending against their will. Perhaps the topic isn't relevant. Perhaps they are negative about life in general and themselves in particular. Perhaps they feel negative toward you or are bothered by the composition of the group.

Moreover, you don't know how widespread the negative is. It's possible that the one or two antagonists are the tip of the iceberg, and that a number of others have similar negative feelings but are not as outspoken as the antagonists.

What Can Be Done

To begin with, you would like to know how widespread the negative attitude is (so you know how much time to devote to dealing with it, or whether there's any chance of changing it). Thus, the moment you get the first few negative comments from your antagonists, turn to the rest of the group and ask, "How do the rest of you feel about Sam's comment?" If they disagree or see Sam as a negative or disruptive influence, their response will tell you whether there is a problem.

Another way of disarming antagonists is to put them to work—taking notes, serving as recorder at the flip chart, or helping you to run an exercise. This serves to channel their thoughts and energy into productive activity.

If these methods don't work, then it might be appropriate for you to take antagonists aside during a break and talk to them. Here's an example: "Sam, I have the feeling that these sessions are not meeting your expectations, or aren't relevant to your needs. I wanted to discuss it with you because I certainly don't want to see you wasting your time here. Am I right?"

The dialogue that follows will lead to one of two outcomes: Either Sam agrees to go along with the objectives and agenda without undermining them, or he drops out of the group, which he really wasn't a part of to begin with.

What Not to Do

It is wise not to take on antagonists. First, you may lose. Second, a verbal fight may be just what antagonists want. Don't reinforce this undesirable behavior by granting them the stage. Third, many such arguments or debates do not have the possibility of a win–win outcome, so there is no way to get closure and wrap them up.

It is also wise not to put down antagonists even if they are annoying others in the group. When you try to get them back in line in front of others, you are only adding to their negative feelings about the meeting and you. Moreover, you are resorting to parent-to-child techniques of discipline rather than dealing with the antagonist on an adult-to-adult basis.

PREVENTION

Here are a few words on how to avoid these problems. The more you can know about your participants in advance of the meeting, the better off you will be in dealing with their problems. Forewarned is forearmed. If you know going in, for example, that Sam doesn't believe in the program but is coming to the meeting because his boss wants him there, you are much better prepared to address his negative feelings. Indeed, you might begin the meeting by noting that, "I know that some of you have reservations about the program we will be discussing today. For example, Sam here feels that [you restate Sam's position], and I suspect others here have similar feelings. Have I stated your view correctly, Sam?"

You have just done two things to avoid having the meeting sink to a gripe session or venting of negative attitudes. First, you stole Sam's thunder and disarmed him. Second, you let the group know that there are two sides to the issues under discussion and that you aren't going to deal with "the party line," "management's side," or whatever.

Another way to prevent problems is to establish ground rules at the start of a meeting so that participants will know a) what is appropriate and inappropriate behavior, and b) that it is the role of everyone present to make the meeting a success in achieving its goals. Anyone who doesn't buy in to the goals has the right to question them and seek clarification or defense of them. Thereafter, each participant should either accept them (and stay) or reject them (and leave).

A set of ground rules or guidelines for everyone, participants and leaders, appears at the end of this guide.

SUMMARY

Guidelines that can be applied to a wide variety of problems can be deduced from the previous examples. They are:

1. *Separate symptoms from problems.* The participant's undesirable actions have to be viewed as symptoms. You are sometimes in danger when you try to treat symptoms without knowing the problem or even whether there is a problem.

2. *Let the group handle the out-of-line participant.* This enables you to maintain a neutral role and still provides feedback for you and the participant.

3. *Save face.* Don't let anyone lose face in the group. When people are diminished in the eyes of other members of the group, their membership is in jeopardy. Your responsibility is to maintain the integrity and unity of the group. This means facilitating the interactions in such a way that all members know the goals and are working together to achieve them.

4. *Maintain adult-to-adult relationships.* Parent-to-child relationships are inappropriate in the workplace. Issues must be dealt with rationally, not emotionally, based on facts and opinions rather than on fictions, assumptions, shaky or incomplete evidence, etc.

GUIDELINES FOR GROUP BEHAVIOR

1. At the start of any meeting, it is essential that the group agree on the objectives (purpose, goal) of the meeting. This often means devoting time to an airing of the expectations of the members and a brief discussion of how the group will know that the objectives have been met. Often it is good to have these expected outcomes written down in brief, crisp wording, on the premeeting announcement, a handout, or a flip chart. At any time during the meeting that any member is confused or has reason to question the relevance of what is being discussed, he or she should ask how it relates to the objectives of the meeting.

2. If participants are new to one another and have not functioned as a group before, it is appropriate to spend a few minutes at the start of a meeting to establish ground rules. They become a tool for reaching agreement on the procedure to be used in dealing with issues and reaching the objectives.

3. Everyone in the group has an equal right to his or her opinion. Members owe one another the courtesy of listening objectively and hearing out all relevant contributions before taking action or attempting to reach consensus.

4. Any member who feels that another member has been cut off, misunderstood, or not given a fair hearing should bring this observation to the group's attention and return the discussion to the member who was cut off.

5. On the other hand, any member who feels that another member's behavior is counterproductive to the group's objectives and goals should attempt to bring the member back into the fold or to find out if other members see the behavior as disruptive.

6. Any member wishing to speak should first be recognized by the leader. This is not always practical (e.g., when discussion is rolling and highly interactive), so the leader and members reserve the right to call time and identify the persons the group wants to hear from. (Without this option of calling time, no one will be heard if the group lapses into a verbal free-for-all.)

7. Feedback is essential if people are to know how their comments are received, especially if there is doubt as to whether the group understood. It is appropriate for any member to give a member feedback. Example: "Let me see if I understand the point you're making, Fred. You seem to be saying three things. First,...."

8. Any member who feels that the process is not supporting the objectives of the meeting should share this observation, whether privately with the leader or publicly with the full group, whichever is appropriate. Example: If the group wants to vote on a decision prematurely (i.e., without airing all the facts, without trying to reach consensus), any member who recognizes this should bring it to the group's attention and not simply go along with the others.

33

USING THE "NOMINAL GROUP PROCESS" TO SOLVE PROBLEMS

Theresa Musser

Overview The Nominal Group Process is a seven-step technique for problem solution and identification. The primary advantages of the process are its time efficiency and effectiveness at encouraging equality among all members of a group. This guide will take you through the process step by step and give you examples of its use.

INTRODUCTION

We have probably all attended meetings either at work or in our communities that never end and never accomplish much. Or perhaps you have been challenged to solve a problem or situation using the committee or team approach but the group seems to never get beyond initial posturing and complaining. No one wants to "waste" time; in our busy lives there is an ever-diminishing amount of time that we can afford to spend frivolously. And yet, the problems still exist and opportunities to generate solutions or new ideas aren't always apparent. With quality improvement techniques and team-building strategies being thrust on us in the workplace, here is an "old" technique that may be helpful in these situations which is generally more efficient and in some cases more effective: the Nominal Group Process, or "NGP."

The NGP, a structured problem-solving process, was specifically designed to generate ideas and produce group consensus. It was originally developed by Delbecq et al. (1975) as an alternative research method to mail and telephone surveys. The technique is actually based on the Delphi process. The process has been most effective in problem-identification or solution-oriented meetings of relatively small groups

Contact Information: Theresa Musser, Penn State University, 224 Grange Building, University Park, PA 16802 814-865-7576, txm4@psu.edu, www.personal.psu.edu/txm4

of people. It has been successfully utilized for research, classroom instruction, assessment, and evaluation activities.

The NGP is a seven-step procedure that allows people to express their individual priorities in the beginning. Group priorities follow with a final list of priorities agreed upon collectively by the group. The major benefit of using the NGP is that it prohibits any single speaker or topic from dominating. It can be conducted, from start to finish, in 1 to 2 hours.

HOW TO USE THE NOMINAL GROUP PROCESS

The meeting should be held in a comfortable room, large enough to hold the expected number of participants in such a manner that one or more tables seating up to 8 persons can be placed apart for independent group activity. There should be one group leader/recorder assigned to each table, and an overall coordinator for the meeting. The following supplies are also needed for each table: one large pad of flip chart paper, four or five 5 × 8-inch cards per person, a broad felt-tip marking pen, masking tape, pencils, and an easel.

There are six basic "rules" dictated by the NGP:

1. Be extremely well prepared and well organized.
2. State the task very clearly and write it down for all to see.
3. Complete each step without any variation that may weaken the process.
4. Hold the group to the time schedule.
5. Be firm yet fair throughout.
6. Only allow participants to make positive, constructive comments during discussion.

The following seven steps of the NGP are based on a 2-hour procedure. A 1-hour process can be conducted by cutting the time for each step in half.

Step 1: Nominal Group Activity (10 minutes)

The group leader states the task in brief, precise terms, and writes it on a blackboard or large sheet of paper for all to see. Each participant receives 5 x 8-inch index cards and is asked to write suggestions and ideas regarding the task in short words or phrases. Everyone is reminded that there are no right or wrong answers, and individuals must work in silence and alone. This is actually a brainstorming activity that is done individually and in silence rather than as a group.

Tip: It is very important that the question or problem be stated clearly and succinctly; you will probably put much thought into exactly what it is you want to accomplish before phrasing the question or statement.

Step 2: Round-Robin Listing of Ideas (20 minutes)

Proceed around the table with each person in turn briefly stating one idea. No discussion other than clarification is permitted. The leader records and numbers each idea on a large pad or chalkboard. This continues until all ideas have been expressed.

Tip: Be sure to number the responses so you can refer to the number during discussion. Tear off each sheet of flip chart paper as it becomes full and tape the sheets around the room so that everyone can refer to them in later steps.

Step 3: Individual Group Discussion (30 minutes)

The group discusses the ideas listed, clarifying, lobbying, and defending the different statements.

Tip: The group may decide that some ideas are so closely related that they should be put together into a category. You may be eliminating some items from your original list to combine them with other items. Use your facilitation skills to make sure everyone who wants has a chance to speak and that the time limit is strictly adhered to.

Step 4: First Vote (10 minutes)

On a new 5 × 8-inch index card, each person writes "First Vote" in the upper right corner. Then, using the numbers assigned to the statements, everyone ranks the top five items listed. Scores for the individually ranked items should be tallied by the group leader. A score of 5 is given to each individual's top priority item, 4 to the second priority, etc. After scores are totaled, items are prioritized by score, highest to lowest.

Tip: If your original list of items is relatively small (fewer than 20 ideas) you may ask participants to vote for only 3 items instead of 5.

Step 5: Group Discussion of First Vote (20 minutes)

The group debates the items on the list. The group leader helps clarify any items.

Tip: You may have to remind participants to keep their comments positive. Make sure to watch the time and keep things moving.

Step 6: Final Group Vote (10 minutes)

On a new 5 × 8-inch index card, members write "Final Vote" in the upper right corner. Everyone then votes for 3 to 5 of the priorities, in an effort to eliminate some of the items and allow for changes in personal views. All must vote in silence and independently.

Tip: You may use the same scoring technique described in Step 4.

Step 7: Wrap-Up (20 minutes)

Final group rankings are tallied and each priority is clarified by the leader so that everyone understands what has been decided by the total assembly. The leader again tells everyone why the information was obtained, and offers praise for what has been accomplished at the meeting.

Tip: Rewrite the final list so that everyone can see the results more clearly. You may find the group wanting to discuss the process as well as the results. When several small groups are reporting to the leader during wrap-up, it is not necessary to rewrite each group's priorities. However, when synthesizing this information after the program is over, add the value scores for each item that is identical across groups to develop a "final" priority listing for the session. You are free to summarize this information any way you see fit. Some groups may have identical or similar items and some may not.

CAUTIONS AND LIMITATIONS

There are a few considerations to take into account when preparing to conduct the Nominal Group Process. Be sure that:

1. Instructions are clear and uncomplicated.
2. Explanation is well organized.
3. Delivery is appropriate (no distractions due to inexperience in public speaking).
4. Confidence is communicated through a combination of firmness and diplomacy.
5. Feedback is encouraged by questions and response to nonverbal signals (posture, facial expressions, gestures) from the audience.
6. Flexibility is shown in responding to the audience but not in bending the rules of the Nominal Group Process.

USES OF THE NOMINAL GROUP PROCESS

Possible uses for the Nominal Group Process are limited only by the imagination. Listed here are some ideas or suggestions for situations in which the process could be effective:

1. Long-range planning.
2. Bringing together people who seldom interact.
3. Generating enthusiasm and commitment.
4. Encouraging interagency cooperation.
5. Helping people with strong opinions on a topic to see different viewpoints.
6. Committee meetings.

CONCLUSION

No one certain group procedure is appropriate and effective for all activities and situations. Focus group interviews, surveys, total quality management, process improvement teams, and committees are some of the group techniques utilized to improve our lives, workplace, productivity, etc. The Nominal Group Process is another technique to add to the facilitator's toolbox. Uses for this simple, effective, efficient process are limited only by the imagination of the manager. Some group activities can be painful and frustrating to participants if good facilitation is not apparent. However, the NGP is quite easy to facilitate with these step-by-step directions and tips. Give the technique a try and find out how positive and fun problem solving can be!

REFERENCE

DelBecq, A. L., A. H. Van de Ven, and D. H. Gustafson. 1975. *Group Techniques for Program Planning: A Guide to Nominal Group and Delphi Processes.* Glenview, IL: Scott, Foresman and Company.

34
IMPROVING PROBLEM SOLVING IN MEETINGS

Edwina Haring

Overview Here is an exercise that serves several objectives simultaneously. First, it allows team members to work with colleagues on the team other than those they interact with on a daily basis. Second, it levels the playing field; all parties are on equal footing in the exercise. Third, it provides practice in using a problem-solving model. Fourth, the exercise gives team members the opportunity to learn how to participate in team problem solving even though the problem may not be specific to their work duties. Fifth, at each round, each small group works with fresh content in another step in the problem-solving model, thereby reinforcing the skill of using the problem-solving model steps and stemming the tide of content saturation (whereby new learners may be tempted to skip steps). Last, it is fun, challenging, and active!

Suggested Time 3 to 3½ hours

Materials Needed
✔ Forms A to D (Problem-Solving Relay), one copy of each form for each small group
✔ One copy of Form E (Problem-Solving Steps), for each learner, preferably printed on brightly colored paper
✔ 4 paper clips
✔ Pencils or pens
✔ Writing surface
✔ Sufficient room for learners to work in small groups without disturbing other small groups

Contact Information: Edwina Haring, Dynamic Performance Consultants, Newark, DE, 19725, 302-455-1727, Eharing@magpage.com

Group Size   Ideal size is 16 to 20 participants in 4 small groups of 4 or 5 learners.

Preparation   Prepare three flip charts in advance with the following information:

Flip chart 1
    Team Meeting Concerns
    Making Team Decisions
    Communication about Decisions
    Professional Style Disagreements
    Consistent Minutes and Distribution

Flip chart 2
Problem-Solving Steps

1.   Identify the Problem

2.   Generate Solutions

3.   Prioritize the Solutions

4.   Create Implementation Plan

Flip chart 3

Topic/Round	Round 1	Round 2	Round 3	Round 4
Making Team Decisions	A	D	C	B
Communication about Decisions	B	A	D	C
Professional Style Disagreements	C	B	A	D
Consistent Minutes and Distribution	D	C	B	A

Note: Insert team names in boxes on your flip chart to replace A, B, C, and D where indicated. Reveal only one round at a time.

Procedure   1.   Introduce the topic: "Today, we are going to learn an easy process for solving problems using the strengths of the team. Our target problem for this exercise will be our team meeting skills. We will work on four team meeting concerns while learning to use the problem-solving steps." (Use your own words.)

2.   Show the prepared flip chart 1.

3.   Divide learners into four small groups. Try to organize the small groups so that people are not working with the same people they work with every day. Ensure that learners have a pencil or pen, one paper clip per group, and a surface for writing. Separate the groups so they can work undisturbed by other small groups.

4.   Ask the newly formed small groups to take one minute to introduce themselves (if necessary) and one minute to choose a team name.

5. At the end of 2 minutes, ask each small group for its team name and record the team names on a separate piece of flip chart paper.

Round One

1. Explain that the exercise begins with each group working on Step One in problem solving: Identify the Problem. Show flip chart 2. (Use the reveal method: Show only "Identify the Problem.")

2. Distribute a copy of Form A to each group, with the group's team name written at the top and its assigned topic circled or highlighted (see flip chart 2).

3. Review the instructions. Give the groups 30 seconds to choose a scribe and ask who the scribes are for this round.

4. Tell learners that you want them to discuss all the reasons why this is a concern and to list all their ideas about what may be causing the problem. Allow 8 to 10 minutes.

5. While small groups are working on Round 1, record the names on flip chart 3 in the appropriate places: Wherever there is a place for A, record the actual name the group has chosen instead. Do the same with the other group names for B, C, and D.

6. At the end of the time, ask each group to spend the next 5 minutes developing a clear, concise problem statement. Have the scribes record the statements at the bottom of the handouts. Collect each team's Form A.

Round Two

1. Reveal Step Two on flip chart 2, Generate Solutions.

2. Say, "The next step in problem solving is to generate solutions to the problem. How many of you have done brainstorming before? What are the rules for brainstorming?" Let them tell you how to conduct a brainstorming session; reinforce correct perceptions and correct or add rules where necessary.

3. Tell learners they will work with another group's problem identification (from Form A) and will have 10 minutes to brainstorm solutions and record them on Form B.

4. Redistribute the completed Forms A, along with a blank Form B, in the following sequence (see flip chart 2):

Distribute Team A's Form A to group B.

Distribute Team B's Form A to group C.

Distribute Team C's Form A to group D.

Distribute Team D's Form A to group A.

5. Resist the temptation to answer questions about why you are doing the exercise this way; that discussion is part of the debriefing.

6. Allow 10 minutes for brainstorming and recording, then call time and collect each team's Forms A and B.

Round Three

1. Reveal Step Three on flip chart 2, Prioritize the Solutions.

2. Say, "The next step in problem solving is to prioritize the solutions. We prioritize because we have to choose something to do first. Prioritization should consider the feasibility of each solution, the effort to implement the solutions, the time it may take, and its likelihood of success in correcting the problem."

3. Redistribute the completed Forms A and B, along with a blank Form C, in the following sequence (see flip chart 2):

   Distribute Team A's forms to group B.

   Distribute Team B's forms to group C.

   Distribute Team C's forms to group D.

   Distribute Team D's forms to group A.

4. Tell learners they will work with another group's solutions generated for another concern and that they will have 10 minutes to prioritize the solutions provided.

5. Call time.

Round Four

1. Reveal Step Four on flip chart 2, Create Implementation Plan.

2. Say, "The last step in problem solving deals with how we are going to implement the prioritized solution. You may not agree with the top solution selected by the previous group, but often we are called upon in the workplace to implement solutions that we did not choose.

   "In this step, you will figure out how to make the solution a reality. List all the tasks that have to be done for this solution to be implemented. Name names or departments where possible. If you are unsure, suggest a name or position that may be responsible. Estimate how long you think it will take to complete each task and assign a tentative completion date. Don't hesitate to be precise—that's how solutions are implemented!"

3. Allow 20 minutes for teams to complete Form C, Prioritized Solutions. Then call time and collect each team's forms.

4. Redistribute the forms, along with a blank Form D, in the following sequence (see flip chart 2):

Distribute Team A's forms to Team B.

Distribute to Team B's forms to Team C.

Distribute to Team C's forms to Team D.

Distribute Team D's forms to Team A.

5. Tell learners they will have 20 minutes to create an implementation plan.

6. Call time after 20 minutes.

7. Distribute flip chart markers. Instruct teams to post their solutions and implementation plans on the flip chart paper provided and hang the flip charts on the wall.

Process Activity

1. Instruct the groups to choose a spokesperson to explain in 5 minutes the information the group received and the implementation plan they devised. Allow learners to ask a few questions of the group's plan.

2. Ask the group when they will make a final decision on what plans to implement and when. Look for commitments to the plans or commitments to the consideration of the plans.

Debriefing Activity

Ask the following questions:

• How did the exercise work for you?

• What did you learn?

• Why do you think the exercise was designed this way?

• Why didn't your small group keep working on the same concern throughout the afternoon?

Closing Activity

Distribute Form E, Problem-Solving Steps, and review the steps one more time. Note that it is printed on bright paper so participants can find it easily when they need it!

Variations
1. Use any topics that surface in your analysis; adapt this exercise framework freely.

2. Reduce or expand the time allotted based on learner needs.

3. Allow small groups to work on the same content issue for all four problem-solving steps.

PROBLEM-SOLVING RELAY (FORM A) DOWNLOADABLE

Round 1	Concern 1
	Concern 2
	Concern 3
	Concern 4

Identify the Problem:	Making Team Decisions
	Communication of Decisions
	Professional Style Disagreements
	Consistent Minutes and
	Distribution

Instructions: Your group has been assigned one of four concerns about how meetings are conducted within teams.
Your small group's assignment is:

1. Choose someone to be the group scribe.

2. Identify the exact nature of this problem using your personal, firsthand knowledge or what you have heard from others on the team. Think about the behaviors that cause this to be a concern. What doesn't work? What happens that prevents the team from being good at the concern noted above?

Note: Do not generate solutions!

Write a problem statement:

_____

_____

_____

_____

PROBLEM-SOLVING RELAY (FORM B) [DOWNLOADABLE]

Round 2   Concern 1
                               Concern 2
                               Concern 3
                               Concern 4

Identify the Problem: Making Team Decisions
                               Communication of Decisions
                               Professional Style Disagreements
                               Consistent Minutes and
                               Distribution

Instructions:

1. Choose someone to be the group scribe.

2. Using the Problem Identification information from the previous group, generate solutions to the problem. Use brainstorming rules:

   - Be in a state of openness and focus.
   - All ideas are valid.
   - All ideas are heard and recorded.
   - Piggyback on each other's ideas.
   - Don't evaluate ideas during brainstorming.

Solutions:

_____

_____

_____

_____

PROBLEM-SOLVING RELAY (FORM C) DOWNLOADABLE

Round 3   Concern 1
                                     Concern 2
                                     Concern 3
                                     Concern 4

Identify the Problem: Making Team Decisions
                                     Communication of Decisions
                                     Professional Style Disagreements
                                     Consistent Minutes and
                                     Distribution

Instructions:

1. Choose someone to be the group scribe.

2. Using the Solutions generated by the previous group, prioritize the solutions, considering the following attributes:

   - Feasibility
   - Likelihood of success
   - Ease of implementation
   - Time available to implement
   - Possible to do

Prioritized Solutions:

1. _____

2. _____

3. _____

4. _____

5. _____

PROBLEM-SOLVING RELAY (FORM D)

Round 4	Concern 1
	Concern 2
	Concern 3
	Concern 4

Identify the Problem:	Making Team Decisions
	Communication of Decisions
	Professional Style Disagreements
	Consistent Minutes and
	Distribution

Instructions:

1. Choose someone to be the group scribe.

2. Use Solution 1 from the previous group to craft an implementation plan. List the tasks necessary for this solution to be implemented. Assign responsibilities wherever possible. Provide estimated dates for completion of tasks. Post your plan on the flip chart.

Write Solution 1 here:

_____

_____

Implementation Plan

Tasks	Responsible person(s)	Estimated completion date
_____	_____	_____
_____	_____	_____
_____	_____	_____
_____	_____	_____

PROBLEM-SOLVING STEPS (FORM E)

When your team is in trouble or just needs to resolve an issue, everyone is responsible for problem solving.

Here are the four steps to problem resolution:

1. Identify the problem...the real problem. Watch out for naming "symptoms" of the problem. Write a concise problem statement. This is necessary!

2. Generate all possible solutions to the problem. Go "outside the box" in your thinking. Use brainstorming rules. The most unlikely solutions are sometimes the best!

3. Prioritize the solutions generated in step 2. Let feasibility, time available, ease, and success factors influence your prioritization. (That's reality!)

4. Create an implementation plan that includes names, dates, and tasks that need to be accomplished. Think W3—**W**ho does **W**hat by **W**hen.

35

BETTERING THE QUALITY OF GROUP DISCUSSION

Malcolm Burson

Overview   Discussions and conversations of all sorts, whether in business or other parts of our lives, benefit when there's a good mixture of statements and assertions, on the one hand, and questions to explore the meaning of what's been said, on the other hand. From a reflective distance, this makes sense to most people. After all, unless you're in a formal debate and a third-party judge is going to decide who piled up the most points, we know that our ability to arrive at a decision or agreement benefits from a certain give and take. And many people admit that they'd like to improve the quality of conversations at work.

But in the urgency of business situations, where the need to get on with the work at hand makes us impatient, our natural desire is to make sure our point gets made. There's little incentive to listen, question, or explore the meaning of what's already been said. It's as if we came into the room, sat down, and stacked up our small pile of verbal hand grenades, to be pitched one at a time into the fray. Even if our team decides to change its behavior in this regard, in the hope of achieving better outcomes than the frustration we often experience in meetings, time pressure makes it nearly impossible to adjourn our work long enough to learn the skills we need.

Improving the quality of business discussions requires the intent to do so, agreed ways of behaving, and a common set of tools. Balancing inquiry and advocacy is a crucial part of this. If each participant in a meeting does little more than make a series of unconnected statements and unexplored assertions (advocacy), that does little to build the shared understanding needed for making good decisions. We can give more weight to the inquiry end of the teeter-totter by making room for questions that explore the implications of what has been said. In this way, we make sure that recognizing different perceptions of an idea or

Contact Information: Malcolm C. Burson, Maine DEP, #17 State House Station, Augusta, ME 04333-0017, 207-287-7755, malcolm.c.burson@state.me.us

issue, for instance, allows the team to build a more complete picture and also increases the likelihood that the team will reach agreement as an outcome.

How to overcome our natural tendency toward assertion and advocacy, so we can step back toward reflection and inquiry? This activity provides a simple and slightly playful (if initially frustrating) way for team members to find a balance for themselves and the group. It works best in the real-time context of an existing team engaged in its usual work. It requires explicit agreement by all team members that improving the quality of discussion and conversation is a goal.

Suggested Time   45 to 60 minutes, in the context of a usual meeting

Materials Needed

✔   Flip chart

✔   3 × 5-inch cards, two for each participant, as follows: a card of one color (e.g., yellow) with **?** on one side; and a card of another color (e.g., blue) with **!** on one side of it. *Note:* Avoid red and green, as these colors convey a message that is at odds with the intent of the exercise.

✔   Form A (Template for Making ! and ? Cards)

Procedure

1. Give the team a brief overview of the usefulness of balancing inquiry and advocacy. Draw a picture of a scale or balance on the flip chart, with the "advocacy" side clearly weighed down. Explain that the team will be learning how to develop inquiry skills (or to move toward a better balance) while getting on with their usual tasks. Note that the purpose of inquiry is to ask questions that explore the implications of what has been said as well as to test assumptions, in order to build meaning that everyone shares.

2. Distribute the cards so that each team member has one of each color. Ask participants to place the cards on the table in front of them where everyone can see them.

3. Determine how the discussion or conversation will begin. It could pick up where the team left off the last time it met, or it could begin with a new topic. In either case, the topic should be written on the flip chart, in the form of either a statement or a question.

4. Explain the rules for discussion, as follows:
    Once the conversation begins, anyone may speak. If that person makes a statement or assertion, she or he turns the ! card over. This person may not make another statement, even to answer a direct question, until she or he recovers the ! card.

The only way to recover the ! (advocacy) card is by asking a question that intends to move the group along; that is, by playing one's ? (inquiry) card.

If the person making a statement is asked a direct question in response, someone else may seek to answer, thereby playing his or her advocacy card. Alternatively, someone could ask a question that probes more deeply into what has been said.

Note that the facilitator has the power to interpret the rules and to determine whether an inquiry or question is really a disguised assertion (against the rules!).

5. When all team members have had multiple opportunities to speak, call time and debrief the activity. Make sure to note on the flip chart the name of the last speaker, and the point to which the discussion has proceeded. This will allow you to provide continuity when the meeting resumes.

6. Close the intentional practice portion of the meeting by reopening the discussion at the point noted on the flip chart. Suggest that team members are no longer limited by the rules of the exercise, but may want to keep the cards in front of them as a reminder. In some teams known to me that meet regularly, I've observed people keeping the cards in the notebooks they usually bring to the meeting.

Debriefing Questions

✔ Ask whether being forced to think of a question that would further the group's work meant that participants had to listen harder to what others were saying instead of planning their next assertion.

✔ Ask how participants experienced the quality of the conversation: Did it seem more or less respectful, productive, or focused than usual?

✔ Acknowledge that this approach may seem artificial at the beginning, but that the goal is to improve the quality of discussion over time. Point out that teams that find a good balance between inquiry and advocacy often observe that their effectiveness improves measurably.

✔ If the team's task was problem solving or decision making, ask whether members think that progress was made.

✔ In general, model inquiry in your own leadership of the debriefing, and see if anyone notices.

Variations

1. It may be useful to model the exercise briefly, using a fishbowl of 3 to 4 team members. With the others looking on, this group

addresses the item from step 3. After 4 or 5 minutes and several interactions by all participants, the leader or facilitator invites the rest of the team to join the discussion. In this case, it's best to give those in the fishbowl two advocacy cards each; otherwise the discussion may be too constrained, especially at the beginning. When the number of participants increases, the extra ! cards are no longer needed.

2. Allow the team to struggle with the limitations imposed by the rules. If and when the discussion lags, don't be in a hurry to break the resulting silence. On the other hand, a sense of humor helps defuse some of the frustration team members will experience when (as most will) they find themselves with something important to say, only to realize they must ask a question in order to earn the right to advocate.

TEMPLATE FOR MAKING ! AND ? CARDS (FORM A)

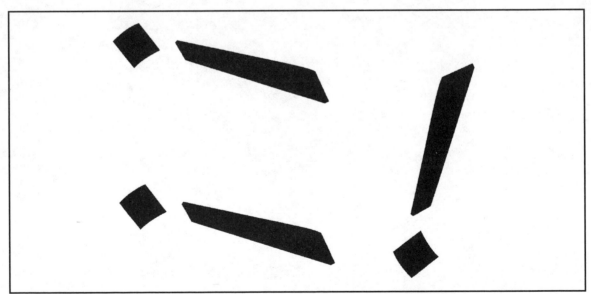

36
BREAKING STALEMATES IN GROUPS

Mel Silberman

Overview
When a conflict completely overtakes a group and each side won't budge, you might try to move the process along by asking all parties to agree to engage in a four-step process called Breaking the Stalemate.

Suggested Time
30 to 45 minutes

Materials Needed
None

Procedure
1. Tell the group that, in your opinion, the conflict has deteriorated into an argument over who's right and who's wrong. Explain that you have a process to attempt to break the stalemate.

2. Ask each side to prepare a four-part presentation:

The Conflict We're Having
Discuss and agree on the positions being taken that oppose each other. Be objective and descriptive, and show that you have listened well to your opponents. Don't disparage their position. Be respectful of it.

For example, consider a conflict over grade inflation between the academic dean of a college and the faculty. The faculty might state: It seems that we have opposite views about grade inflation. You want a greater distribution of grades so that we appear to have higher standards than are reflected in the current grade distribution. We think that the higher grades reflect well on us as a faculty. We must be doing something right.

Contact Information: Mel Silberman, Active Training, 303 Sayre Drive, Princeton, NJ 08540, 609-987-8157, mel@activetraining.com, www.activetraining.com

What Concerns Us

Ask each party to share feelings, concerns, and needs about the issue in conflict.

The faculty might say: We are concerned that students will become obsessed with how they are graded rather than how they can be effective learners. We also worry that focusing on grade inflation emphasizes making things tougher for students...not rethinking what our basic teaching goals are and what we can do to facilitate them.

What We'd Like to Suggest

Each party shares a creative suggestion to get beyond the point where the group is stuck.

The faculty might now say: It would be ideal if we could agree to be more explicit about the performance criteria for different grading outcomes. If most students do well, there's no reason to have a grading curve.

What We're Willing to Do about It

Each party makes a statement about the actions it is prepared to take to create a better situation.

The faculty might conclude: We're willing to submit our current grading criteria to the Academic Dean and obtain recommendations on how they can be made clearer.

3. Invite each side to make its presentation.

4. Ask each side to comment on the presentations:

   - How understanding was the other side?

   - What suggestions hold promise?

   - Is there a basis for moving to a win–win resolution of the problem?

Variation Sometimes, an issue is so explosive or the meeting is so tense that a full group discussion of a conflict seems unproductive. The best approach may be to adopt a small-group approach that minimizes open conflict and maximizes collaboration.

1. Devise three questions to ask participants about the conflict affecting the group. Here are three possibilities:

   - How important is it that we resolve this conflict?

   - What is the ideal resolution to this conflict?

- What practical ideas do you have to resolve this conflict?

Write the questions so that concrete answers are attainable. Avoid highly open-ended questions.

2. Inform participants that you would like the group to try a collaborative approach to conflict resolution that avoids extended discussion or public fighting.

3. Divide participants into trios. Give each participant one each of the three conflict assessment questions you have created. Ask each trio member to interview the other participants and obtain (and record) answers to his or her assigned question.

4. Convene in subgroups all the participants who have been assigned the same question. For example, if there are 18 participants, arranged in trios, 6 of them will have been assigned the same question.

5. Ask each subgroup to pool its data and summarize it. Then, ask each subgroup to report to the entire group what they have learned about the group's response to the question assigned to it.

6. Ask the group to reflect on the data that has emerged and assess what to do next.

37

PROMOTING THE VALUE OF "YES"

Kat Koppett

Overview An important communication rule is to "yes, and" rather than "yes, but." "Yes, and…" means that you accept an idea or "offer" and add to it. For example, a member of a team says, "Let's redesign the Web site to make it more user-friendly." Other team members might say, "Yes, but it'll be too much work." Or "Yes, but that will cost too much money." Or "Yes, but we're not experts on that." While all of those things might be true, they might not. Imagine how much more productive it would be to say, "Yes, and I'll investigate ways to do it inexpensively," or "Yes, and I'll contact Greg in the IT department for advice."

    Here is a simple activity that illustrates in an experiential way the value of saying "yes" to ideas. Although many of us are familiar with the rules of brainstorming—separating idea generation from idea evaluation, quantity over quality—in practice, it can be very difficult not to censor, judge, and dismiss ideas before they are fully explored. There are all sorts of reasons we say "no" to ideas, and some of those reasons are valid. However, often we say "no" when it would behoove us to say "yes." Some of the most pervasive and detrimental reasons we reject ideas include:

- The idea means more work for me.
- Someone else had the idea.
- We don't know immediately how it will work.
- The idea seems risky or frightening.
- We think being critical equals being intelligent.
- Saying "no" is a habit.

    Many of us say "no" much more often than we realize. We might not say the word "no"; we say, "yes, but…" and have the same effect. The

Contact Information: Kat Koppett, StoryNet, LLC, 774 Great Highway 4A, San Francisco, CA 94121, 415-752-0217, www.thestorynet.com, kat@thestorynet.com

practice does more damage than might be evident at first glance. This activity illustrates the value of accepting an idea and building on it. In the activity, two groups set about the task of planning a company party. The first group will struggle to achieve anything. The second will generate ideas much more easily.

Suggested Time 4 to 8 minutes

Materials Needed None

Procedure **Round 1**

1. Ask for 3 to 5 volunteers.

2. Tell the group that they are in charge of planning the company holiday party.

3. Each person must contribute an idea. There is no specific order, but no one may contribute more than one idea in a row.

4. Anyone may start, and each successive idea must begin with the words, "Yes, but...."

5. Allow the exercise to continue for 2 to 3 minutes, or until it degenerates beyond repair.

Round 2

6. Ask for 3 to 5 new volunteers.

7. Set up the same activity, with one adjustment: This time, each new sentence must start with the words, "Yes, and...."

8. Allow the activity to continue for 2 to 3 minutes, or until the group seems satisfied and delighted.

Tips • Continue to remind participants to use the words "Yes, and..." or "Yes, but...."

• End the rounds when the ideas trail off (usually in the first round) or on an explosion of approval (usually in the second round).

• Pay attention to the intention of the statements. If the demonstration does not work, it may be because the participants are actually blocking even though they are saying "Yes, and..." or vice-versa.

Suggested Debriefing Questions

- How does it feel to have your ideas rejected? Accepted?
- How did this experience compare to real life?
- Why do we block other people's ideas?
- How can we increase our willingness and ability to accept ideas?

Variations

1. Play simultaneously in pairs or groups of up to 5. Allow each group to try both the "Yes, but..." and the "Yes, and..." versions.
2. Assign a different task (e.g., create a meeting agenda; design a new product).
3. Have the same group of 5 conduct both rounds.
4. Role play with some people saying "Yes, and..." and some saying "Yes, but...."

38

STARTING A PLANNING PROCESS STRATEGICALLY

Becky Mills and Chris Saeger

Overview What is it about planning? It seems to hold much promise. We all talk about it, and most people think it is important; yet when we sit down to do planning the mood of the group often shifts to one of resignation. The Planning Game is an excellent start to any strategic planning session. It provides an interesting and informative way to explore organizational issues of trust, shared commitment, and customer focus.

The game does this by placing the participants in a simulated organization with a stovepipe departmental structure and a lack of customer focus. Over several rounds, the participants attempt to coordinate action and produce products to serve the customer. From the simulation, participants can:

- Observe the effects of trust on planning.

- Observe the effects of planning on customer service, team performance, and use of resources.

- Observe the benefits of involving the customer in planning.

- Identify improvements in the planning process and workplace applications.

Suggested Time 60 to 90 minutes (depending on the depth of the debriefing)

Materials Needed

✔ A table with six chairs for each set of players. Players must be within arm's reach of each other and the middle of the table.

✔ A deck of UNO cards, sorted to include only numbers 1 through 6 in green and yellow, and numbers 1 through 7 in blue and red.

Contact Information: Becky Mills and Chris Saeger, Learning Landscapes, 9824 Fairfax Square #381, Fairfax, VA 22031, 703-836-6776, Info@learninglandscapes.com, www.learninglandscapes.com

✔ Instruction sheets, Forms A to F, for each of the six players. Place the appropriate instruction sheet face down at each seat.

✔ A piece of flip chart paper and a marker.

Setup Shuffle the cards well and deal out three cards for each of the four places along the sides of the table. Seat players at the table so that the Department Heads are along the sides (where there are three cards set out for each); the Customer is at one end; and the Investor is at the other. Give each person an instruction sheet: four Department Heads, one Customer, and one Investor. Give the Investor the rest of the sorted UNO deck.

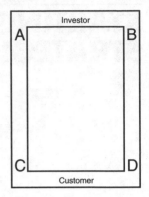

Procedure 1. Give these initial instructions:

Please read the instruction sheet in front of you. Do not discuss your instructions. Each of the four players with cards represents a Department Head of a service organization. This is the start of the fiscal year, and the cards you already hold represent the resources you already have. All of the department heads are new to your jobs, but you have some idea of what you are to do.

The player at this end of the table is the Investor. The Investor holds a lot more resources, and will be giving them to your organization during the course of the game. The player at the other end of the table is the Customer. The Customer desperately needs the services (represented by sets of cards) provided by your organization.

When the game begins, the Investor will start contributing resources to the Department Heads, who will assemble the resources into sets (or services) and then deliver them to the Customer.

For this first round of the game, no talking among you is allowed before we start. As in so many organizations, new employees are expected to "roll up their sleeves," "hit the ground running," and "just get the job done."

Investor, are you ready to deal? Department Heads, are you ready to assemble and deliver your sets of cards? Customer, are you ready to receive the services? Go!

2. Conduct a discussion after the first round. During this and other discussions, participants will report the number of acceptable ser-

vices produced and the waste rate for each table. Record these on the flip chart.

Ask the Customers: Did you get what you needed? Are you satisfied with the service you received? How many usable services did you receive? (Count the acceptable card sets.)

Ask the Department Heads: You were certainly working hard. How do you feel about the work you've done? How many resources went unused? (Count any cards that were not passed on to the client and any cards the client could not use.)

Ask the Investors: What do you think about how the company used the resources you invested?

Tell all participants: I'm sure you have some ideas about how your organization could do better in using Investor resources to meet Customer needs. You have five minutes to discuss how you want to do things differently, and then we will play through the next fiscal year. Investors, please collect all the cards, shuffle them, and redeal three to each of the Department Heads. In five minutes, we will begin the game again.

3. Conduct a discussion after the second round.

   Ask the Customers: How do you feel about the services you received this time? How many usable services did you receive? (Count the card sets.)

   Ask the Department Heads: How do you think it went this time? (Count the unused cards and cards that were unusable to the Customer. Compare this to the first round.)

   Ask the Investors: How do you feel about the organization now?

   Ask all participants: What differences did you see between the first and second rounds? Do you believe that you can further improve your services or improve relationships with customers and investors?

   Note: The best possible score is four complete product sets and four waste cards. If the groups are close to this outcome, you may want to stop the simulation here. Otherwise, give the participants another 5 minutes to discuss process improvements, and then proceed with round three.

4. Conduct a discussion after the third round.

   Ask the Customers: How do you feel about the services you received this time? How many usable services did you receive? (Count the cards.)

Ask the Department Heads: How do you think it went this time? (Count the unused and unusable resources. Compare with previous rounds.)

Ask the Investors: How do you feel about the organization now?

Ask all participants: What differences did you see between the second and third rounds?

Debriefing Questions

Conduct a final debriefing by asking:

- How did you feel about the simulation play?
- How was the simulation play similar to or different from your experience at work?
- How did you improve service delivery during the simulation?
- Ask for discussion (and make a list on newsprint): What do you see are the benefits of planning? (E.g., makes better use of resources, helps to meet customer needs, encourages cooperation and communication.)

Debriefing Topics

Effects of Trust on Planning:

During the first round, participants will grab for resources without regard for the resource needs of the other departments. Players will sometimes hoard cards in the hope of meeting their departmental objectives. There is no focus on the customer. Players compete simply to meet their own departmental objectives. As the rounds progress, players begin to cooperate and have a sense of trust that the other players are engaged with them in meeting the customer needs, not simply meeting departmental objectives.

Effects of Planning on Customer Service, Team Performance, and Use of Resources:

A dramatic aspect of the game occurs after the participants play a second and possibly third fiscal year. As they implement their strategy and engage in conversation and cooperation throughout the fiscal year, the number of useful products increases dramatically. Teams often go from producing no useful products to producing the maximum number of useful products. The teams are accomplishing more, yet they are using exactly the same deck of cards, and hence, exactly the same resources they used in the first fiscal year. The difference can be found in the waste rate. The waste rate is the number of cards left unused at the end of each fiscal year. Even the most efficient teams will still have four cards that are not in a completed product at the end of the year, since it is impossible to delete all waste from a system.

If the participants have input into the budget process for your organization, they may see parallels in resource use and allocation. During the first fiscal year, each department tries to grab as many resources as possible. The process becomes more orderly and productive once the team formulates a strategy for allocating resources. Rather than stockpiling, departments take only the resources they can effectively use. Perhaps more importantly, participants clearly demonstrate for themselves that meeting departmental goals is not enough to ensure the success of the organization. After developing a shared vision of success, they cooperate with one another to employ each particular resource so that it most effectively meets the goals of the organization.

The Benefits of Involving the Customer in Planning:

The key to improving organizational performance is to determine the customer's expectations. The team does not receive credit for products that fail to address the needs of the Customer, no matter how much energy or enthusiasm went into producing them. In a real competitive market, customers will switch to another organization's services or products if their current provider cannot meet their expectations, so it is important to determine current customer expectations.

Unfortunately, customer expectations aren't static. In fact, as quality improves, customer requirements often become more stringent. When an organization takes a product or service to a new level, customers expect future products to meet or exceed the new, higher standard. In the game, the initial customer requirements may simply be to receive the packs of cards in the necessary order. In later rounds, customers may demand that the cards in each pack be in numerical order or that the packs be delivered in a particular manner.

Improvements in the Planning Process:

Improvements in the planning process that past participants have identified include: taking a multidepartmental approach; tying objectives to the real results expected in the organization; building a shared vision; and implementing workflow improvements. Over the rounds, players have usually modified the workflow procedures in the game. We use the game workflow and the changes participants have made to begin to talk about the organization's workflow and coordination.

WELCOME TO THE PLANNING GAME! (FORM A)

Your role in the game today is Head of Department A. Please do not show these instructions or your cards to the other players in the game.

The Planning Game is about a service organization. Other players in the game are:

Three other Department Heads.

A Customer, who depends on receiving services from you.

An Investor, who provides the resources you use to develop services.

You are new on the job at the organization. Your department's role has been to assemble sets of three cards—numbered 1, 2, and 3 (any colors)—and deliver the sets to your Customer.

On the table in front of you are three cards. These are the resources you start with at the beginning of the fiscal year. When the game begins, the Investor will start to issue new cards at a steady rate to the center of the table. Get the cards you need, assemble the sets, and deliver them to the Customer right away.

When the Investor has given away all the resources, the first round of the game is over.

WELCOME TO THE PLANNING GAME! (FORM B)

Your role in the game today is Head of Department B. Please do not show these instructions or your cards to the other players in the game.

The Planning Game is about a service organization. Other players in the game are:

Three other Department Heads.

A Customer, who depends on receiving services from you.

An Investor, who provides the resources you use to develop services.

You are new on the job at the organization. Your department's role has been to assemble sets of three red cards (any numbers) and deliver the sets to your Customer.

On the table in front of you are three cards. These are the resources you start with at the beginning of the fiscal year. When the game begins, the Investor will start to issue new cards at a steady rate to the center of the table. Get the cards you need, assemble the sets, and deliver them to the Customer right away.

When the Investor has given away all the resources, the first round of the game is over.

WELCOME TO THE PLANNING GAME! (FORM C)

Your role in the game today is Head of Department C. Please do not show these instructions or your cards to the other players in the game.

The Planning Game is about a service organization. Other players in the game are:

Three other Department Heads.

A Customer, who depends on receiving services from you.

An Investor, who provides the resources you use to develop services.

You are new on the job at the organization. Your department's role has been to assemble sets of three blue cards (any numbers) and deliver the sets to your Customer.

On the table in front of you are three cards. These are the resources you start with at the beginning of the fiscal year. When the game begins, the Investor will start to issue new cards at a steady rate to the center of the table. Get the cards you need, assemble the sets, and deliver them to the Customer right away.

When the Investor has given away all the resources, the first round of the game is over.

WELCOME TO THE PLANNING GAME! (FORM D)

Your role in the game today is Head of Department D. Please do not show these instructions or your cards to the other players in the game.

The Planning Game is about a service organization. Other players in the game are:

Three other Department Heads.

A Customer, who depends on receiving services from you.

An Investor, who provides the resources you use to develop services.

You are new on the job at the organization. Your department's role has been to assemble sets of three cards—numbered 4, 5, and 6 (any colors)—and deliver the sets to your Customer.

On the table in front of you are three cards. These are the resources you start with at the beginning of the fiscal year. When the game begins, the Investor will start to issue new cards at a steady rate to the center of the table. Get the cards you need, assemble the sets, and deliver them to the Customer right away.

When the Investor has given away all the resources, the first round of the game is over.

WELCOME TO THE PLANNING GAME! (FORM E)

Your role in the game today is the Customer. Please do not show these instructions to the other players in the game.

The Planning Game is about a service organization. Other players in the game are:

> Four Department Heads from the organization (whom you depend on to provide the services you need); and

> An Investor, who provides the resources they use to develop services.

As the Customer, you can use as many units of useful services as the group produces. A useful service consists of twelve cards (four sets of three cards each). To count as one useful service, sets must be received in the following order:

> three cards numbered 1, 2, 3 (any color);

> three cards numbered 4, 5, 6 (any color);

> three blue cards with any number;

> three red cards with any number.

When the game starts, the Department Heads will begin assembling sets of cards. When you receive the first set of 1, 2, and 3, place them in front of you. Then watch for a set of 4, 5, and 6. Place these in front of you. Do the same for the blue set and the red set. Any sets not received in order cannot be used. You should set these to the side.

You have a need for as many useful services as the company can provide. If you complete a group of four sets, start a new group of four, beginning with the set of 1, 2, and 3.

When the Investor has given away all the resources, the first round of the game is over.

WELCOME TO THE PLANNING GAME! (FORM F)

Your role in the game today is the Investor. Please do not show these instructions or your cards to the other players in the game.

The Planning Game is about a service organization. Other players in the game are:

Four Department Heads from the organization; their job is to turn the resources you invest into services for the Customer; and

A Customer, who depends on receiving services from the organization.

On the table in front of you is a deck of cards. These are the resources you will invest in the organization. When the game begins, deal the cards, one at a time and face up, onto the center of the table at a steady rate (about one per second).

When you have given away all the resources (cards), the first round of the game is over.

REPRODUCIBLE TOOLS FOR LEADING CHANGE

39

HOW READY ARE YOUR PEOPLE FOR CHANGE?

Randall Buerkle

Overview How ready are your people to face change? In times of rapid change, it becomes necessary to acknowledge that all individuals do not adjust to transition similarly. Resiliency, or the ability to confront change and adapt to new ways of performing work, is dependent upon a variety of factors. These include personal history, one's perception of change, and the capacity to flex with changes of varying magnitude.

The Change Resiliency Profile is an instrument designed to assess change resiliency and may be used in a variety of industries. Though originally designed for individual use, it may be used within a work team as well.

Contact Information: Randall Buerkle, Flagship Consulting, 107 Kings Chapel Drive, Troy, OH 45371, 937-335-0797, flagship@wesnet.com

CHANGE RESILIENCY PROFILE

Purpose: The Change Resiliency Profile (CRP) was designed to help you and your work team identify your outlook on change. Upon completion, all should discuss the results in order to establish the general change resiliency of the team. In essence, the team's resiliency to change is perhaps more critical than that of any one individual.

Directions: Read each statement and circle your response, using the key given at the top of the columns:

	Strongly Agree	Agree	Neutral	Disagree	Strongly Disagree
1. I think the world has many facets and that relationships overlap.	5	4	3	2	1
2. I expect the world to have many shifting variables.	5	4	3	2	1
3. I view disruption as a natural phenomenon.	5	4	3	2	1
4. I see major change as uncomfortable, but I believe that hidden benefits usually exist.	5	4	3	2	1
5. I believe there are usually important lessons to be learned from challenges.	5	4	3	2	1
6. I see life as generally rewarding.	5	4	3	2	1
7. I believe I am able to reestablish my perspective following a significant disruption.	5	4	3	2	1
8. I believe change is a manageable process.	5	4	3	2	1
9. I have a high tolerance for ambiguity.					
10. I need only a brief time to recover from disappointment.	5	4	3	2	1
11. I feel empowered during change.	5	4	3	2	1
12. I know my own strengths and weaknesses and can accept my own internal and external limits.	5	4	3	2	1
13. I am able to challenge and modify my own assumptions about change.	5	4	3	2	1
14. I rely on nurturing relationships for support.	5	4	3	2	1
15. I display patience, insight, and humor when confronted with change.	5	4	3	2	1
16. I recognize the underlying themes in confusing situations.	5	4	3	2	1
17. I am able to organize several unrelated projects into a central theme.	5	4	3	2	1
18. I am able to renegotiate priorities during change.	5	4	3	2	1
19. I can handle many tasks and demands at the same time.	5	4	3	2	1
20. I can compartmentalize stress so it doesn't overlap into other areas of my life.	5	4	3	2	1

CHANGE RESILIENCY PROFILE (CONT.)

Scoring and Interpretation

Add the total of all the numbers you circled.

Enter the total after item 20 and here: _____.

If your score is:

88–100   You perceive yourself as being highly flexible in change situations. You are an exemplary role model for change.

76–87   You perceive yourself as being relatively flexible in most change situations. You are comfortable in most change situations.

64–75   You perceive yourself as being flexible in some change situations. Depending on your existing state and the nature of the change, you may or may not find change comfortable.

52–63   You perceive yourself as being relatively inflexible in change situations. You are not comfortable in many change situations and tend to hang on to established ways of doing things until you see the value of a change.

Below 52   You perceive yourself as being very inflexible in change situations. You may feel helpless or victimized when faced with change. Your personal resources for adjusting to change are easily drained.

40

IS YOUR ORGANIZATION READY FOR CHANGE?

Duane Tway

Overview The Organizational Change Characteristics Survey is used to identify your organization's readiness for or progress in implementing second-order planned change. First-order change is a modification of the organization's structure, the organization's processes, or the organization's internal relationships that does not affect the core of the organization. Second-order change goes straight to the core processes, structures, and relationships. Second-order change is self-sustaining in that no further action is necessary to keep the change "changed."

The survey is a set of questions that will allow you to gauge whether the organization is experiencing first- or second-order change. This can be extremely useful as a change program is taking place. It can be used as a diagnostic tool before attempting change, as a "how's it going" survey during change, and as a final evaluation of a change effort. The author has found that it provides excellent feedback to senior leadership teams throughout planned change processes.

Contact Information: Duane Tway, C.O.R.E., 7022 E. Hacienda Reposo, Tucson, AZ 85715-4919, 520-721-6642, dtway@waldenu.edu, www.coreconsultants.com

ORGANIZATIONAL CHANGE CHARACTERISTICS SURVEY

Directions: The Organizational Change Characteristics Survey is a 22-question survey that asks about several aspect of change within your organization. Answer each of the questions based on your experience within this organization.

1. In this organization, change happens in only a few dimensions, components, or aspects.

1	2	3	4	5	6	7	8	9
almost never				sometimes				almost always

2. In this organization, change results in a new state of being (thinking and acting).

1	2	3	4	5	6	7	8	9
almost never				sometimes				almost always

3. We tend to change things on only one or a few levels, i.e., the individual or group level rather than the organizational level.

1	2	3	4	5	6	7	8	9
almost never				sometimes				almost always

4. In this organization, change results in a new worldview, a new paradigm or model.

1	2	3	4	5	6	7	8	9
almost never				sometimes				almost always

5. We change only one or two behavioral aspects, like attitudes or values.

1	2	3	4	5	6	7	8	9
almost never				sometimes				almost always

6. In this organization, change is seemingly irrational and based on a different logic.

1	2	3	4	5	6	7	8	9
almost never				sometimes				almost always

7. In this organization, we make quantitative changes.

1	2	3	4	5	6	7	8	9
almost never				sometimes				almost always

ORGANIZATIONAL CHANGE CHARACTERISTICS SURVEY (CONT.)

8. In this organization, change is irreversible.

1	2	3	4	5	6	7	8	9
almost never				sometimes				almost always

9. We make changes in the content rather than the context.

1	2	3	4	5	6	7	8	9
almost never				sometimes				almost always

10. In this organization, change happens in revolutionary jumps.

1	2	3	4	5	6	7	8	9
almost never				sometimes				almost always

11. When we change we have continuity, we make improvements, and we develop in the same direction.

1	2	3	4	5	6	7	8	9
almost never				sometimes				almost always

12. In this organization, change involves discontinuity and taking new directions.

1	2	3	4	5	6	7	8	9
almost never				sometimes				almost always

13. We make incremental changes.

1	2	3	4	5	6	7	8	9
almost never				sometimes				almost always

14. We make changes in the context as well as in the content.

1	2	3	4	5	6	7	8	9
almost never				sometimes				almost always

15. The changes that we make can be reversed.

1	2	3	4	5	6	7	8	9
almost never				sometimes				almost always

16. We make changes that are qualitative as well as quantitative.

    1　　　2　　　3　　　4　　　5　　　6　　　7　　　8　　　9
    almost　　　　　　　　　sometimes　　　　　　　　almost
    never　　　　　　　　　　　　　　　　　　　　　　always

17. In this organization, change is logical and rational.

    1　　　2　　　3　　　4　　　5　　　6　　　7　　　8　　　9
    almost　　　　　　　　　sometimes　　　　　　　　almost
    never　　　　　　　　　　　　　　　　　　　　　　always

18. We all change all behavioral aspects, i.e., attitudes, norms, values, perceptions, beliefs, worldview, and behaviors.

    1　　　2　　　3　　　4　　　5　　　6　　　7　　　8　　　9
    almost　　　　　　　　　sometimes　　　　　　　　almost
    never　　　　　　　　　　　　　　　　　　　　　　always

19. In this organization, we make changes that do not alter our worldview or our culture.

    1　　　2　　　3　　　4　　　5　　　6　　　7　　　8　　　9
    almost　　　　　　　　　sometimes　　　　　　　　almost
    never　　　　　　　　　　　　　　　　　　　　　　always

20. We tend to change at all levels: individuals, groups, and the whole organization.

    1　　　2　　　3　　　4　　　5　　　6　　　7　　　8　　　9
    almost　　　　　　　　　sometimes　　　　　　　　almost
    never　　　　　　　　　　　　　　　　　　　　　　always

21. We tend to change within the old state of being, thinking, and acting.

    1　　　2　　　3　　　4　　　5　　　6　　　7　　　8　　　9
    almost　　　　　　　　　sometimes　　　　　　　　almost
    never　　　　　　　　　　　　　　　　　　　　　　always

22. In this organization, change is multidimensional; we change many components and aspects.

    1　　　2　　　3　　　4　　　5　　　6　　　7　　　8　　　9
    almost　　　　　　　　　sometimes　　　　　　　　almost
    never　　　　　　　　　　　　　　　　　　　　　　always

SCORING

To score this survey, score the even-numbered questions as you would a normal Likert scale question: If the respondent circles eight, the score is eight. For odd-numbered questions, subtract the respondent's answer from ten to compute the score. For example, if the respondent circles eight, subtract that answer from ten to get the score of two.

INTERPRETATION

Very high scores, 150 and above, indicate an organization that is exceptionally ready for, or going through, second-order planned change. Scores between about 100 and 150 indicate an organization that is well placed to begin second-order planned change, or if it has already begun, that needs to readdress and reinforce change preparation. Scores below 100 but above 50 indicate that the organization's people are probably aware of the change effort but that much work remains to be done. If the change effort has already begun, it would be best to stop and reevaluate the program. Some key element, perhaps overt management support, is missing. Scores below 50 indicate that second-order change will be difficult and that much planning and preparatory work must be done before embarking on a change program.

41

COACHING EMPLOYEES THROUGH CHANGE

Nancy Jackson

Overview   This guide will help managers identify stages of change that employees must go through to resolve ambivalence and change behavior. Using the model, they can apply the necessary supports to help each person discover his or her own motivation for change. The six stages are Precontemplation, Contemplation, Determination, Action, Maintenance, and Recycle. Effective coaching can help people go through the change process more comfortably and effectively by giving employees what they need when they need it.

Over and over again we hear the charge, "Things are changing faster than ever." And our experience confirms it—changes in what we do, how we do it, and who we do it with leave us breathless and overwhelmed.

What is happening to employees caught in the middle of all these changes? Stress, poor morale, attitudes of noncommitment and reactance—employees everywhere feel that teams and the zap of empowerment are just so many words to justify more work for less pay. Yet the need for change is evident. Companies have to change their focus to survive—from the mass production models of the industrial revolution to complex information systems in a global economy. We are overwhelmed and stressed; we want to go forward, but fear we are slipping back.

What is needed is a systematic way to help tired, angry employees deal with the realities of the workplace of today.

THE CHANGE CYCLE

Borrowing from the realm of psychotherapy, we can adopt a model of motivation for change that has been used and researched. It is readily

Contact information: Nancy Jackson, 592 S. Victor Way, Aurora, CO 80012, 303-363-1930, Nansolo@aol. com

adaptable for use in organizations to help employees and managers cope with the upheavals they face in the workplace.

The Change Cycle was developed by psychologists Prochaska, Norcross, and Diclemente watching what they called "successful self-changers." Since its development, the six-stage model has been used with thousands of changers in several countries. The results have been amazing. When changers are helped to identify their readiness and given the support they need, they are enabled and motivated to change, and they maintain the change over time. This model can be used in organizations to help employees respond more comfortably to the changes they face.

In this guide, the six stages of change and typical statements of a person who is in that stage will be described. Next, descriptions of some interventions that a coach may use to help the person resolve ambivalence and progress to the next stage will be described. To use the Change Cycle model, the coach needs to identify what stage the changer is in, to know where to begin the process. So it is important to understand what each stage looks like, and then what a person in that stage needs.

IDENTIFYING THE PHASES

Stage One-Precontemplation

The first stage is *Precontemplation*. A person in this stage may say, "They can't make me learn that program," "I have seniority, I'll be here forever," or, "Oh, other companies are going to TQM, but we never will." Precontemplation is denial or unawareness of the need for change. There may be rumors floating about the big move or downsizing, but the individual in the precontemplation stage denies, ignores, or avoids the information.

Stage Two-Contemplation

When individuals have passed precontemplation, they are in the second stage, which is *Contemplation*. In the contemplation stage, the individual considers the information and begins to think about it. "Some day I suppose I'll have to learn that program..." or, "Perhaps I'll have to take a class..." or, "I suppose our company will have to change its process ...." Like the government, which seems to be in a perpetual contemplation phase, a contemplator will say, "Some day we'll have to do something about inefficiency and waste." In this stage, commitment to change increases and ambivalence decreases until a decision is made and the next stage begins.

Stage Three-Determination

The third stage is *Determination*. The person has decided to change and begins to make plans and envision the future. The person begins time management strategies, scheduling, training, and other "preaction" activities in preparation for the change.

Stage Four-Action

Action is the next stage, in which the individual is actually performing, practicing, or executing the change. For example, the person might be using the new program, or new teams have been formed and are meeting, or the new marketing plan is in effect. (This is usually when most change efforts begin. Unfortunately, the first two steps are frequently omitted; there is often no warm-up, only action. But without warm-up, the action is incomplete and the changes may not last.)

Stage Five-Maintenance

The change process is not over with the action stage. The change won't really feel comfortable or "natural" for a period of months, or even years. Individuals need to go through a period of *Maintenance* in which new skills may be needed to manage a new way of behaving and to handle old habits that begin to creep back. The change cycle may end here, or may go to the next step.

Stage Six-Recycling

Finally, but not necessarily, there may be relapse or *Recycling*. Perhaps there was not enough support from upper management, perhaps it was a halfhearted implementation, or perhaps the training was inadequate; for whatever reason, the individual slips back and goes through the cycle again, as in: "I've quit smoking ... ten times!"

The six steps must be gone through in succession. Too fast a progression sends the person back to "go" and he or she has to begin again. Real change takes time and commitment.

COACHING MOTIVATION FOR CHANGE

As individuals go through the Change Cycle, they need different strategies for each stage, so training for coaches is needed to identify stages in the cycle and to know how to provide what is needed at the appropriate time. Skills practice in active listening, problem solving, and effective communication can greatly enhance the process.

What follows is a brief description of the interventions required at each stage of change. These interventions or supports can be given by trained coaches, change groups, or coworkers.

Precontemplation

In the first stage, precontemplation, the individual isn't even aware of the need for change, or may be in denial. "I don't even want to think about it!" To directly insist on change at this point is an invitation for resistance. In order to help a person see the need for change, information is needed. "Why this change? How will it impact me, what will happen if we don't change?" Information about why the individual *ought* to change is not helpful, but "just the facts" to clarify the situation.

Examples of "just the facts" might be:

✓ "This company has adopted this policy for this reason."
✓ "ABC company has taken over our market share and we have to respond."
✓ "By next year, management's goal is that all technicians will be certified in XYZ."
✓ "Here's where you are now. This is the goal. What will you do?"
✓ "This training will benefit you by ...."
✓ "It will take three weeks to change the equipment."
✓ "Your speed will be increased by 40 percent after training."

When people are in precontemplation, they may be defending against change. It is best not to directly attack a defended person, but to increase trust and approach the need for change in a matter-of-fact way. "Here is the situation. What do you want to do?" It is also important to let people know that they have a choice—no matter how limited that choice may be.

Contemplation

As the recognition begins to dawn that they may want to (or need to) change, people move into contemplation. At this stage, they need someone to listen to their ambivalence, and to reinforce their motivation. What are the pros and cons of the new way? What are the pros and cons of the old way? What are your hopes and fears? As people become aware of their ambivalence and fear, there is opportunity to listen and reinforce the motivation for change. There should be no forcing of people, only the opportunity to exercise whatever control over the process they may legitimately claim, and their concerns should be listened to sincerely. It can be helpful to remember that a person does not have to be 100 percent motivated to change, just more motivated than not motivated to begin changing.

Determination

In the determination stage, people are beginning to think about the future. What will the new offices look like? How will the team meetings be conducted? Can you see yourself as a coach and not a manager? Again, the person in the determination phase needs to be listened to and supported. Although it may be tempting to try to tell people in this phase how they ought to proceed and what they ought to do, it has been found to be more helpful to let them construct their plans and make their own choices. Of course, individuals need to know the parameters of their empowerment—"Which training session would you prefer, morning or afternoon?" rather than "You take the afternoon training so you can get your work done first." Choices made by the employee are motivating.

Another useful tool is visualization, or the envisioning of the future state. In this stage, the person is helped to identify potential roadblocks, try to solve problems and resolve difficulties before they actually arise. "What changes do you see in how you spend your day?" or, "How do you see the new technology affecting your interaction with the customer?" or, "What problems do you think you'll encounter with the other members of the team?" As individuals visualize themselves in the change, ambivalence may crop up. It is always helpful to listen to the changers' ambivalence, and to support them in a positive way.

Action

Last is the action phase—the implementation. At this stage, the individual may need very little in the way of support, especially if the previous stages have been thorough. Perhaps occasional "how's it going" check-ups and short discussions of problem solving will be all that are needed.

Maintenance

Just because things have been smooth for a while does not mean that the Change Cycle has been completed. Maintenance is critical. It takes a long while to truly change behavior, and the care and nurturing of a new behavior can make the difference between success and a relapse.

One great help to maintenance may be training in "soft skills" that will help individuals continue to cope with the current change as well as new changes they face. Individuals may profit from training in communication, problem solving, and other interpersonal skills, that can be reinforcing for all levels. Soft-skill training gives individuals new ways to look at their jobs, and new tools with which to manage their lives. At the risk of using the overused but truly wonderful concept, soft skills are empowering, and will help people cope with the next round of changes that is sure to develop.

Recycle

Finally, sometimes a recycle—a slip-up or relapse—may occur. This is not cause for despair. A relapse means that there were lapses in the commitment, the support, or the development of the cycle. The Change Cycle can be thought of as a spiral rather than a circle. Each time you go around, the trip is shorter, your ambivalence decreases, your commitment increases, and you will reach the goal.

When a relapse occurs, people need to examine their commitment. Where are they now? Probably back in contemplation—"I know I should, but ...." Excuses and delaying tactics appear again. People need more listening, perhaps some skill-building, and help with resolving their ambivalence. "Do I want to change? Why or why not?..." And off they go again, through the cycle. It is not uncommon for people to recycle many times. But with persistence and understanding, real, permanent change does happen.

APPLYING THE CHANGE CYCLE TO ORGANIZATIONS

The Change Cycle can be applied to the organization as a whole system, or on the individual level. There might be departments of a large organization in different phases of the cycle, while individuals within those departments may be at different phases depending upon their personalities, experiences, and adaptability.

Frequently, perfectly good programs are cut because the organization seems to be in a muddle. It has often been said that many of the failures of TQM, quality, work teams, or other programs were not caused by poor ideas, but by poor implementation. We simply did not know how to help people go through change.

Now, using the cycles of change, trainers, managers, and employees have a systematic way to diagnose the stage of change and apply the necessary supports to help people discover their own motivation for change.

Notice that the emphasis is on the level of the individual and not the implementation of the organization. One of the important findings of the research is that people respond with resistance (reactance) when they perceive that they are being forced to change. "Push me and I push back." Therefore, people have to be helped to resolve their own ambivalence and to find their own motivation to change. These strategies are effective with heroin addicts and smokers, and will help employees who don't like the idea of teams (for example) come to terms with their ambivalence.

SUMMARY

Organizations go through changes constantly, some of which are purposely imposed, some of which "just happen," and some of which sneak in the back door. We are engulfed by reengineering, process changes, and technological and cultural changes. It's about time that we had a method to help us cope and resolve the difficulties that change brings.

The six-step Cycle of Change used by therapists to help people change addictive behaviors can be used in organizations to relieve stress, avoid costly implementation disasters, and help motivate employees. In the long run it is more productive and less costly to give people what they need rather than forcefully impose new systems, structures, and technologies that leave people in the dust, tired and stressed.

REFERENCES

Miller, William and Stephen Rollnick. 1991. *Motivational Interviewing.* Guilford Press.

Prochaska, John, John Norcross, and Carlo Diclemente. 1994. *Changing for Good.* William Morrow and Company.

THE CYCLES OF CHANGE AND COACHING INTERVENTIONS

Phase	Precontemplation	Contemplation	Determination	Action	Maintenance	Recycle
Response	Denial	Ambivalence	Anxiety & stress	Action	Vigilance	Backslide
Need	Information	Resolve ambiguity	Deal with stress	Support	Support	Reinforcement
Statement	I don't have a problem, my problem is you.	Maybe I have a problem …	I've got to do something …	I'm ready to start.	How do I keep this up?	I tried and failed.
Coach	Give information, create doubt, establish trust	Listen, identify + and – of change	Help plan, give resources	Support, affirm motivation	Support, provide skills training	Evaluate problems and obstacles, check intentions
Questions to ask	What's wrong with the way things are now?	Will it be worth it?	What will you do?	How is it going?	What helps?	What's your intention today?

42

SEEKING EMPLOYEE OPINION

Kammy Haynes and Warren Bobrow

Overview   Attitude surveys are useful data collection tools that can lead to meaningful organizational change when developed, administered, analyzed, and used in the proper way. However, they can be detrimental to an organization if the data is misused or if the information is not used to make appropriate changes. There are fewer things worse than asking your employees for their opinions and then ignoring them. When you conduct an employee survey, you set up an expectation that action will be taken as a result. If no action is taken after the survey, any dissatisfaction that existed before will be magnified. This guide will provide you with methodologies to use and questions to ask your client in order to ensure that the survey meets its objectives and helps to move the client's organizational change efforts forward.

INTRODUCTION

Several factors have an impact on the successful design and implementation of an employee survey, including:

- Climate (trust, confidentiality, participation).
- Support from management at all levels.
- Clearly defined purpose (limit the scope).
- Choosing the right administration and analysis methodologies.
- Presenting the results in a meaningful, easy-to-understand, and actionable manner.
- Following through on action items and relating implementation to the survey results.

Contact Information: Kammy Haynes, The Context Group, 2073 Lake Shore Drive, Suite A, Chino Hills, CA 91709, 909-591-2848, kammyh@contextgroup.com, www.contextgroup.com

Warren Bobrow, The Context Group, 5812 W. 76th Street, Los Angeles, CA 90045, 310-670-4175, warrenb@contextgroup.com, www.contextgroup.com

Whether you are an internal or external consultant, the remainder of this guide will help you think through your survey project and make wise decisions.

Why Conduct an Employee Attitude Survey?

Several organizational issues could prompt you to conduct an employee attitude survey. Based on our experience, some of the most common reasons are:

- high turnover
- low productivity
- to measure understanding or opinions on a new program or process
- difficulty recruiting new employees

- low morale
- safety concerns
- to monitor progress as part of a process improvement program
- to justify changes in a program or process

In the end, the reason for conducting an employee survey is to answer a question. By asking the question(s), you create expectations that changes will be made and create an implicit commitment to respond. Unless the client organization is willing to take action on (at least some of) the results, you should not expend the time and effort to administer the survey. You can gather information on an informal basis to drive your decisions.

SURVEY DESIGN

It is important to have a clear understanding of the purpose of your survey before you design it. The choices you make regarding what is included in and what is left out of the survey will have a major impact on your ability to answer key questions down the line. It is critical that you discuss these issues with your client up front so there is no confusion at the end of the survey, when the data do not answer certain questions. For example, if the client were concerned about confidentiality or anonymity, minimal demographic information would be collected from each participant. As a result, you would be unable to determine whether there are significant differences between genders or age groups because you do not have that information.

Several elements go into survey design including the use of focus groups, item writing, negatively worded items, open- and closed-ended questions, demographic information for analysis, follow-up interviews, and number of items plus completion time. Each of these elements is discussed below.

Focus Groups. Focus groups are very effective for determining critical areas to include on a survey. By involving some employees in the survey design process, you can develop an increased level of support and buy-in for the survey. Employees are able to see that their issues (in their words, if possible) are on the survey. The goodwill this creates is extremely helpful when conducting surveys in environments where there is a lack or low level of trust between employees and management.

In practice, allowing participants to brainstorm the issues is more effective than reviewing an existing survey. When deciding which issues to include on the survey, you need to determine whether management is prepared to investigate or address them as a result of the survey findings. One issue that often appears is pay. In most cases, employees feel that they are underpaid. If management has no intention of researching pay disparity or making any attempt to rectify the issue (assuming there is disparity in the industry or within the company), you should consider eliminating that issue from the survey. On the other hand, you may decide to keep the issue(s) to determine the level of dissatisfaction and identify whether there are some departments or job positions that are harder hit by the pay issue. It's a judgment call that is, as always, influenced by the climate and the level of management support.

Focus groups can also be useful for getting employees involved in the action-planning phase of the project. Once the results have been presented, focus groups can be used to prioritize action items or to begin brainstorming solutions. The continuing involvement of employees in the project will reinforce the organization's commitment to employee participation.

Item Writing. When developing survey items, it is important to limit each statement or question to one idea. That is, avoid items that ask about two or more concepts. An example of a poorly written (double-barreled) statement is: "My supervisor is available and willing to help me solve problems." This item will be difficult to answer unless the participant feels the same way about both halves of the statement (availability and willingness). However, if one half is true and the other is false, the participant is likely to choose a middle rating, as if to average the two ideas together. It is better to ask the two halves as separate questions: a) "My supervisor is available to help me solve problems." b) "My supervisor is willing to help me solve problems."

It is helpful if you can pilot the items with a small sample of employees to ensure that there is consistent interpretation of the questions and to catch confusing or double-barreled questions before you begin administering the survey.

Negatively Worded Items. In order to prevent participants from getting into a response pattern (e.g., always marking the "strongly agree" option), item writers use negatively worded items such as: "My coworkers do not take pride in their work." These items cause the participant to pay closer attention to the question and to consider using other points on the rating scale. It is important to make these items easy to understand so that you do not create confusion about how employees should respond to convey their opinions. For example, "There is not poor communication between divisions" requires too much processing ("poor" is negative, and "not" negates the negative, which makes it positive). That statement will create confusion and inaccurate results. Keep your negatively worded items simple, and do not use many of them in your survey.

Closed-Ended Questions. In order to collect a large amount of data while minimizing the amount of time it takes to complete surveys, use closed-ended statements. Examples of closed-ended statements are "I like my coworkers" and " I receive adequate training to perform my job."

When using closed-ended items, develop rating scales (most often to measure agreement or satisfaction) geared to the particular topic of the statement. It is important to clearly define each scale point so that everyone is rating items the same way. Participants need a frame of reference so they are using the same "ruler" to measure their level of agreement or satisfaction. For example, rather than giving participants directions that say "1 = Strongly Disagree and 5 = Strongly Agree," it is important to define what the points in the middle (2, 3, and 4) mean.

Open-Ended Questions. Open-ended questions allow participants to say what's on their minds, using their own words. Examples of open-ended questions are: "What do you like best about working at MNO Industries? What three things could be done to improve working conditions at RS Corporation in the next 12 months? What are the top five reasons that would cause you to leave JJ Inc.?" Remember that you are directing the participants to focus on the positive or negative depending on the way you phrase the questions. Take that focus into account when you begin to blend the results from the open-ended questions with those from the closed-ended questions to draw conclusions or make recommendations.

When using open-ended questions, you need a plan for interpreting the data. We have found that coding comments is a useful approach. Some common themes that emerge in most surveys are communication, pay, advancement opportunities, quality of supervision, training, and fairness. By grouping comments into these areas and assigning codes, we can integrate the content with the rest of the item responses and present the results in an organized and easy-to-understand format for the client.

It is important to limit the number of responses you want for each open-ended question. In most cases, three to five answers are sufficient (consider the number of employees you have and the data entry and analysis that will be required to process the responses).

Demographics. Depending on the question(s) you are attempting to answer in your survey, here is a list of demographic information that you may want to collect from your participants:

- department or division
- supervisor or manager
- ethnicity
- age
- gender
- tenure with the company

Remember, the more demographic information you collect, the more likely participants are to feel that you can identify them as individuals. Consider including only the items that will enable you to perform the needed analyses without compromising the confidentiality of your survey.

We do not recommend "coding" surveys in a surreptitious manner (e.g., assigning different dates or footnotes to different departments). This tactic is most often used in environments where there is little trust or confidence in management. When the coding is discovered (and it will be because your participants are already suspicious), you will have reinforced the distrust and undermined the project.

Follow-Up Interviews. Post-survey interviews can be useful in clearing up seemingly contradictory results and adding detail to general findings. While you may plan for these interviews in your overall project plan, you need not be wedded to completing the interviews if the preliminary survey results do not warrant the need for additional detail. Again, refer to your survey objective to determine whether the extra time, cost, and imposition on the participants is worth it. In some cases, you may decide that follow-up interviews are of little value in the overall scheme of the project.

There are two basic options for follow-up interviews: face-to-face or phone interviews. Like other decisions, this one will be affected by the organizational climate. If there is a high level of trust, then either format will be accepted and the final decision is likely to be based on scheduling and locations. If there is not a high level of trust, the interviewer may be more successful in getting candid responses by phone (particularly if the client organization is not privy to the list of interviewees and interviewees are promised that their names will not be revealed).

There appears to be a bimodal distribution of employees who agree to participate in follow-up interviews. They are either relatively dissatisfied with the way things are going and want to discuss their key issues or relatively satisfied and want to say something nice about the company or some specific employees. The employees in the middle seem to be less inclined to participate in follow-up interviews. Keep an eye out for this type of division in the interview responses, and take it into account as you begin to synthesize interview and survey data. Be careful not to let the opinions of these follow-up groups override those of the larger group.

Number of items plus completion time. Another consideration when designing a survey is the number of items, the depth and breadth of topics, and the expected completion time. In today's work environment, there is considerable pressure to collect as much data as you can in a short period of time. Focus on closed-ended questions whereby employees are asked to indicate their level of agreement with (and perhaps the importance of) a particular statement. Then ask for the participant's top three responses to three or four open-ended questions. This format allows you to cover a wide variety of topics, in some depth, in approximately 30 minutes of each participant's time.

SURVEY ADMINISTRATION

Depending on the objective of your survey, there are options regarding data collection. As with any methodology, there are advantages and disadvantages to each approach.

Survey Frequency. When determining how frequently to administer a survey, remember that the time lapse between data gathering and action should be short, and there needs to be enough time between surveys to measure changes. Also, it can be expensive to administer surveys to everyone in your company on a frequent basis. We recommend that if you are surveying frequently (e.g., once per quarter), you give the survey to only a sample of your workforce at a time, but ensure that everyone has the chance to complete it every few administrations.

If the survey is going to be given less frequently (e.g., once per year), administer it to everyone. The decision regarding frequency and follow-up should be included in your initial project plan to the client.

Sampling. If you elect not to survey everyone, several sampling options are available.

- *Random Sampling.* This involves using a computer or other neutral process to choose a certain percentage of employees. The advantage of this process is that, more often than not, you will have a good cross section of employees take the survey at any given time. The downside is that random samples are not always representative of your population, which may lead some people to feel that they are unfairly picked on or that some groups are over- or underrepresented.

- *Stratified Sampling.* This type of sampling involves randomly sampling within certain parameters. For instance, you may want the sample to accurately reflect the proportion of males and females within each department. This process guarantees a more accurate representation, but it adds an administrative burden. Stratified sampling is most often used when you are interested in looking for differences between groups of participants.

- *Targeted or Non-Random Sampling.* You may choose to survey everyone in a certain group (e.g., the accounting department). This approach is good for getting at specific issues, but the results may not be generalizable to the rest of the organization (although it has been found that what is going on in one area is often going on in others).

Internal versus External Administration. External administration has the advantage of the appearance of neutrality, while internal consultants are often automatically seen as biased toward either management or the employees. Whether you are an internal or external consultant may determine which of the drawbacks and potential solutions apply to your situation. In either case, the client's organizational climate will have an impact on how you proceed.

DATA COLLECTION

Many of your decisions about the data collection process will be driven by the purpose of the survey and the client's organizational culture. While there are no hard-and-fast rules, there are options that you need to discuss with your client.

Mass administration. Group administration sessions (gathering groups in a central location for a scheduled period of time) provide several positive outcomes:

- Return rate is increased (80 to 100%, well above the rate for mail-out surveys).

- Participants see that the organization is serious about getting input since they are being paid to take time out of the regular workday.

- Administrators can answer questions about the survey.

- The data is collected over a short period of time, so processing can begin sooner.

- Postage costs are lowered.

Potential Drawbacks	Potential Solutions
A perception of less confidentiality since you could be sitting next to your supervisor.	Ask supervision to complete their surveys at their desks or in another location.
Someone at the company is charged with collecting the surveys, which could compromise confidentiality.	Make a neutral party responsible for collecting and forwarding the surveys for data processing.
Resistance to shutting down the company to complete the survey.	Administer the survey in small groups so that someone is always on duty.
Concern that employees might be absent that day and not be able to participate.	Track participants and allow individuals who were absent on the day of administration to mail the completed survey directly to the data processing group.

Administered by mail (to homes or via internal company mail). The mail-in option is useful for clients who have few employees at a large number of geographically dispersed locations or do not have a work location to which employees report (e.g., salespeople and telecommuters). It is also used by companies that are not interested in the mass administration option. Advantages of this option include:

- It provides the highest perceived level of confidentiality, since no one in the client organization touches the survey (assuming it is mailed directly to an outside vendor for data processing and analysis).

- It requires less active participation from the client organization (no need to schedule meeting rooms, provide refreshments, etc.).

Potential Drawbacks	Potential Solutions
Poor response rate because participants get busy, forget, or don't see the survey as a priority. (Response rates can be as low as 35%.)	Send reminder notes (from the CEO or COO) to encourage participation, and stating the importance of participation. However, this follow-up is time-consuming and may result in only a small increase in the return rate.
Because the organization is completely "hands-off," there may be an impression that there is little support or interest from the top management echelons.	Hold meetings prior to the survey to explain the purpose of the survey and express its importance.

Administered via computer (e.g. intranet, Internet). In an effort to reduce paper handling and data processing, many clients prefer to administer their surveys via electronic media. Advantages of this method include:

- Data is automatically sent to a database, reducing the time and cost associated with data entry.
- The survey distribution process is simplified (e.g., survey can be attached in an e-mail, at a Web site link, or its file name and location referenced in a memo).
- Matches the nature of the organization (i.e., technologically savvy audience, reinforcing the need to be more computer literate).
- May create the impression that the survey is easier to complete than a hard copy version (i.e., complete it and hit the Send button).

Potential Drawbacks	Potential Solutions
Perceived lack of confidentiality if company officials have access to the files and individual responses.	Set up additional passwords or firewalls to minimize security breaches.
	Don't associate names or other identifying information with individual surveys.

Potential Drawbacks	Potential Solutions
Cost and time needed to set up the technology.	Work with Information Technology department or rely on outside vendors for support. Look at which process fits with your existing infrastructure.
Lack of comfort with a computerized process (intimidated by technology).	Offer the survey in hard copy format or provide some training on the process prior to administering the survey.
Poor response rate because participants get busy, forget, or don't see the survey as a priority, or the survey gets lost in the vast number of e-mails received each day.	Send reminder notes (from the CEO or COO), to encourage participation, stating the importance of participation. However, this follow-up is time-consuming and may result in only a small increase in the rate of return.

Confidentiality. Individual surveys should be confidential (e.g., no one from the client organization will read an individual's survey and know that it is his or hers). However, the degree to which people are asked to identify themselves for the sake of group analysis should be considered carefully. It is common to ask people which department or area they work in and how long they have been with the organization. But more identifying questions may lead to more raised suspicions. In trusting cultures, this is not as much of a problem as it is in more toxic cultures. Be aware of the trade-off between doing more detailed analyses and receiving less candid responses from the participants. Experience shows that there are rarely as many group differences as management thinks there will be (i.e., the culture of the company cuts across most groups).

DATA ANALYSIS

It is important to reach an agreement with the client during the design phase as to what the final feedback will look like. While there may be some adjustments based on the findings, this up-front agreement will minimize a number of costly and time-consuming fishing expeditions when the client asks for more and more breakdowns that do not contribute to the original purpose of the survey.

Methodologies. The analysis methodologies will be driven by the objectives of the survey. You want to be able to answer the key questions posed in the survey without overwhelming the client with details and statistics (which are best saved for appendices). If you want to report on individual items, keep the statistics simple (e.g., average scores and frequencies). If you want to report on overall themes, more sophisticated statistical analyses (correlations and factor analysis) may be required. You will also want to create an objective way of classifying responses to open-ended questions.

Data Interpretation. The numbers don't mean much by themselves. You have to be clear in explaining what the data means and how it relates to the question(s) you are trying to answer. Here are some common errors to help your clients avoid:

- Interpreting correlations as causation (e.g., "low satisfaction leads to a high intention to leave the company").

- Overemphasizing small score differences (e.g., "My division got a 3.4 and yours got a 3.2, so I'm a better manager than you are").

- Assuming that satisfaction or agreement equates with importance or criticality. Just because the participants feel strongly about an issue doesn't mean it is important to them. In fact, there is often a low correlation between the two, so if you want to know importance, add that rating scale to the survey.

- Overreacting to open-ended comments (e.g., "Anything you would like to add?") that tend to bring out more negative than positive responses. If things are going well or at least okay, participants aren't as compelled to make additional comments.

PRESENTING RESULTS

Narrative. Tell a story that has a beginning (this is why we are doing the survey), a middle (what the data tells us), and an end (this is what we recommend). In order to keep this portion of the report manageable, try the following tips:

- Be concise and stay focused on one point at a time.

- End each section with a recommendation that will move the client forward (including "Keep up the good work," since the tendency for consultants and clients is to focus on fixing whatever is broken).

- Be able to fully back up your conclusions and recommendations with data.

- Don't make excuses or try to explain away unexpected results. This is particularly true for surveys with high response rates, because the data speaks for itself. Simply present the data and proposed action items.

- Use numbers to illustrate and support your conclusions, but save the details for appendices.

Graphs and Charts. Present results in meaningful and manageable chunks. Presenting a sea of numbers in graphs, charts, and tables usually makes people's eyes glaze over and creates more confusion than it alleviates. The object is to get people to understand the results and their implications. The audience will often dictate the mode or style of presentation (e.g., their interest in detail and level of sophistication or their preference for written or oral reports).

What to Present. By conducting a survey, you are committing to a certain amount of openness regarding the results. However, there are cultural and practical considerations regarding who gets the information and the amount of detail included. It is common practice to give the details of the survey to the project sponsor to be used in formulating recommendations and action plans, while presenting the overall results and action plans to the participants. Depending on the structure and climate of the organization, you may want to make more detail available to everyone (on hard copy or via intranet, with or without verbatim open-ended comments) to increase their level of buy-in and commitment to making the necessary changes. This information-sharing needs to be considered in light of concerns about anonymity and confidentiality. If participants feel singled out or exposed, they will not participate (candidly) in future survey efforts. You also run the risk of analysis paralysis when employees are busy reinterpreting the data, making excuses, or pointing fingers rather than taking action.

Preserving Anonymity. Open-ended comments are invaluable in understanding the ratings on a survey. If you ask people their opinions in a confidential setting, you will get them. It's a good idea to share verbatim comments with those involved in interpreting the survey. However, some comments compromise the anonymity of the survey: "My boss treats me unfairly because I'm the only Hispanic in the department." Even if the writer is unconcerned about his or her identify becoming known, you won't be able to guarantee anonymity in future surveys if anyone is identified in the current one. Our guideline is to read the comments first, then edit out information that may lead to a participant being identified. We would edit the previous comment to read, "My boss treats [some people] unfairly" before compiling the final report. This retains the content of the comment without compromising the identity of the participant or the supervisor.

MAKING RECOMMENDATIONS

The kinds of recommendations you make will depend on how much you know about the organization and what your role is on the project. If the survey is part of a larger organizational change effort, you may be directly involved in implementing the changes that are indicated in the survey results. In other cases, you may be making recommendations that other consultants will carry out, or leaving the results of the survey in the hands of the client to implement. In any case, the following need to be included in your recommendations in order to increase the likelihood that action will be taken in response to the survey results:

- Tie the recommendation to a specific result in the survey. This strengthens the link between what the employees said and whatever action you are suggesting.
- Suggest tools or procedures that could be used to easily accomplish the task you have recommended.
- Link the recommendation to the survey objective.

For example, "Given that 68% of employees did not receive performance feedback last year [*result*], we suggest that you enforce the performance appraisal meeting guidelines that you already have in your management plan. Perhaps a checklist of meetings completed (and signed by each employee) that is submitted to Human Resources on a monthly basis would be a useful tool for ensuring compliance [*tool or procedure*]. This action item will directly affect the performance management system and improve productivity [*survey objective*]."

DEVELOPING ACTION PLANS

In addition to making recommendations, which are often presented in narrative form, you may want to consider developing a project plan with tentative timelines and resource needs to help your client get started. Despite the best intentions of most clients, there is often a letdown after the results of an employee survey come back. An action plan can help maintain the motivation level needed to respond to the results and create "immediate" improvements. The longer the time lapse between the administration, the presentation of results, and resulting action, the less confidence the employees will have that their input was taken seriously and valued. In order to have a positive impact on morale, timely action is required.

SUMMARY

Key points to remember when designing and implementing your employee attitude survey are:

- Keep your objective in mind during each phase.

- Maintain confidentiality.

- Consider the implications of your design and implementation decisions.

- Pay attention to the survey design.

- Monitor data collection.

- Consider the level of data analysis.

- Present results thoughtfully.

- Make careful recommendations.

- Take prompt action whenever possible to demonstrate the organization's commitment to improvement.

- Publish actions that are taken in response to the survey, so employees know that you have heard them and took their opinions seriously.

- Make the survey a positive experience (an open channel of communication, a step toward progress).

Each client and organization is unique. A survey process that works well for one client may be inappropriate for another. By examining the advantages and drawbacks at each decision point, you will be able to deliver a well-crafted and useful organizational diagnostic tool that will help the client answer important questions and will better meet the client's business objectives.

43

INITIATING AND MANAGING CHANGE

Nora Carrol

Overview Today's combination of external and internal workplace pressure guarantees that every organization must face change. Because change represents some element of the unknown, it implies risk. The organization undergoing change can risk its human, physical, and technological resources, its collective knowledge, even its competitive marketplace position in attempting to handle change.

Risk demands that organizations plan for change, rather than waiting for it to happen and then trying to cope after the fact. This guide is a step-by-step chronology, presenting the seven key processes necessary for planning and managing change, regardless of the industry, sector, or region in which the organization operates. Because each process is addressed in question-and-answer format, the guide serves as a workbook, and the organization's stakeholders are the primary resources for providing effective, applicable answers to the questions posed.

STEP ONE: ESTABLISHING YOUR MISSION AND PURPOSE

Any organization or component of an organization must agree upon its overall mission and purpose before any change planning begins. The process of asking and answering the following questions will help lay the foundation for a successful change process.

- Do you already have a formal mission statement?

- If you do, does it accurately reflect your organization and what it offers? If not, why not? Does it need to change?

Contact Information: Nora Carrol, The First Forward Institute, Inc., 5836 Orchard Hill Court, Clifton, VA 20124-1072, 703-266-1266, ncarrol@ffinst.com, www.ffinst.com

- If you do not have one, what actions are necessary in order to formulate and approve a mission statement?

- Can you formulate a mission statement strictly within your unit, department, or division, or does formulation require participation and approval of other parts of the organization?

- Are there legal and institutional ramifications to any statement you formulate?

- How much time do you think you need to formulate a statement of mission?

STEP TWO: AUDITING YOUR CURRENT ORGANIZATION

Products and Services

Your mission and purpose should be reflected in the products or services that you offer to your markets.

- Do the products or services you offer reflect your mission and purpose? If yes, how? If no, why not?

- If there is a conflict or conflicts, how can you resolve it or them? What people or processes need to be involved?

Market Identification and Development

Markets constitute your primary source of revenue, but the type and characteristics of the markets you serve should match your mission and purpose.

- Do you already have a formal statement of the markets you serve now? The markets you want to serve in the future?

- If yes, does the statement differentiate between market segments in a way that allows you to identify each segment and understand the distinctions between them?

- If you do not have a formal statement of markets, what must you do to create it?

- How many levels of authority are involved in setting market development goals?

- Do you believe that your market development expectations are realistic as related to your mission and goals?

- If not, what is necessary to make them attainable?

Unit or Organization

Your own unit's mission and purpose should relate to or reflect the mission and purpose of the organization as a whole. It is important, therefore, to compare them.

- Do your mission and purpose match, complement, or conflict with those of the organization?
- If you cannot tell, why not? If you aren't sure, what processes are needed to recognize the larger mission and purpose?

Capacities and Capabilities

Your capacities and capabilities represent what you currently can do, using existing resources. Assessing both is essential to identifying gaps that must be filled in order to handle change while respecting your mission and purpose.

- Does your unit have the capacity and capability to handle its responsibilities? If yes, in what manner? If no, why not?
- If there are gaps in capacity or capability, what are they?
- What is the impact of those gaps on your unit? What must you do to close those gaps?
- How do your unit's capacities and capabilities affect the organization as a whole? Are they complementary or in conflict?
- What must you do to achieve a maximum match between capacities, capabilities, and meeting your organizational mission and purpose?

Cost and Revenue Performance

While revenue is clearly a function and result of products or services and market development and may not be a mission in itself, it must be considered in order to determine its impact on the organization and its interaction with change efforts.

- Are there formal, enforced revenue expectations within your unit? If so, are you meeting those expectations?
- If there are no formal expectations, do you expect them to be introduced, and when?
- How often do you report your revenues to the supervising authority, and who is that supervising authority?

- Do you have the flexibility to make revenue adjustments during the fiscal year?

- Do you submit your own budget showing projected revenues and costs, with approval granted for both at once?

- If you do not get approval on revenues and costs at the same time, what process is followed?

- Are you satisfied with your budgeting process and your involvement in it?

- If you are not, what changes do you want to occur?

- Are your revenue expectations in line with or at odds with your mission and purpose?

STEP THREE: SCANNING YOUR EXTERNAL ENVIRONMENT

The third phase of preparation for planned change is the conducting of an environmental or external scan. This step is particularly important in that it provides points of comparison between what you are doing, what competitors are doing, and what you want to be doing.

An external scan should explore the following issues:

- direct competition,

- indirect competition,

- concepts of competition,

- markets being served by competitors, and

- regulatory or external requirements and influences impacting your organization.

Direct Competition

Direct competitors have products or services that parallel yours and have a clearly discernible similarity in the eyes of the marketplace.

- Who are your direct competitors?

- What is it in their products or services that makes them direct competitors?

Indirect Competition

Indirect competition may exist in the form of products or services that overlap in some way with yours.

- Who are your indirect competitors and what do they offer?
- If you do not know, what resources and information do you need to find out?

Markets

The concept of markets (rather than market) is based on the belief that there are distinct differences separating markets from each other, and that those differences represent the most important characteristics for marketers to consider.

- Do you serve individual or organizational (business-to-business) markets, or both?
- Who are your markets, in descending order of importance? (If you have both individual and organizational markets, list them separately.)
- What are the most important behavioral characteristics of each market you have listed?
- Which of those markets are served by direct competitors? By indirect competitors?

Regulatory or External Requirements and Influences

- What regulatory or external requirements have an impact on your **organization**?
- Which have an impact on your direct and indirect competitors?
- Do external influences vary by the type of organization your competitors are?

STEP FOUR: CONDUCTING MARKET RESEARCH

Before selecting market research options, it is necessary to know both the research purpose and the research stages or formats.

- Do you want to do an introductory investigation, establish patterns of behavior among markets, or confirm earlier findings?
- Does it make sense to collect quantitative (volume) or qualitative (in-depth) data, or both?

Capability

- Do you have the capability to conduct research, or should you hire an outside source?

- How much analyzed data already exist to act as a foundation for further research?

STEP FIVE: CREATING A CONTINUUM—SHORT-TERM AND LONG-TERM GOALS

You have now determined your mission and purpose, conducted your internal and external investigation, assessed your products, services, and markets, and made some determinations about market research in preparation for further development. Now it's time to begin planning for change!

Planning and implementing change cannot and should not occur all at once: It makes far more sense to divide your efforts into short- and long-term activities. This strategy will enable you to test and analyze different ideas, and make refinements before investing in major long-term change.

Begin by deciding the following:

- What do you want changed?
- When do you want the change(s) to occur, with timetables for each?
- Who can champion those changes?
- What resources will be needed to accomplish the desired change(s)?
- What processes or structural components are needed to implement the change(s)?
- What is the content of what you want to change?
- What is its depth (penetration of organization) and scope (breadth of impact)?
- What is the underlying process that must support it?
- In what order of priority should desired changes occur?

Change Agents

Change is best accomplished when specific people, who have already been convinced of the need for change, take on the responsibility for planning and implementation. They are typically called change agents and champion the effort internally.

As you examine your priority list of desired changes, it is necessary to decide:

- Who will be most effective in leading everyone toward the change you want?
- What roles do those people currently serve?
- What responsibilities and authority must your change agents have to be effective in implementing the changes desired?
- Are these change agents internal (within the immediate organization) or external (outside the immediate organization)?

Organizational and Cultural Change

- What needs to happen at the organizational level to implement the desired changes? Reallocation of resources? New job descriptions? New reporting lines? New structure? Time set aside for planning, decision making, and approvals?
- What kind of organizational culture do you have, and how might it interact with change?
- Is your organization's structure formal or informal? A hierarchy, a matrix, or something else?
- Are decisions made from the top down, bottom up, or laterally? Is your decision-making process authoritative, consensus or collective, or individualistic?
- What kind of management style exists? Is it management by directive, by objectives, participatory, or other?

STEP SIX: DEVELOPING AND IMPLEMENTING AN ACTION PLAN

Implementation is the most difficult phase of an action plan, because it requires the selection, allocation, and oversight of resources to accomplish the desired changes.

Action Planning

- What are your priorities for change?
- How can you operationalize them? Can you depend entirely on internal resources and processes, or do you need assistance from external resources?
- How can you transfer the operationalized change goals into an interactive timetable?

- How can you assess and evaluate your efforts to implement and manage change?

STEP SEVEN: INTEGRATING CHANGE PLANNING INTO YOUR SYSTEM

Change planning is an ongoing, proactive process and way of thinking, not something that is done only once. As such, it is most effective when built into your organization as a permanent part of its strategic processes.

Change Triggers

There are conditions and situations under which change is most likely; these should be considered triggers that act as early warnings and can alert you to the need for heightening your analytic and planning efforts. These triggers are usually caused by:

- internal organizational change, in mission, goals, or objectives; or
- external change, in markets, technological developments, or condition and status of competitors or competitors' offerings.

Early-Warning System

It is critical to perceive triggers through an early-warning system, allowing you to recognize impending change internally and externally before changes are beyond your control.

- Who, in each of your functional or structural areas, is best able to scan the internal and external environments and report on early signals of change in that area?
- Who, in a supervisory role, is best able to authorize a response to warnings of change?
- What is the most efficient way to communicate needed changes?
- What processes need to occur to react to early warnings of change?
- When must you go outside of your immediate domain to respond to early warnings of change?
- Who can be assigned to coordinate your recommended responses to upcoming change? To implement those recommendations?

- Who is an effective negotiator and spokesperson to represent your area when response to upcoming change requires the cooperation of other organizational units?

- What can be done to recruit support among management and non-management personnel for the change(s) proposed?

Feedback System

An early-warning system will not resolve problems unless warnings are communicated to the appropriate personnel in a timely manner and then acted upon. Once you have developed your early-warning process, you are ready to construct a feedback system.

- To whom should your scanners or agents go for the greatest volume of internal feedback? The greatest depth of feedback?

- Do you currently have a mechanism for acquiring and recording market (customer) comments and responses on your products or services and organizational image? If yes, what is that mechanism? Is it actively used? If no, what do you need to do to create and approve such a mechanism?

- Do you communicate with professional colleagues at other organizations? If yes, do you have a mechanism for integrating the results into your feedback?

- Do you serve as a formal or informal communications link with other units on change-related issues? If yes, how can you integrate the effort into feedback? If no, how do you think you can establish such a link?

- At this time, can you create an organizational diagram for a feedback system that will serve your needs? If no, do you have internal resources to assist you in creating it?

- What processes need to occur for you to be able to react to early warnings of change?

- When must you go outside of your immediate domain to respond to early warnings of change?

- Who can be assigned to coordinate your recommended responses to upcoming change? To implement those recommendations?

- Who is an effective negotiator and spokesperson to represent your area when response to upcoming change requires the cooperation of other organizational units?

- What can be done to recruit support among management and non-management personnel for the change(s) proposed?

CONCLUSION

The processes of planning for and managing change impact every part of the organization, and thus require the involvement of every organizational stakeholder or interested party. It is essential that each organization be honest with itself and identify who those stakeholders are, recognizing which stakeholders:

- have a critical versus marginal impact on the organization;
- have a temporary versus permanent relationship with the organization;
- hold a stakeholder role inside versus outside the organization; and
- have direct versus indirect influence, outside the organization, on markets and competition.

Is this analysis really necessary? It cannot be underestimated in importance! There are too many cases of otherwise well-designed change efforts that have gone awry because the organization did not acknowledge, understand, or include some stakeholder group in its change planning and management initiative.

44

UNDERSTANDING CHANGE THROUGH OTHER PEOPLE'S EYES

Vicki Schneider

Overview By the time leaders ask their organizations to change, they have already analyzed the situation, determined the best course of action to take, and are standing, banner in hand, wondering why their team isn't charging up the hill behind them.

The reason is rather simple. In the process of contemplating the change, the leaders came to grips with the personal losses they would incur and had identified, at least on a visceral level, the rewards that would replace them. To the leaders, who have already gone through the thought process, the need for the change is obvious and the sacrifices that have to be made are accepted as necessary and reasonable.

What leaders often fail to realize is that change, especially significant change, will force others to give up things they value greatly. Until the leader recognizes and understands what each person is being asked to give up, the change, no matter how essential, will likely be met with crippling resistance. The loss each team member anticipates may seem insignificant to an outsider; but it may be important enough to cause the individual to resist or even undermine the change.

This interactive exercise helps leaders and associates look at change and its related losses through other people's eyes; understand better why they and others resist change; and develop insights that will lead to a more sensitive and successful change climate.

Suggested Time 30 to 60 minutes

Materials Needed
✔ Three pennies
✔ Three stick-figure drawings or colorful scribbles
✔ Three $20 bills

Contact Information: Vicki Schneider, Vantage Solutions, 4434 Waveland Court, Hamburg, NY 14075-2003, 716-627-3345, VSTECNY@aol.com

325

    ✔   Form A (Instructions for "contestants")

    ✔   Form B (One set of cards for each member of the "audience")

Procedure

1. Select three members from the audience to be contestants in "The Great Giveaway."

2. Give each contestant one of the cards from Form A, one penny, one drawing, and one $20 bill. Tell the contestants to read their instructions to themselves and stay apart from the other contestants.

3. Divide the audience into thirds. Assign one-third of the audience (left, center, right) to each of the three contestants.

4. Distribute one set of cards from Form B to each member of the audience.

5. Tell the audience that each contestant will be asked to give up one of the three objects in order to move forward. The contestant will eventually give up two of the three objects. The audience members' job is to predict which object their contestant will have left at the end of the game—the penny, the drawing, or the $20 bill. (Show the audience the three objects.)

6. Ask the audience to make their predictions. Instruct them to keep the card that has that item written on it. Caution the audience not to show their cards to anyone until they are asked to.

7. Collect the rest of the cards from the audience members, taking care to keep the audience and the contestants from seeing what's on them.

8. Have the three contestants line up next to one another across the front of the room.

9. Ask the contestants to decide which of their three objects they want to give you. Take that object from the first contestant, announce the object, and have the contestant take one step forward. Repeat this process for the other two contestants.

10. Ask the contestants to decide which of the remaining two objects they want to give you. Take that object from the first contestant, announce the object, and have the contestant take one step forward. Repeat this process for the other two contestants.

    The three contestants are now at the finish line. In all likelihood, they have kept different objects.

11. Ask the first one-third of the audience (right side) to hold up their cards, showing which object they thought their contestant would have kept.

12. In all likelihood, some of the audience will be correct and some will be wrong. Ask volunteers to explain why they chose what they chose.

13. Ask the first contestant why he or she kept that object.

14. Repeat steps 11 to 13 for the second contestant (middle section of audience), and again for the third contestant (left section of audience).

15. Debrief by asking:

- What did the contestants know that you didn't? What effect did your differing perspectives have on the outcome? How could you have had a better chance of predicting the right object?

- As we ask people to change, we ask them to leave things behind —both tangibles and intangibles. Many times people resist change because we are asking them to leave behind something of value to them that we value differently. How can we use what we learned from this activity to better understand why people (or why you) resist change?

Select from among the following questions, depending on your learning objectives, and have participants share their experiences in groups of 2 to 5. After 20 minutes, ask for volunteers to provide insights into what they have learned about themselves and others.

- Think of a major change you are going through right now. What are you being asked to leave behind? If you embrace the change, what things of equal or greater value to you might replace that loss?

- Think of a change you've gone through in your life that you resisted. What were you being asked to leave behind? Why was that such a difficult loss for you? How did you overcome your resistance? If you successfully implemented that change, what replaced the thing(s) you lost?

- Think of someone who is resisting change. What do you think the person is being asked to leave behind? How can you find out? How can you help the person identify something to replace that loss?

Reinforcing Activity

Conduct a "brain dump" at the end of the session: Ask participants to state the insights they gained from the session. You or a scribe should write them, without discussion, on a chart. Keep adding comments until all comments have been exhausted.

THE GREAT GIVEAWAY (FORM A)

Instructions to Trainer: Cut these cards apart and give a different card to each of the contestants.

Instructions to Contestant A:

During this game you will be asked to give away two of the objects you start the game with.

In making your decisions, keep in mind that the penny is worth $.01, the drawing is a worthless scribble, and the $20 bill is worth twenty dollars.

None of the objects has any unusual significance or value.

Instructions to Contestant B:

During this game you will be asked to give away two of the objects you start the game with.

In making your decisions, keep in mind that the drawing is a worthless scribble and the $20 bill is worth twenty dollars.

The penny, however, is a very rare coin that completes your collection and is worth a lot of money.

Instructions to Contestant C:

During this game you will be asked to give away two of the objects you start the game with.

In making your decisions, keep in mind that the penny is worth $.01 and the $20 bill is worth twenty dollars.

The drawing was the first piece of artwork your autistic child ever drew, and it has a great deal of sentimental value for you.

THE GREAT GIVEAWAY (FORM B)

Instructions to Trainer: Copy this entire form for each member of the audience. Cut the sections apart into three cards before distributing a full set to each audience member.

At the end of The Great Giveaway,
I believe my contestant will be left with

A Penny

At the end of The Great Giveaway,
I believe my contestant will be left with

A $20 Bill

At the end of The Great Giveaway,
I believe my contestant will be left with

A Drawing

45

DISCUSSING CHANGE AND INNOVATION

Scott Simmerman

Overview Managing and leading change requires both influence and involvement. It helps to know the desired direction of the initiative, it's important to have a sense of the process of change, and it's imperative that change masters involve and engage people in the transformation process as it occurs. People involved in the process understand the real expectations and are less surprised as things change.

This exercise includes one of my favorite metaphors and is packaged to be quite flexible in delivery. It is easy to lead, engages people in a discussion of "The Answer," and lends itself to the discovery that teams create a far better set of possibilities than any one individual can. The exercise is meant to be done "with" people rather than "to" them, so that we minimize resistance to change and generate active participation within the metaphor and among participants.

Suggested Time 20 minutes

Materials Needed
- ✓ Form A (Square Wheels One)
- ✓ Form B (It is dangerous to know The Answer)
- ✓ Optional: A wide variety of butterfly stickers, pins, balloons, stuffed toys, calendars, and other colorful images

Procedure
1. Distribute Form A or present the image as an overhead transparency.
2. Explain that you heard a good joke. Say:

   "There were two caterpillars riding on a wagon and a beautiful butterfly floats by.

Contact Information: Scott Simmerman, Performance Management Company, 3 Old Oak Drive, Taylors, SC 29687, 864-292-8700, Scott@SquareWheels.com, www.SquareWheels.com

One caterpillar looks up and says to the other,

'You'll never get me up in one of those things' "

3. Now, ask people if they "get the joke" and even ask for a show of hands. [This is a simple joke, but it is more than the punch line that is important here. I had been telling this joke for about two years when I told it in Hong Kong to a group of English-speaking Chinese people. The reaction was a bit mixed, so I simply asked them to discuss the joke among themselves so that they could tell me The Answer. They did this with an increasing amount of laughter and interaction between tables. When I asked them to share their thinking, they gave me 32 different answers to the joke. All this time, I had been telling the joke thinking that the answer was "Resistance to Change." I would never have realized that there are many answers to the joke if I had not been paying attention to the reactions of others.]

4. Now, share the following comments:

"In the U.S. Open Tennis Tournament, John McEnroe, the retired tennis star, once said in a press conference upon losing: 'That taught me a lesson, but I am not sure what it is.'

"There was a lesson in the telling of this joke. Take two minutes to discuss this with your associates and see if you can discover 'The Lesson' in the joke."

5. Have participants discuss "The Lesson" in small groups. As the energy level dies down among the participants, call a halt and ask people for "The Lesson."

6. Invariably, they will share various lessons, such as:

- Change is inevitable.

- It's important to have a vision of the future.

- It's better to ride on the wagon than crawl in the dirt.

7. Respond that each of these lessons can be derived from the joke, but none of them is The Lesson.

8. Say:

"The lesson is simple:

'It is dangerous to know The Answer.' "

[Present Form B as an overhead transparency.]

- "Leadership, innovation, teamwork, and change all require us to realize that there are lots of possibilities and lots of perspectives, and just knowing The Answer tends to limit our thinking. In the initial telling of the joke, people invariably get The

Answer and quit thinking about other possibilities, and thus limit their thinking and perspective. Different people see and understand things differently. Only by talking about these differing perspectives can we become more aware."

9. You can also link these points to a model of change using this script:

"There are four components to teamwork and change. By increasing any one of them, we increase the likelihood that change may occur. The four components are:

- The current level of discomfort with the way things are now.
- The attractiveness of the vision of the future.
- The individual's or group's previous success with change.
- The peer or workgroup support for the change.

"By increasing the understanding of the change process key factors, we can help people become less comfortable with maintaining the status quo and help them perceive a more attractive vision of what we can become. By allowing them to feel creative and come up with new ideas and work together to generate ideas for improvement in the workplace, we make them more likely to succeed.

"One key is to recognize that there are different perspectives. People cannot consider what they do not contemplate. By working with others to generate different ideas in relation to the joke, we open them up to consider different ideas of what they can choose to do differently in the future.

"For managers and talent alike, it is important to recognize that knowing The Answer is limiting one's discoveries."

See the article, "Teaching the Caterpillar to Fly," at www.squarewheels.com/content/teaching.html for a more detailed description of the metaphor, delivery ideas, and the change model presentation.

SQUARE WHEELS ONE (FORM A)

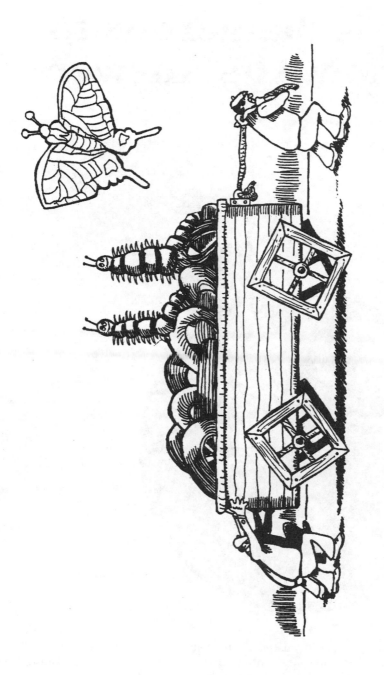

It is dangerous to know The Answer.

INDEX